# LIBER AMORIS
*and*
# DRAMATIC CRITICISMS

# LIBER AMORIS
*and*
# DRAMATIC CRITICISMS

*by*

WILLIAM HAZLITT

*with an essay of introduction by*
CHARLES MORGAN

PETER NEVILL LIMITED
*London*

PETER NEVILL LTD
50 Old Brompton Road
London SW7

Made and printed in Great Britain by Thomasons Ltd Cedar Press Hounslow
Bound by S. E. Bray Ltd Boscombe Bournemouth
MCMXLVIII

## *Contents*

# INTRODUCTION TO THE LIBER AMORIS

by

CHARLES MORGAN

[1]

Hazlitt's *Liber Amoris or The New Pygmalion* was published in May, 1823. It was anonymous, but wore a disguise so thin as to deceive no one. It was an account of Hazlitt's frustrated passion for a girl, Sarah, the second daughter of a tailor named Walker, in whose house in London Hazlitt lodged.

The first of the book's three parts was made up of a group of dialogues between the girl and the author; the second was a series of letters, describing the writer's agony and devotion, addressed to " C.P. Esq.", easily identifiable with P. G. Patmore, father of the poet; and the third consisted of letters to another friend, now known to have been the dramatist, Sheridan Knowles, giving the dénouement of the unhappy tale. The manuscript of the book and the originals of the letters to Patmore from which Hazlitt made selection were preserved. In 1894, the whole material was gathered together and privately printed in a volume introduced by Richard Le Gallienne.

Since then P. P. Howe's authoritative *Life* has greatly added to our knowledge of Hazlitt, but Howe's view of his duty was scholarly rather than interpretative, or—to speak more precisely—he preferred to keep himself in the background and to present Hazlitt's life, as far as possible, in the words of those who were witnesses of it. The method had great advantages. It made the biography " authoritative " in the strictest sense of the word. But it withheld the biographer from any attempt to correct the prejudice by which the *Liber Amoris* has always been surrounded or to re-assess its value.

Such a re-assessment is overdue. In spite of persistent attack, the *Liber Amoris* has stubbornly survived. It was called " disgusting " by Crabb Robinson, using the word, not in its earlier sense of " distasteful," but as we use it, violently, to mean " revolting " or " repulsive." Le Gallienne called it " silly." and, even as late as 1947, so wise and humane a critic as Mr. Frank Swinnerton, spoke of it as " that tragic piece of futility." And yet it lives with its own life, and not merely because the great essayist wrote it. No one who reads ever forgets it.

One reason is that it constitutes what a lawyer might call a leading case in the psychology of love. It said on the subject something that had not been said before in English prose, and has not been said since with the same directness and candour. What it said, and the value of the evidence it gave, we, in the midst of the Twentieth Century, are better able to discern than were those Victorians and pre-Victorians to whom its truth was unfamiliar and disturbing. Either they had not read Stendhal or they discounted him as French.

Love has never been, and is not now, an accurate translation of *amour*. Nevertheless ideas, even of love, cross the Channel at last. Stendhal is now familiar to us, and a comparison of the date, 1822, of Stendhal's *De L'Amour*, with that of the *Liber Amoris*, is illuminating. These dates prove beyond doubt that Stendhal wrote independently of Hazlitt, and there is every reason to believe that Hazlitt wrote independently of Stendhal.

[2]

The " book of our conversations (I mean mine and the statue's) which I call *Liber Amoris* " was begun at Stamford and dated 29th

January, 1822. The author was on his way to Edinburgh where, with the assistance of Scottish law more compliant than the English, he and his first wife were to be collusively divorced. In February and March he was at the Renton Inn, Berwickshire, (called the Bees Inn in his book), writing " ten pages a day, which mounts up to thirty guineas' worth a week," of those essays, including *Patronage and Puffing* and *On the Fear of Death,* which were to be the second volume of *Table Talk.* At the end of March he went to Edinburgh. Held by the law's delays, beset by agonized hopes and doubts concerning Miss Walker, writing to her and receiving replies (when he received any at all) as non-committal as only a statue's or a cautious servant-girl's could be, writing to Patmore, lecturing, walking in the Highlands with Sheridan Knowles, fencing with his wife who, he feared, might not go through with the divorce after all, Hazlitt loitered in Scotland.

In the latter half of May, he was in London, a lodger again in Southampton Buildings, distracted by Sarah's coldness, even more by her inarticulateness. " She turned her head and shrunk from my embraces, as if quite alienated or mortally offended . . . I could get only short, sullen, disconnected answers, as if there were something labouring in her mind which she either could not or would not impart." This astonished him in the girl who for so many months, when he had formerly lodged under her parents' roof, had spent hours of every day in his room and had permitted and delighted in every intimacy except that last which, because he idealized her and wished to become her husband, he had not pressed upon her. He did not understand it. " I asked what could it mean ? "—and Sarah Walker did not enlighten him, partly because she had other fish to fry, partly also, we may hazard, because she was bewildered by a passion she did not share and, in face of Hazlitt's appalling eloquence and intensity, fell back upon the little, stiff conventions, half-pert, half-formal, of her class when ill at ease. Hazlitt was baffled, furious and enchanted. Aware of his humiliation but accepting it, he begged crumbs of reassurance even from the girl's mother, who was clearly a bawd. " I took her wrinkled, withered, cadaverous, clammy hand at parting and kissed it. Faugh ! "

This stage of the struggle endured nearly a fortnight. Hazlitt then returned to Scotland where, on 17th July, the divorce proceedings ended. He was now free to offer marriage to Miss Walker. Meanwhile he had taken soundings. Was it worth his while to make a formal offer ? The girl's brother-in-law could give no better answer than that he thought Hazlitt might try his fortune. This he promptly did " with joy, with something like confidence," and with what consequences of disillusionment the end of the *Liber Amoris* tells us.

For a period which began long before Hazlitt's going to Scotland, she had been playing with another lodger, Mr. C., the same game that she had played with him. Now Mr. C. lived no longer in the house but at a little distance, and Hazlitt came upon the two walking together. His description of the encounter has the straightness of Defoe, and, at the end a touch—the recording that they passed *twice*—so brilliant, so unlikely and so persuasive, so unemphatic and yet so strikingly true, that it takes the breath away : " I passed a house in King-street where I had once lived, and had not proceeded many paces, ruminating on chance and change and old times, when I saw her coming towards me. I felt a strange pang at the sight, but I thought her alone. Some people before me moved on, and I saw another person with her. It was a tall, rather well-looking young man, but I did not at first recollect him.

We passed at the crossing of the street without speaking . . . She went by me without even changing countenance, without expressing the slightest emotion . . . I turned and looked—they also turned and looked—and as if by mutual consent, we both retrod our steps and passed again, in the same way. I went home." What do men mean who say that a book which contains such passages as this is " silly " ? The firmness, speed and veracity of it send us all to school.

Worse was to come. Hazlitt and Mr. C. afterwards compared notes. Miss Walker's duplicity was clear. It was not that she had favoured each in turn, but that she had systematically and simultaneously deceived both, while maintaining, as an excuse for keeping Hazlitt in agony, the fiction—was it a fiction ?—of a lost adorer to whom her very soul was devoted. Hazlitt abandoned hope, was deluded no more—was deluded no more, that is to say, by Miss Walker herself. " If there had been the frailty of passion, it would have been excusable ; but it is evident she is a practised, callous jilt." And again : " Her unmoved indifference and self-possession all the while, shew that it is her constant practice. Her look even, if closely examined, bears this interpretation. It is that of studied hypocrisy or startled guilt, rather than of refined sensibility or conscious innocence." Disillusionment could go no further. " Were she even to return to her former pretended fondness and endearments, I could have no pleasure, no confidence in them." And yet, though the girl was nothing, the ideal love, which had (to use Stendhal's word) been crystallized in her, lived on. " She is dead to me," Hazlitt wrote in his conclusion, " but what she once was to me, can never die ! "

The whole story of the *Liber Amoris* is a flawless

example of Stendhal's theory of crystallization, the more valuable because it was almost certainly written without knowledge of that theory. In 1824, probably in April, Hazlitt married again and on 1st September set out upon a journey through France and Italy. In Paris he met Stendhal for the first time, and Howe tells us, "Stendhal's *De L'Amour* formed Hazlitt's travelling companion during his tour, and was brought by this means to the knowledge of readers of the *Morning Chronicle.*" It is, of course, not impossible that he had received an earlier copy of the book, but 1824 looks like the date of his first reading it. With thoughts of Miss Walker in his mind, he must have read it with deep attention, for he himself, in the heat of blood, had set down his experience, asking again and again: "What does it mean? Why am I, who see so clearly, yet so bewitched?" and here was Stendhal telling him precisely why.

Almost too precisely. *De L'Amour* was brilliant analysis. It isolated, and held up for intellectual observation, a truth about love which, though others had expressed it often enough—Shakespeare in his *Sonnets*, for example, and Montaigne in his *Essays*—had never been so isolated before. We know more of ourselves (when we have leisure to examine ourselves) because Stendhal wrote, but we have not, in time of trouble, the mental detachment and coolness necessary to be his pupils. Hazlitt's book, without so well understanding what it says, says the same thing in such a way that passionate youth, or passionate middle-age for that matter, may see, reflected in its pages, an aspect of love which the aloof world calls "disgusting" or "silly" or "futile" and which the passion-stricken one half-knows to be so in himself. Yet he may find, in these same pages, that assuagement which is given by imagination shared, and is, to the tormented and enraptured, more precious than counsel.

[3]

What is this truth that Montaigne knew, and Stendhal reiterated, and Hazlitt exemplified? That we project our own imagining of Love on to her whom we say we love. We re-create her in an ideal shape—Hazlitt called Miss Walker "the statue"—and worship her in that shape, and struggle to bring the statue to life. "Like the passion of Love," said Montaigne, "that lends Beauties and Graces to the person it does embrace; and that makes those who are caught with it, with a depraved and corrupt Judgment, consider the thing they love other and more perfect than it is."*

Hazlitt goes further than this, further than Montaigne, further even than Stendhal, in his laying bare of the process of crystallization. He shows, because he is a supreme realist and is unafraid to give himself away, that the crystallizing lover is by no means the blind fool that he is traditionally supposed to be. He thus deprives himself of the only romantic defence with which an aloof and self-righteous world might be disposed contemptuously to cover him. The lover, Hazlitt says in effect, is not even a dupe; he is worse, he is a half-dupe, and yet persists; his desire is, as Shakespeare has said, "*past reason* hunted . . .

All this the world well knows, yet none knows well
To shun the heaven that leads men to this hell."

Hazlitt made no attempt to dignify his obsession. His division of mind between knowledge of Miss Walker's inadequacy and passionate exaltation of the ideal she represented is made plain in his terrible

* I am indebted for this reference to Montaigne, II, 17 (Cotton's translation) to P. and C. N. S. Woolf's translation of *De L'Amour* (London: Duckworth, 1915).

alternation of blame and praise, of angry distrust and wild confidence, of sickening triviality and high romance. In the *Liber Amoris* as it was published, there is evidence enough of this; in the original letters even more. He urged Patmore to employ a friend, E., to seduce the girl if he could in order that his, Hazlitt's, doubts might be quenched. "Get someone to try her," he wrote on 4th July, "or I am destroyed for ever. To go and see E., then after he (*words obliterated*) her for the asking, would lift my soul from Hell. It would be sweet and full revenge. *You* may try her, if you like . . . Life is hideous to me, and death horrible. Oh! that I knew she was a strumpet, and that she knew I did." And four days later, having received news from Patmore which he took to be reassuring, this: "She is an angel from heaven . . . She is a saint, an angel, a love. I now worship her, and fall down on my knees in thankfulness to God and Nature for this reprieve at least . . . I have been thinking of her little face these last two days, looking like a marble statue, as cold, as fixed and graceful as ever statue did, and I could not believe the lies I told of her."

It is not, to use *Blackwood's* word, "manly." The letters, even as they were published, expose their writer to all the shafts of ridicule and contempt. But they are an invaluable document because they are not dressed-up, because they are fearless of being laughed at, because they pour out the vast and the petty inconsistencies of the truth. If they are read contemptuously or in moral indignation, they will yield nothing. If they are read pitifully, they will yield not much more. But if they are read compassionately, in a spirit of "feeling with," they respond with compassion. That is why no lover who opens the *Liber Amoris* puts it down easily, and why no one who reads—though he resist and hate—ever forgets it.

[4]

It is an extreme book. For that reason, and because its extremism is sexual, and because it was written by genius and, therefore, not palely but with blood, it has hitherto been a cause either of rage or of bridling and embarrassment in many readers. Even to-day, after the lapse of a century and a quarter, it will not be received dispassionately; nor should it be; it is not a dispassionate book: you pick up what might, after so many years, be a spent ember, and it burns.

Nevertheless, we may hope, as our predecessors could not, to see the *Liber Amoris* as it is in itself and to judge it by its faults and virtues in its own kind. Our intolerances, even when political, are not those of Hazlitt's age, and, even when sexual, are no longer of the sort that made Crabb Robinson cry out, after reading the book, that "it ought to exclude the author from all decent society."

The reasons for its having been attacked with so much vehemence are plain. They were at first political; then, in the Victorian age, conventionally moral.

Hazlitt was an independent. Neither in life nor in literature did he run for shelter into any school, and he had no organized claque to support him. His opinions, tenaciously maintained, conformed to no system recognized by his contemporaries. Though conservative by temperament, a lover of the past, a profound loyalist to the memories of his childhood and youth, he was an unswerving hater of the Bourbons. An admirer of Burke's *Reflections*, he yet regarded himself as a child of the French Revolution. An apostle of Freedom in the abstract, he adored Napoleon. "I am no politician," he wrote, "and still less of a party man," but party-men, then as now, were determined to engage artists on one side or the other, and the anti-Jacobins were out for Hazlitt's blood. The appearance of the *Liber Amoris* was a heaven-sent opportunity to his enemies. *Blackwood's* reviewer let himself go. The book, he observed with delight, was "not a creation of mere Cockney imagination, but a *veritable* transcript of the feelings and doings of an individual living LIBERAL." He then quoted the passages which seemed to him the most damagingly licentious, identified the publisher, John Hunt, as the publisher of the *Liberal* and the *Examiner* and as the brother of Leigh Hunt, and, with a triumphant flourish, left the examples quoted—as final damnation of the Cockney School—"in the hands of every single individual, however humble in station, however limited in knowledge or acquirement, who has elevation enough to form the least notion of what 'virtue,' 'honour' and 'manliness,' and, we may add, 'love' mean—and penetration enough to understand a plain English story told in plain English."

This is fustian, but there is no denying that, *Blackwood's* being then what *Blackwood's* was, Hazlitt had asked for it. The *Liber Amoris* is a vulnerable book. Nothing is easier than to quote from it derisively. Even to the point of self-humiliation in the little shames, Hazlitt, following Rousseau, had not hesitated to give himself away, and the reviewer did only what was to be expected of him. There is, moreover, a sense in which it is true to say that the *Liber Amoris* is a failure. It is not, even within its own intention, the great book it might have been; it does not take rank—and no one can have been more bitterly aware of this than its author—with or near the *Confessions* of Rousseau or *La Nouvelle Heloise*. It was written too close in time to the experience from which it sprang. The period of distillation was too short, and its shortness prevented Hazlitt from entering imaginatively into Sarah Walker's mind.

[5]

It was a mind which presents interesting problems to an imaginative reader of Hazlitt's book, above all to a novelist; and it is worth while to turn aside for a moment to examine what evidence there is about Sarah Walker. What was her own point of view? Why did she behave as she did, and what account of her behaviour did she give to herself?

Her appearance is relevant, and of this we have some knowledge. She had a rare grace of movement, an air of gliding or wafting herself across a room without visibly taking steps. Procter, quoted by Birrell, speaks of her snake-like walk, and Hazlitt, evidently thinking of her when he wrote his essay *On Living to One's Self*, quoted Procter's *Mirandola:*

> "With what a waving air she goes
> Along the corridor. How like a fawn!
> Yet statelier! Hark! No sound, however soft,
> Nor gentlest echo telleth where she treads,
> But every motion of her shape doth seem
> Hallowed by silence—"

and we receive an impression continually of a girl whose bodily movement had in it a quality of reticence, beautiful but mysterious, as though she were trying to make herself invisible.

Her face seems not to have been beautiful by any standard ordinarily accepted then or now. It was small and round—so far, perhaps, so good; but the eyes were bad. "Glassy," says an independent witness, and Hazlitt, having spoken of them as "timidly cast upon the ground," makes us feel that they were exceedingly uncomfortable when they looked up. There was then, he said in his *Table Talk*, "a cold, sullen, watery, glazed look about the eyes, which she bent upon vacancy, as if determined to avoid all explanation with yours." The charitable may say that the girl needed spectacles, but there seems to have been more in it than that. "Glassy" and "glazed" are not pleasant words. Hazlitt speaks also of "their glittering, motionless surface." Such eyes accord too well with the snake-like movement.

And yet she was "demure, pretty, modest-looking," and, above all, gave Hazlitt the impression that she genuinely loved him. This, to him, was of supreme importance. He was a suspicious, shy man who, though his intimate friends, such as Lamb, were fond of him, did not make easy first impressions and believed himself to be disliked. In his youth, Crabb Robinson tells us, Hazlitt "was excessively shy, and in company the girls always made game of him. He had a horror of the society of ladies, especially of smart and handsome and modest young women." Add to this that he was of sensual temperament, deeply serious and conscious of his own powers. The desire not to be "teased" by pretty girls, as Crabb Robinson's friend Miss Kitchener teased him, is comprehensible.

Sarah Walker was not "smart" or, in the formidably social sense of the word, "handsome." It was at any rate not by chatter that she teased him. She was accessible to caresses, she spent hours with him willingly; she did not madden him with that clamorous frivolity of which Miss Kitchener may be suspected. On the contrary she was silent by habit. While sitting on his knee and embracing him, she listened—as though it were the words she enjoyed—at the talk of the man who could hold the audience to Lamb's; she kissed him and yet was demure; he quoted and she let him quote; he worshipped and she let him worship. She was neither so chaste as to freeze, nor so unchaste as to alarm, him. Her passivity and listlessness prevented her from giggling genius down. It was easy for him to believe that she, alone among women, appreciated and loved him.

The simple and probably inadequate explanation

of Miss Walker is that she was an early nineteenth century equivalent of what is nowadays called a "good-timer"—a girl, that is to say, with no rule except her own pleasure but without the capacity or courage to drink pleasure deep; a weak creature seeking always the petty re-assurances of vanity; anaemically indifferent rather than callous; desiring change not for adventure's sake but to cheat the natural emptiness of her mind; conventional, defensive, always afraid of missing something, an intuitive hater of distinction, vulgarly refined. Miss Walker had some of these qualities, but the character does not fit her. It does not fit her because it is a mass-product, and she, whatever her faults, was not mass-produced.

It seems by no means improbable that, before she met Hazlitt, she had loved in her fashion a man who had vanished from her life. She said so; she gave it as her reason for holding Hazlitt back; and the man is more likely to have existed than to have been invented by her. That he was altogether a fiction, it is hard to believe, and, if he existed, she may well have crystallized in him her idea of love, and so have become, as it were, chilled against all but the minor sensualities in which she indulged with Hazlitt and Mr. C. All that we are told of her suggests that she was in some sense numb rather than naturally cold or deliberately cruel.

Haydon says that the dialogues given in the *Liber Amoris* were "literal." They bear the stamp of truth. Consider then, these passages:

> H. Tell me why you have deceived me, and singled me out as your victim?
> S. I never have, Sir. I always said I could not love . . . I have always been consistent from the first.

Hazlitt demands why, then, she had kissed him at first asking. She had seemed "so reserved and modest" that "whatever favours you granted must proceed from pure regard." To a long tirade, she answers only: "I am no prude, Sir." Then, later:

S. I'll stay and hear this no longer.
H. Yes, one word more. Did you not love another?
S. Yes, and ever shall most sincerely.

Hazlitt himself believed it at the time, for he replied: "Then, *that* is my only hope." Sarah never swerved from it.

Hazlitt came afterwards to believe that she had lied. It was an explanation supplied by rage and disappointment. If he had waited until he was able to recollect his emotion in tranquillity and had then re-imagined Miss Walker, he might have seen himself as she, perhaps, saw him: a man different from any she had formerly known, belonging to a world she had never guessed at, having powers she had never felt. His imagination, the force of crystallization that drove him mad, could not be without its effect on her. She was, or thought of herself as being, ordinary; but imagination has creative power, and this extraordinary man was imagining her as an extraordinary girl. She was on her own ground with Mr. C. across the passage; he passed the time; but what was she to do with Mr. Hazlitt? Not love him—as well love a whirlwind. Not marry him—as well marry a creature from Mars. And not abruptly repel him for many reasons—mixed reasons, good and bad: that he was a profitable lodger and she her mother's daughter; that she had, in any case, to wait on him and life had to be lived; that she was more than a little in awe of him; and, to do her credit, that he was often kind, and gave her presents, and she did not wish to offend him. Moreover, she was, in some obscure way, grateful to him—not, as he once implied, for the presents only, but because he made her feel important. She could not explain; she had not the language; she had not even the consecutive thought in which to explain herself to herself. What, then, should she do? She could, if he liked it, put her arms round him, and kiss him, and, being an animal, like it too. Perhaps she was deceiving him about Mr. C., but, at the same time, she was not deceiving him, for Mr. C. belonged to a different compartment of her mind.

Whether, if he had given himself time, Hazlitt would have interpreted her in this way or another, he would certainly, being an artist, have interpreted her from the inside. That he did not do so unbalances his book if we consider it as we might consider a novel. From that point of view, it is incomplete. But this very one-sidedness, this extreme subjectivity, gives it rare value as a document written at white-heat by a man of genius at the height of passionate obsession. At the time, Hazlitt was afflicted by the terrible loquaciousness which is often a consequence of spiritual loneliness and despair. Being a man, he did what many a man before him has done in his condition: he went from friend to friend, from acquaintance to acquaintance, boring them all, telling his story—to him a tragedy, to them almost a farce—again and again. Finding Haydon from home, he poured it all out to Haydon's manservant, Sammons; then, on the same day, going to inspect lodgings in Pimlico and meeting a landlady who said he did not look well—"the devil take me, if I did not let out the whole story from beginning to end!"

So the man, suffering to the point of insanity. But Hazlitt was also a writer. The *Liber Amoris* was his relief. It has the defect of being unbalanced in its treatment, or in its failure to treat with interior sympathy the other protagonist of the tale. But balance, except in very dull leading articles and very pedestrian men, is not all. Pressure is one of the evidences of genius, and another, when you can write Hazlitt's prose, is a complete carelessness for the moderate and unsentimental sneer that will greet the end of your sentence. Hazlitt wrote this : " . . . I am now inclosed in a dungeon of despair. The sky is marble to my thoughts ; nature is dead around me, as hope is within me ; no object can give me one gleam of satisfaction now, nor the prospect of it in time to come. I wander by the sea-side ; and the eternal ocean and lasting despair and her face are before me. Slighted by her, on whom my heart by its last fibre hung, where shall I turn ? I wake with her by my side, not as my sweet bed-fellow, but as the corpse of my love, without a heart in her bosom, cold, insensible, or struggling from me ; and the worm gnaws me, and the sting of unrequited love, and the canker of a hopeless, endless sorrow. I have lost the taste of my food by feverish anxiety ; and my favourite beverage, which used to refresh me when I got up, has no moisture in it. Oh ! cold, solitary, sepulchral breakfasts . . . " Who will may smile at that. It is extreme, unbalanced, and, fortunately, without a sense of humour. But it is true with a truth that a regulated and discreet sanity could not have communicated. " The sky is marble to my thoughts," wrote Hazlitt, and the saying is of Shakespeare's breed. It has the terrible flash of *Troilus and Cressida*.

But it was neither Hazlitt's failure to re-imagine Miss Walker nor his " sepulchral breakfasts " that provoked *Blackwood's* rage. The reviewer condemned the book for its principal merit—its treatment of love. He may say what he pleases about " virtue," " honour " and " manliness." They are words used by him to create fashionable prejudice, and, at this distance of time, are not worth disputing, but to say that Hazlitt did not know the meaning of love, and to say no more than this, was to beg the whole question that the *Liber Amoris* presents for judgment.

[6]

Whether *Blackwood's* reviewer was as shocked as he pretended to be we may a little doubt; he was, presumably, a child of the Eighteenth Century; but that the Victorians were genuinely shocked is certain and understandable. Stevenson abandoned a project of writing Hazlitt's Life because Hazlitt had written the *Liber Amoris*, and when, at the end of the century, Augustine Birrell wrote on Hazlitt in the English Men of Letters Series, he approached Miss Walker with contortions of reluctance and held out the *Liber Amoris* with a pair of tongs. "The loves of the middle-aged," he began, forgetful of Antony, "are never agreeable subject-matter for the pens of third parties. 'A fool at forty is a fool indeed,' and this affair of Hazlitt's must be briefly handled." He then rehearsed the facts which were, he said, by now "offensively familiar," and concluded: "Anyhow, the whole sentimental structure of the *Liber Amoris* now sinks below the stage, and joins the realm of things unspeakable—'vile kitchen stuff,' fit only for the midden."

This is fierce prejudice; if we can understand it, we may the better understand the book which provoked it, for the value of the *Liber Amoris* is that it expresses a kind of love—no less love for being also a kind of madness—which a great part of Victorian opinion persisted in regarding as inhuman baseness, so vile and so exceptional that it was not a fit subject for literature or even for thought. From this point of view, passion—of which the existence could scarcely be denied by readers of *Romeo and Juliet*—was seen as a lamentable intrusion upon the ordered decencies of society. It was, therefore, carefully distinguished, as an aberration, from that love which conformed to the social rule. When it appeared in the very young, it was treated, unless it led to extra-matrimonial disaster, as a naïveté to be wryly smiled at, and, if it could not be suppressed, to be tolerated under the name of calf-love. In all other circumstances, it was ruthlessly hunted, as it was in Parnell ; and, in order that it might be hunted, it had first to be outlawed—that is to say, it had to be proclaimed as something freakish and unnatural, abnormal as crime is abnormal. This attitude towards passion, and a corresponding attitude towards crystallization, were expressed by Richard Le Gallienne (1894) with the ingenuous candour of the period. "Though, as we have seen, the illusion did credit to Hazlitt's heart, it is impossible not to feel that no man of forty should be able to mistake a woman for a goddess or an angel . . . It is unnatural, uncanny, in the bearded man. Naïveté is charming up to twenty, but the naïveté of middle-age is unattractive, and the *Liber Amoris* is full of that unattractive quality—much like the naïveté we sometimes find in the poetical effusions of criminals."

It is an adroit piece of special pleading. To mistake a woman for a goddess would indeed be naïve, but this precisely is what Hazlitt did not do. He saw the woman and the goddess at the same time ; was agonizingly aware both of the distinction between them on one plane of his consciousness and of their identity on another plane ; was unceasingly observant of his self-division ; was the sane, unsparing analyst of his own madness, and, therefore, racked.

[7]

That this was possible and in the nature of passion, the upholders of Victorian convention would not admit. They would not admit it because to have done so would have been to let in a flood which must destroy, and has since destroyed, their world. They were not, as their detractors are at last beginning to understand, blind. Still less were they complacent. They saw what was coming. As the century drew towards its end, they fought, in fear for their society, a long defensive battle for the values upon which it was based. It was as clear to them as it is to us that sexual passion is a dominant force which in a stable society must be harnessed. Their method of harnessing it was to equate love with respect, respect with reason, reason with constancy; and to discountenance all love, and all books about love (except Shakespeare's), which did not conform to this theory.

Two things necessarily followed of which the rigidity, often unjustly called the hypocrisy, of their matrimonial code was only an outward manifestation: first, the outlawing of passion felt to be subversive; second, a refusal to recognize that it is possible and even natural to respect and not respect at the same time, to despise and worship, to be mean and generous, cruel and kind, a sensual slave and a true lover, not only in turns but *at the same time*. The wiser among them were not ignorant of this; they had read their Shakespeare and had lived their own lives; but they would not give their knowledge recognition because they feared that to give social effect to the tendency of the human personality to fragment would be to disintegrate society itself. That they were unjustified in their fear, we, in whom they would see the justification of it, dare not assert. We examine the fragments of the human personality as they did not, but the Twentieth Century has found no alternative to their admittedly artificial integration.

This is not to say that no alternative exists. If it can be found, and when it can be found, the breakdown of the Victorian artifice may be counted as a gain. Not until then; but we are, at any rate, to this extent liberated : that we no longer fear to read Shakespeare in the context of our own lives.

> " My love is as a fever, longing still
> For that which longer nurseth the disease ;
> Feeding on that which doth preserve the ill,
> The uncertain sickly appetite to please.
> My reason, the physician to my love,
> Angry that his prescriptions are not kept,
> Hath left me, and I desperate now approve
> Desire is death, which physic did except.
> Past cure I am, now reason is past care,
> And frantic-mad with ever more unrest ;
> My thoughts and my discourse as madmen's are,
> At random from the truth vainly express'd ;
> For I have sworn thee fair, and thought thee bright,
> Who art as black as hell, as dark as night."

It is a sonnet that might have stood as epigraph to the *Liber Amoris* which also tells a little of what suffering humanity has to learn of its own unreason.

> " Who taught thee how to make me love thee more,
> The more I hear and see just cause of hate ? "

It is Shakespeare's question and Hazlitt's too. Is it criminal naïveté ? Is it, even, a rare question ? Happy the man or woman who never has cause to ask it ! Happy—or dead. Happy as the Brownings were—or dead as they were not.

CHARLES MORGAN

# LIBER AMORIS

## *PART I*

## *The Picture*

H. Oh! is it you? I had something to show you—I have got a picture here. Do you know any one it's like?

S. No, Sir.

H. Don't you think it like yourself?

S. No: it's much handsomer than I can pretend to be.

H. That's because you don't see yourself with the same eyes that others do. *I* don't think it handsomer, and the expression is hardly so fine as yours sometimes is.

S. Now you flatter me. Besides, the complexion is fair, and mine is dark.

H. Thine is pale and beautiful, my love, not dark. But if your colour were a little heightened, and you wore the same dress, and your hair were let down over your shoulders, as it is here, it might be taken for a picture of you. Look here, only see how like it is. The forehead is like, with that little obstinate protrusion in the middle; the eyebrows are like, and the eyes are just like yours, when you look up and say 'No—never!'

S. What then, do I always say 'No—never?' when I look up?

H. I don't know about that—I never heard you say so but once; but that was once too often for my peace. It was when you told me, 'you could never be mine.' Ah! if you are never to be mine, I shall not long be myself. I cannot go on as I am. My faculties leave me: I think of nothing, I have no feeling about anything but thee: thy sweet image has taken possession of me, haunts me, and will drive me to distraction. Yet I could almost wish to go mad for thy sake: for then I might fancy that I had thy love in return, which I cannot live without!

S. Do not, I beg, talk in that manner, but tell me what this is a picture of.

H. I hardly know; but it is a very small and delicate copy (painted in oil on a gold ground) of some fine old Italian picture, Guido's or Raphael's, but I think Raphael's. Some say it is a Madonna; others call it a Magdalen, and say you may distinguish the tear upon the cheek, though no tear is there. But it seems to me more like Raphael's St. Cecilia, 'with looks commercing with the skies,' than anything else.—See, Sarah, how beautiful it is! Ah! dear girl, these are the ideas I have cherished in my heart, and in my brain; and I never found anything to realise them on earth till I met with thee, my love! While thou didst seem sensible of my kindness, I was but too happy: but now thou hast cruelly cast me off.

S. You have no reason to say so: you are the same to me as ever.

H. That is, nothing. You are to me everything, and I am nothing to you. Is it not too true?

S. No.

H. Then kiss me, my sweetest. Oh! could you see your face now—your mouth full of suppressed sensibility, your downcast eyes, the soft blush upon that cheek, you would not say the picture is not like because it is too handsome, or because you want complexion. Thou art heavenly-fair, my love—like her from whom the picture was taken—the idol of the painter's heart, as thou art of mine! Shall I make a drawing of it, altering the dress a little, to show you how like it is?

S. As you please.

## *The Invitation*

H. But I am afraid I tire you with this prosing description of the French character and abuse of the English? You know there is but one subject on which I should ever wish to talk, if you would let me.

S. I must say, you don't seem to have a very high opinion of this country.

H. Yes, it is the place that gave you birth.

S. Do you like the French women better than the English?

H. No: though they have finer eyes, talk better and are better made. But they none of them look like you. I like the Italian women I have seen much better than the French: they have darker eyes, darker hair, and the accents of their native tongue are much richer and more melodious. But I will give you a better account of them when I come back from Italy, if you would like to hear it.

S. I should much. It is for that I have sometimes had a wish for travelling abroad, to understand something of the manners and characters of different people.

H. My sweet girl! I will give you the best account I can—unless you would rather go and judge for yourself.

S. I cannot.

H. Yes, you shall go with me, and you shall go with honour—you know what I mean.

S. You know it is not in your power to take me so.

H. But it soon may: and if you would consent to bear me company, I would swear never to think of an Italian woman while I am abroad, nor of an

English one after I return home. Thou art to me more than thy whole sex.

S. I require no such sacrifices.

H. Is that what you thought I meant by sacrifices last night? But sacrifices are no sacrifices when they are repaid a thousand fold.

S. I have no way of doing it.

H. You have not the will.—

S. I must go now.

H. Stay, and hear me a little. I shall soon be where I can no more hear thy voice, far distant from her I love, to see what change of climate and bright skies will do for a sad heart. I shall perhaps see thee no more, but I shall still think of thee the same as ever—I shall say to myself 'Where is she now? what is she doing?' But I shall hardly wish you to think of me, unless you could do so more favourably than I am afraid you will. Ah! dearest creature, I shall be 'far distant from you' as you once said of another, but you will not think of me as of him, 'with the sincerest affection.' The smallest share of thy tenderness would make me blessed; but couldst thou ever love me as thou didst him, I should feel like a god! My face would change to a different expression: my whole form would undergo alteration. I was getting well, I was growing young in the sweet proofs of your friendship: you see how I droop and wither under your displeasure! Thou art divine, my love, and canst make me either more or less than mortal. Indeed, I am thy creature, thy slave—I only wish to live for your sake—I would gladly die for you—

S. That would give me no pleasure. But indeed you greatly overrate my power.

H. Your power over me is that of sovereign grace and beauty. When I am near thee, nothing can harm me. Thou art an angel of light, shadowing me with thy softness. But when I let go thy hand, I stagger on a precipice: out of thy sight the world is dark to me and comfortless. There is no breathing out of this house : the air of Italy will stifle me. Go with me and lighten it. I can know no pleasure away from thee :

> But I will come again, my love,
>     An' it were ten thousand mile !

S. Mrs. E—— has called for the book, Sir.

H. Oh! it is there. Let her wait a minute or two. I see this is a busy day with you. How beautiful your arms look in those short sleeves!

S. I do not like to wear them.

H. Then that is because you are merciful, and would spare frail mortals who might die with gazing.

S. I have no power to kill.

H. You have, you have—your charms are irresistible as your will is inexorable. I wish I could see you always thus. But I would have no one else see you so. I am jealous of all eyes but my own. I should almost like you to wear a veil, and to be muffled up from head to foot; but even if you were, and not a glimpse of you could be seen, it would be to no purpose—you would only have to move, and you would be admired as the most graceful creature in the world. You smile—Well, if you were to be won by fine speeches—

S. You could supply them!

H. It is, however, no laughing matter with me; thy beauty kills me daily, and I shall think of nothing but thy charms, till the last word trembles on my tongue, and that will be thy name, my love—the name of my Infelice! You will live by that name, you rogue, fifty years after you are dead. Don't you thank me for that?

S. I have no such ambition, Sir. But Mrs. E—— is waiting.

H. She is not in love, like me. You look so

handsome to-day, I cannot let you go. You have a colour.

S. But you say I look best when I am pale.

H. When you are pale, I think so ; but when you have a colour, I then think you still more beautiful. It is you that I admire ; and whatever you are, I like best. I like you as Miss L——, I should like you still more as Mrs——. I once thought you were half inclined to be a prude, and I admired you as a ‘ pensive nun, devout and pure.’ I now think you are more than half a coquet, and I like you for your roguery. The truth is, I am in love with you, my angel ; and whatever you are, is to me the perfection of thy sex. I care not what thou art, while thou art still thyself. Smile but so, and turn my heart to what shape you please !

S. I am afraid, Sir, Mrs. E—— will think you have forgotten her.

H. I had, my charmer. But go, and make her a sweet apology, all graceful as thou art. One kiss ! Ah ! ought I not to think myself the happiest of men ?

## *The Flageolet*

H. Where have you been, my love!

S. I have been down to see my aunt, Sir.

H. And I hope she has been giving you good advice.

S. I did not go to ask her opinion about anything.

H. And yet you seem anxious and agitated. You appear pale and dejected, as if your refusal of me had touched your own breast with pity. Cruel girl! you look at this moment heavenly-soft, saint-like, or resemble some graceful marble statue, in the moon's pale ray! Sadness only heightens the elegance of your features. How can I escape from you, when every new occasion, even your cruelty and scorn, brings out some new charm. Nay, your rejection of me, by the way in which you do it, is only a new link added to my chain. Raise those downcast eyes, bend as if an angel stooped, and kiss me. . . Ah! enchanting little trembler! if such is thy sweetness where thou dost not love, what must thy love have been? I cannot think how any man, having the heart of one, could go and leave it.

S. No one did, that I know of.

H. Yes, you told me yourself he left you (though he liked you, and though he knew—Oh! gracious God!—that you loved him) he left you because 'the pride of birth would not permit a union.'—For myself, I would leave a throne to ascend to the heaven of thy charms. I live but for thee, here—I only wish to live again to pass all eternity with thee. But even in another world, I suppose you would turn from me to seek him out who scorned you here.

S. If the proud scorn us here, in that place we shall all be equal.

H. Do not look so—do not talk so—unless you would drive me mad, I could worship you at this moment. Can I witness such perfection, and bear to think I have lost you for ever ? Oh ! let me hope ! You see you can mould me as you like. You can lead me by the hand, like a little child ; and with you my way would be like a little child's :—you could strew flowers in my path, and pour new life and hope into me. I should then indeed hail the return of spring with joy, could I indulge the faintest hope—would you but let me try to please you !

S. Nothing can alter my resolution, Sir.

H. Will you go and leave me so ?

S. It is late, and my father will be getting impatient at my stopping so long.

H. You know he has nothing to fear for you—it is poor I that am alone in danger. But I wanted to ask about buying you a flageolet. Could I see that which you have ? If it is a pretty one, it would hardly be worth while ; but if it isn't, I thought of bespeaking an ivory one for you. Can't you bring up your own to shew me.

S. Not to-night, Sir.

H. I wish you could.

S. I cannot—but I will in the morning.

H. Whatever you determine, I must submit to. Good-night, and bless thee !

[*The next morning S. brought up the teakettle as usual ; and looking towards the tea-tray, she said ' Oh! I see my sister has forgot the tea-pot.' It was not there, sure enough ; and, tripping down stairs, she came up in a minute, with the teapot in one hand, and the flageolet in the other, balanced so sweetly and gracefully. It would have been awkward to have brought up the flageolet in the tea-tray, and she could not have well gone down again on purpose to fetch it. Something, therefore, was to be omitted as an excuse. Exquisite witch! But do I love her the less dearly for it? I cannot.*]

## *The Confession*

H. You say you cannot love. Is there not a prior attachment in the case? Is there any one else that you did like?

S. Yes, there was another.

H. Ah! I thought as much. Is it long ago then?

S. It is two years, Sir.

H. And has time made no alteration? Or do you still see him sometimes?

S. No, Sir! But he is one to whom I feel the sincerest affection, and ever shall, though he is far distant.

H. And did he return your regard?

S. I had every reason to think so.

H. What then broke off your intimacy?

S. It was the pride of birth, Sir, that would not permit him to think of a union.

H. Was he a young man of rank, then?

S. His connections were high.

H. And did he never attempt to persuade you to any other step?

S. No—he had too great a regard for me.

H. Tell me, my angel, how was it? Was he so very handsome? Or was it the fineness of his manners?

S. It was more his manner; but I can't tell how it was. It was chiefly my own fault. I was foolish to suppose he could ever think seriously of me. But he used to make me read with him—and I used to be with him a good deal, though not much neither—and I found my affections entangled before I was aware of it.

H. And did your mother and family know of it?

S. No—I have never told any one but you ; nor I should not have mentioned it now, but I thought it might give you some satisfaction.

H. Why did he go at last ?

S. We thought it better to part.

H. And do you correspond ?

S. No, Sir. But perhaps I may see him again some time or other, though it will be only in the way of friendship.

H. My God ! what a heart is thine, to live for years upon that bare hope !

S. I did not wish to live always, Sir—I wished to die for a long time after, till I thought it not right ; and since then I have endeavoured to be as resigned as I can.

H. And do you think the impression will never wear out ?

S. Not if I can judge from my feelings hitherto. It is now sometime since—and I find no difference.

H. May God for ever bless you ! How can I thank you for your condescension in letting me know your sweet sentiments ? You have changed my esteem into adoration.—Never can I harbour a thought of ill in thee again.

S. Indeed, Sir, I wish your good opinion and your friendship.

H. And can you return them ?

S. Yes.

H. And nothing more ?

S. No, Sir.

H. You are an angel, and I will spend my life, if you will let me, in paying you the homage that my heart feels towards you.

## *The Quarrel*

H. You are angry with me?

S. Have I not reason?

H. I hope you have; for I would give the world to believe my suspicions unjust. But, oh! my God! after what I have thought of you and felt towards you, as little less than an angel, to have but a doubt cross my mind for an instant that you were what I dare not name—a common lodging-house decoy, a kissing convenience, that your lips were as common as the stairs—

S. Let me go, Sir!

H. Nay—prove to me that you are not so, and I will fall down and worship you. You were the only creature that ever seemed to love me; and to have my hopes, and all my fondness for you, thus turned to a mockery—it is too much! Tell me why you have deceived me, and singled me out as your victim?

S. I never have, Sir. I always said I could not love.

H. There is a difference between love and making me a laughing-stock. Yet what else could be the meaning of your little sister's running out to you and saying, 'He thought I did not see him!' when I had followed you into the other room? Is it a joke upon me that I make free with you? Or is not the joke rather against *her* sister, unless you make my courtship of you a jest to the whole house? Indeed, I do not well see how you can come and stay with me as you do, by the hour together, and day after day, as openly as you do, unless you give it some such turn with your family. Or do you deceive them as well as me?

S. I deceive no one, Sir. But my sister Betsy was always watching and listening when Mr. M—— was courting my eldest sister, till he was obliged to complain of it.

H. That I can understand, but not the other. You may remember, when your servant Maria looked in and found you sitting in my lap one day, and I was afraid she might tell your mother, you said 'You did not care, for you had no secrets from your mother.' This seemed to me odd at the time, but I thought no more of it, till other things brought it to my mind. Am I to suppose, then, that you are acting a part, a vile part, all this time, and that you come up here, and stay as long as I like, that you sit on my knee and put your arms round my neck, and feed me with kisses, and let me take other liberties with you, and that for a year together; and that you do all this not out of love, or liking, or regard, but go through your regular task, like some young witch, without one natural feeling, to shew your cleverness, and get a few presents out of me, and go down into the kitchen to make a fine laugh of it? There is something monstrous in it, that I cannot believe of you.

S. Sir, you have no right to harass my feelings in the manner you do. I have never made a jest of you to anyone, but always felt and expressed the greatest esteem for you. You have no ground for complaint in my conduct; and I cannot help what Betsy or others do. I have always been consistent from the first. I told you my regard could amount to no more than friendship.

H. Nay, Sarah, it was more than half a year before I knew that there was an insurmountable obstacle in the way. You say your regard is merely friendship, and that you are sorry I have ever felt anything more for you. Yet the first time I ever asked you, you let me kiss you; the first time I ever saw you, as you went out of the room, you turned full round at the door, with that inimitable grace with which you do everything, and fixed your eyes full upon me, as much as to say 'Is he caught?'—that very week you sat upon my knee, twined your arms round me, caressed me with every mark of tenderness consistent with modesty; and I have not got much farther since. Now if you did all this with me, a perfect stranger to you, and without any particular liking to me, must I not conclude you do so as a matter of course with everyone?—Or, if you do not do so with others, it was because you took a liking to me for some reason or other.

S. It was gratitude, Sir, for different obligations.

H. If you mean by obligations the presents I made you, I had given you none the first day I came. You do not consider yourself *obliged* to everyone who asks you for a kiss?

S. No, Sir.

H. I should not have thought anything of it in anyone but you. But you seemed so reserved and modest, so soft, so timid, you spoke so low, you looked so innocent—I thought it impossible you could deceive me. Whatever favours you granted must proceed from pure regard. No betrothed virgin ever gave the object of her choice kisses, caresses more modest or more bewitching than those you have given me a thousand and a thousand times. Could I have thought I should ever live to believe them an inhuman mockery of one who had the sincerest regard for you? Do you think they will not now turn to rank poison in my veins, and kill me, soul and body? You say it is friendship—but if this is friendship, I'll forswear love. Ah, Sarah! it must be something more or less than friendship. If your caresses are sincere, they shew fondness—if they are not, I must be more than indifferent to you. Indeed you once let some words drop, as if I were out of the question in such matters, and you could trifle with me with impunity. Yet you complain at other times that no one ever took such liberties with you as I have done. I remember once in particular your saying, as you went out at the door in anger, 'I had an attachment before, but that person never attempted anything of the kind.' Good God! How did I dwell on that word *before*, thinking it implied an attachment to me also; but you have since disclaimed any such meaning. You say you have never professed more than esteem. Yet once, when you were sitting in your old place, on my knee, embracing and fondly embraced, and I asked you if you could not love, you made answer 'I could easily say so, whether I did or not—YOU SHOULD JUDGE BY MY ACTIONS!' And another time, when you were in the same posture, and I reproached you with indifference, you replied in these words, 'DO I SEEM INDIFFERENT?" Was I to blame after this to indulge my passion for the loveliest of her sex? Or what can I think?

S. I am no prude, Sir.

H. Yet you might be taken for one. So your mother said 'It was hard if you might not indulge in a little levity.' She has strange notions of levity. But levity, my dear, is quite out of character in you. Your ordinary walk is as if you were performing some religious ceremony: you come up to my table of a morning, when you merely bring in the tea-things, as if you were advancing to the altar. You move in minuet-time: you measure every step, as if you were afraid of offending in the smallest things. I never hear your approach on the stairs, but by a sort of hushed silence. When you enter the room, the Graces wait on you, and Love waves round your person in gentle undulations, breathing balm into the soul! By Heaven, you are an angel! You look like one at this instant! Do I not adore you—and have I merited this return?

S. I have repeatedly answered that question.

You sit and fancy things out of your own head, and then lay them to my charge. There is not a word of truth in your suspicions.

H. Did I not overhear the conversation downstairs last night, to which you were a party? Shall I repeat it?

S. I had rather not hear it!

H. Or what am I to think of this story of the footman?

S. It is false, Sir, I never did anything of the sort.

H. Nay, when I told your mother I wished she wouldn't * * * * * * * * (as I heard she did), she said 'Oh, there's nothing in that, for Sarah very often * * * * * and your doing so before company, is only a trifling addition to the sport.

S. I'll call my mother, Sir, and she shall contradict you.

H. Then she'll contradict herself. But did not you boast you were 'very persevering in your resistance to gay young men,' and had been 'several times obliged to ring the bell'? Did you always ring it? Or did you get into these dilemmas that made it necessary, merely by the demureness of your looks and ways? Or had nothing else passed? Or have you two characters, one that you palm off upon me, and another, your natural one, that you resume when you get out of the room, like an actress who throws aside her artificial part behind the scenes? Did you not, when I was courting you on the staircase the first night Mr. C—— came, beg me to desist, for if the new lodger heard us, he'd take you for a light character? Was that all? Were you only afraid of being *taken* for a light character? Oh, Sarah!

S. I'll stay and hear this no longer.

H. Yes, one word more. Did you not love another.

S. Yes, and ever shall most sincerely.

H. Then, *that* is my only hope. If you could feel this sentiment for him, you cannot be what you seem to me of late. But there is another thing I had to say—be what you will, I love you to distraction! You are the only woman that ever made me think she loved me, and that feeling was so new to me, and so delicious, that it 'will never from my heart.' Thou wert to me a little tender flower, blooming in the wilderness of my life; and though thou should'st turn out a weed, I'll not fling thee from me, while I can help it. Wert thou all that I dread to think—wert thou a wretched wanderer in the street, covered with rags, disease, and infamy, I'd clasp thee to my bosom, and live and die with thee, my love. Kiss me, thou little sorceress!

S. NEVER!

H. Then go: but remember, I cannot live without you—nor I will not.

## *The Reconciliation*

H. I have then lost your friendship?

S. Nothing tends more to alienate friendship than insult.

H. The words I uttered hurt me more than they did you.

S. It was not words merely, but actions as well.

H. Nothing I can say or do can ever alter my fondness for you—Ah, Sarah! I am unworthy of your love: I hardly dare ask for your pity; but oh! save me—save me from your scorn: I cannot bear it—it withers me like lightning.

S. I bear no malice, Sir; but my brother, who would scorn to tell a lie for his sister, can bear witness for me that there was no truth in what you were told.

H. I believe it; or there is no truth in woman. It is enough for me to know that you do not return my regard; it would be too much for me to think that you did not deserve it. But cannot you forgive the agony of the moment?

S. I can forgive; but it is not easy to forget some things!

H. Nay, my sweet Sarah (frown if you will, I can bear your resentment for my ill behaviour, it is only your scorn and indifference that harrow up my soul)—but I was going to ask, if you had been engaged to be married to any one, and the day was fixed, and he had heard what I did, whether he could have felt any true regard for the character of his bride, his wife, if he had not been hurt and alarmed as I was?

S. I believe, actual contracts of marriage have

sometimes been broken off by unjust suspicions.

H. Or had it been your old friend, what do you think he would have said in my case?

S. He would never have listened to anything of the sort.

H. He had greater reasons for confidence than I have. But it is your repeated cruel rejection of me that drives me almost to madness. Tell me, love, is there not, besides your attachment to him, a repugnance to me?

S. No, none whatever.

H. I fear there is an original dislike, which no efforts of mine can overcome.

S. It is not *you*—it is my feelings with respect to another, which are unalterable.

H. And yet you have no hope of ever being his? And yet you accuse me of being romantic in my sentiments.

S. I have indeed long ceased to hope; but yet I sometimes hope against hope.

H. My love, were it in my power, thy hopes should be fulfilled to-morrow! Next to my own, there is nothing that could give me so much satisfaction as to see thine realized! Do I not love thee, when I can feel such an interest in thy love for another? It was that which first wedded my very soul to you. I would give worlds for a share in a heart so rich in pure affection!

S. And yet I did not tell you of the circumstance to raise myself in your opinion.

H. You are a sublime little thing! and yet, as you have no prospects there, I cannot help thinking, the best thing would be to do as I have said.

S. I would never marry a man I did not love beyond all the world.

H. I should be satisfied with less than that—with the love, or regard, or whatever you call it, you have shown me before marriage, if that has only been sincere. You would hardly like me less afterwards.

S. Endearments would, I should think, increase regard, where there was love beforehand ; but that is not exactly my case.

H. But I think you would be happier than you are at present. You take pleasure in my conversation, and you say you have an esteem for me ; and it is upon this, after the honeymoon, that marriage chiefly turns.

S. Do you think there is no pleasure in a single life ?

H. Do you mean on account of its liberty ?

S. No, but I feel that forced duty is no duty. I have high ideas of the married state !

H. Higher than of the maiden state ?

S. I understand you, Sir.

H. I meant nothing ; but you have sometimes spoken of any serious attachment as a tie upon you. It is not that you prefer flirting with 'gay young men' to becoming a mere dull domestic wife ?

S. You have no right to throw out such insinuations : for though I am but a tradesman's daughter, I have as nice a sense of honour as anyone can have.

H. Talk of tradesman's daughter ! You would ennoble any family, thou glorious girl, by true nobility of mind.

S. Oh ! Sir, you flatter me. I know my own inferiority to most.

H. To none ; there is no one above thee, man nor woman either. You are above your situation, which is not fit for you.

S. I am contented with my lot, and do my duty as cheerfully as I can.

H. Have you not told me your spirits grow worse every year ?

S. Not on that account : but some disappointments are hard to bear up against.

H. If you talk about that, you'll unman me. But tell me, my love—I have thought of it as something that might account for some circumstances; that is, as a mere possibility. But tell me, there was not a likeness between me and your old lover that struck you at first sight? Was there?

S. No, Sir, none.

H. Well, I didn't think it likely there should.

S. But there was a likeness.

H. To whom?

S. To that little image! (*looking intently on a small bronze figure of Bonaparte on the mantelpiece.*)

H. What, do you mean to Bonaparte?

S. Yes, all but the nose was just like.

H. And was his figure the same?

S. He was taller!

[*I got up and gave her the image, and told her it was hers by every right that was sacred. She refused at first to take so valuable a curiosity, and said she would keep it for me. But I pressed it eagerly, and she took it. She immediately came and sat down, and put her arm round my neck, and kissed me, and I said 'Is it not plain we are the best friends in the world, since we are always so glad to make it up?' And then I added how odd it was that the god of my idolatry should turn out to be like her Idol, and said it was no wonder that the same face which awed the world should conquer the sweetest creature in it! How I loved her at that moment! Is it possible that the wretch who writes this could ever have been so blest! Heavenly delicious creature! Can I live without her?—Oh! no—never—never.*

What is this world? What asken men to have,
Now with his love, now in the cold grave,
Alone, withouten any compagnie!

*Let me but see her again! She cannot hate the man who loves her as I do.*]

## *Letters to the Same*

*Feb.*, 1822.

You will scold me for this, and ask me if this is keeping my promise to mind my work. One half of it was to think of Sarah: and besides, I do not neglect my work either, I assure you. I regularly do ten pages a day, which mounts up to thirty guineas' worth a week, so that you see I should grow rich at this rate, if I could keep on so; *and I could keep on so*, if I had you with me to encourage me with your sweet smiles, and share my lot. The Berwick smacks sail twice a week, and the wind sits fair. When I think of the thousand endearing caresses that have passed between us, I do not wonder at the strong attachment that draws me to you; but I am sorry for my own want of power to please. I hear the wind sigh through the lattice, and keep repeating over and over to myself two lines of Lord Byron's tragedy:

> So shalt thou find me ever at thy side.
> Here and hereafter, if the last may be,

applying them to thee, my love, and thinking whether I shall ever see thee again. Perhaps not—for some years at least—till both thou and I are old—and then, when all else have forsaken thee, I will creep to thee, and die in thine arms. You once made me believe I was not hated by her I loved; and for that sensation, so delicious was it, though but a mockery and a dream, I owe you more than I can ever pay. I thought to have dried up my tears for ever, the day I left you; but as I write this, they stream again. If they did not, I think my heart would burst. I walk out here of an afternoon, and hear the notes of the thrush, that comes up from a sheltered valley below, welcome in the spring ; but they do not melt my heart as they used ; it is grown cold and dead. As you say it will one day be colder.—Forgive what I have written above ; I did not intend it ; but you were once my little all, and I cannot bear the thought of having lost you forever, I fear through my own fault. Has anyone called ? Do send any letters that come. I should like you and your mother (if agreeable) to go and see Mr. Kean in Othello, and Miss Stephens in Love in a Village. If you will, I will write to Mr. T——, to send you tickets. Has Mr. P—— called ? I think I must send to him for the picture to kiss and talk to. . Kiss me my best beloved. Ah ! if you can never be mine, still let me be your proud and happy slave.

H.

## *To the Same*

*March*, 1822.

You will be glad to learn I have done my work—a volume in less than a month. This is one reason why I am better than when I came, and another is, I have had two letters from Sarah. I am pleased I have got through this job, as I was afraid I might lose reputation by it (which I can little afford to lose)—and besides, I am more anxious to do well now, as I wish you to hear me well spoken of. I walk out of an afternoon, and hear the birds sing as I told you, and think, if I had you hanging on my arm, *and that for life*, how happy I should be—happier than I ever hoped to be, or had any conception of till I knew you. '*But that can never be*'—I hear you answer in a soft, low murmur. Well, let me dream of it sometimes—I am not happy too often, except when that favourite note, the harbinger of spring, recalling the hopes of my youth, whispers thy name and peace together in my ear. I was reading something about Mr. Macready to-day, and this put me in mind of that delicious night, when I went with your mother and you to see Romeo and Juliet. Can I forget it for a moment—your sweet modest looks, your infinite propriety of behaviour, all your sweet winning ways—your hesitating about taking my arm as we came out till your mother did—your laughing about nearly losing your cloak—your stepping into the coach without my being able to make the slightest discovery—and oh! my sitting down beside you there, you whom I had loved so long, so well, and your assuring me I had not lessened your pleasure at the play by being with you, and giving me your dear hand to press in mine! I thought I was in heaven—that slender, exquisitely-turned form contained my all of heaven upon earth; and as I folded you—yes, you, my own best Sarah, to my bosom, there was, as you say, *a tie between us*—you did seem to me, for those few short moments, to be mine in all truth and honour and sacredness—Oh! that we could be always so—Do not mock me, for I am a very child in love. I ought to beg pardon for behaving so ill afterwards, but I hope the *little image* made it up between us, etc.

[To this letter I have received no answer, not a line. The rolling years of eternity will never fill up that blank. Where shall I be? What am I? Or where have I been?]

# LIBER AMORIS

## *PART II*

## *Written in a Blank Leaf on Endymion*

I want a hand to guide me, an eye to cheer me, a bosom to repose on ; all which I shall never have, but shall stagger into my grave, old before my time, unloved and unlovely, unless S.L. keeps her faith with me.

* * *

—But by her dove's eyes and serpent shape, I think she does not hate me ; by her smooth forehead and her crested hair, I own I love her ; by her soft looks and queen-like grace (which men might fall down and worship), I swear to live and die for her !

# *A Proposal of Love*

[*Given to her in our early acquaintance*]

Oh ! if I thought it could be in a woman
(As, if it can, I will presume in you)
To feed for aye her lamp and flames of love,
To keep her constancy in plight and youth,
Outliving beauties outward with a mind
That doth renew swifter than blood decays :
Or that persuasion could but thus convince me,
That my integrity and truth to you
Might be confronted with the match and weight
Of such a winnowed purity in love—
How were I then uplifted ! But, alas,
I am as true as truth's simplicity,
And simpler than the infancy of truth.

TROILUS AND CRESSIDA.

# *Letters to C.P.—Esq.*

*Bees-Inn.*

My Good Friend,

Here I am in Scotland (and shall have been here three weeks, next Monday) as I may say, *on my probation.* This is a lone inn, but on a great scale, thirty miles from Edinburgh. It is situated on a rising ground (a mark for all the winds, which blow here incessantly)—there is a woody hill opposite, with a winding valley below, and the London road stretches out on either side. You may guess which way I oftenest walk. I have written two letters to S. L. and got one cold, prudish answer, beginning *Sir,* and ending *From yours truly,* with *Best respects from herself and relations.* I was going to give in, but have returned an answer, which I think is a touch-stone. I send it you on the other side to keep as a curiosity, in case she kills me by her exquisite rejoinder. I am convinced from the profound contemplations I have had on the subject here and coming along, that I am on the wrong scent. We had a famous parting-scene, a complete quarrel and then a reconciliation, in which she did beguile me of my tears, but the deuce a one did she shed. What do you think ? She cajoled me out of my little Bonaparte as cleverly as possible in manner and form following. She was shy the Saturday and Sunday (the day of my departure) so I got in dudgeon, and began to rip up grievances. I asked her how she came to admit me to such extreme familiarities, the first week I entered the house. 'If she had no particular regard for me, she must do so (or more) with everyone : if she had a liking to me from the first, why refuse me with scorn and wilfulness ? ' If you had seen how she flounced, and looked, and went to the door, saying ' She was obliged to me for letting her know the opinion I had always entertained of her '—then I said, ' Sarah ! '—and she came back and took my hand, and fixed her eyes on the mantelpiece—(she must have been invoking her idol then—if I thought so, I could devour her, the darling—but I doubt her).—So I said ' There is one thing that has occurred to me sometimes as possible, to account for your conduct to me at first—there wasn't a likeness, was there, to your old friend ? ' She answered ' No, none—but there was a likeness.' I asked to what ? She said, ' to that little image ! ' I said ' Do you mean Bonaparte ? ' She said ' Yes, all but the nose.' ' And the figure ? ' ' He was taller,'—I could not stand this. So I got up and took it, and gave it her, and after some reluctance, she consented to ' keep it for me.' What will you bet me that it wasn't all a trick ? I'll tell you why I suspect it, besides being fairly out of my wits about her. I had told her mother half an hour before, that I should take this image and leave it at Mrs. B.'s, for that I didn't wish to leave anything behind me that must bring me back again. Then up she comes and starts a likeness to her lover : she knew I should give it her on the spot—' No, she would keep it for me ! ' So I must come back for it. Whether art or nature, it is sublime. I told her I should write and tell you so, and that I parted from her, confiding, adoring !—She is beyond me, that's certain. Do go and see her, and desire her not to give my present address to a single soul, and learn if the lodging is let, and to whom. My letter to her is as follows. If she shews the least remorse at it, I'll be hanged, though it might move a stone, I modestly think. (*See before, Part I, Page* 29).

N.B.—I have begun a book of our conversations

(I mean mine and the statue's), which I call *Liber Amoris*. I was detained at Stamford and found myself dull, and could hit upon no other way of employing my time so agreeably.

# *Letter II*

Dear P——,

Here, without loss of time, in order that I may have your opinion upon it, is little YES and NO's answer to my last.

Sir,

'I should not have disregarded your injunction not to send you any more letters that might come to you, had I not promised the gentleman who left the enclosed to forward it the earliest opportunity, as he said it was *of consequence*. Mr. P—— called the day after you left town. My mother and myself are much obliged by your kind offer of tickets to the play, but must decline accepting it. My family send their best respects, in which they are joined by

Yours truly,

S. L.,

The deuce a bit more is there of it. If you can make anything out of it (or anybody else) I'll be hanged. You are to understand, this comes in a frank, the second I have received from her, with a name I can't make out, and she won't tell me, though I asked her, where she got franks, as also whether the lodgings were let, to neither of which a word of answer * * * is the name of the frank: see if you can decypher it by a Red-book. I suspect her grievously of being an arrant jilt, to say no more—yet I love her dearly. Do you know I'm going to write to that sweet rogue presently, having a whole evening to myself in advance of my work? Now mark, before you set about your exposition of the new Apocalypse of the new Calypso, the only thing to be endured in the above letter is the date. It was written the very day after she received mine. By this she seems willing to lose no time in receiving these letters 'of such sweet breath composed.' If I thought so—but I wait for your reply. After all, what is there in her but a pretty figure, and that you can't get a word out of her? Hers is the Fabian method of making love and conquests. What do you suppose she said the night before I left her?

'H. Could you not come and live with me as a friend?

S. I don't know: and yet it would be of no use if I did, you would always be hankering after what could never be!'

I asked her if she would do so at once—the very next day? And what do you guess was her answer: 'Do you think it would be prudent?' As I didn't proceed to extremities on the spot, she began to look grave, and declare off.—'Would she live with me in her own house—to be with me all day as dear friends, if nothing more, to sit and read and talk with me?'—'She would make no promises, but I should find her the same.'—'Would she go to the play with me sometimes, and let it be understood that I was paying my addresses to her?'—'She could not, as a habit—her father was rather strict, and would object.'—Now what am I to think of all this? Am I mad or a fool? Answer me that, Master Brook! You are a philosopher.

## *Letter III*

DEAR FRIEND,

I ought to have written to you before; but since I received your letter, I have been in a sort of purgatory, and what is worse, I see no prospect of getting out of it. I would put an end to my torments at once; but I am as great a coward as I have been a dupe. Do you know I have not had a word of answer from her since! What can be the reason? Is she offended at my letting you know she wrote to me, or is it some new affair? I wrote to her in the tenderest, most respectful manner, poured my soul at her feet, and this is the return she makes me! Can you account for it, except on the admission of my worst doubts concerning her? Oh God! can I bear after all to think of her so, or that I am scorned and made a sport of by the creature to whom I had given my whole heart?—Thus has it been with me all my life; and so will it be to the end of it!—If you should learn anything, good or bad, tell me, I conjure you: I can bear anything but this cruel suspense. If I knew she was a mere abandoned creature, I should try to forget her; but till I do not know this, nothing can tear me from her, I have drank in poison from her lips too long—alas! mine do not poison again. I sit and indulge my grief by the hour together; my weakness grows upon me; and I have no hope left, unless I could lose my senses quite. Do you know I think I should like this? To forget, ah! to forget—there would be something in that—to change to an idiot for some few years, and then to wake up a poor wretched old man, to recollect my misery as past, and die! Yet, oh! with her, only a little while ago, I had different hopes, forfeited for nothing that I know of! * * * If you can give me any consolation on the subject of my tormentor, pray do. The pain I suffer wears me out daily. I write this on the supposition that Mrs.—— may still come here, and that I may be detained some weeks longer. Direct to me at the Post-office; and if I return to town directly, as I fear, I will leave word for them to forward the letter to me in London—not at my old lodgings. I will not go back there: yet how can I breathe away from her? Her hatred of me must be great, since my love of her could not overcome it! I have finished the book of my conversations with her, which I told you of: if I am not mistaken, you will think it very nice reading.

Yours ever.

Have you read Sardanapalus?—How like the little Greek slave, Myrrha, is to *her*!

## *Letter IV*

[*Written in the winter*]

My Good Friend,

I received your letter this morning, and I kiss the rod not only with submission, but gratitude. Your reproofs of me and your defences of her are the only things that save my soul from perdition. She is my heart's idol; and believe me those words of yours applied to the dear saint,—'To lip a chaste one and suppose her wanton,' were balm and rapture to me. I have *lipped her*, God knows how often, and, oh, is it even possible that she is chaste, and that she has bestowed her loved 'endearments', on me (her own sweet word) out of true regard? That thought, out of the lowest depths of despair, would at any time make me strike my forehead against the stars. Could I but think the love 'honest' I am proof against all hazards. She by her silence makes my *dark hour;* and you by your encouragements dissipate it for twenty-four hours. Another thing has brought me to life. Mrs.—— is actually on her way here about the divorce. Should this unpleasant business (which has been so long talked of) succeed, and I should become free, do you think S. L. will agree to change her name to——? If she *will*, she *shall*; and to call her so to you, or to hear her called so by others, would be music to my ears, such as they never drank in. Do you think if she knew how I love her, my depressions and my altitudes, my wanderings and my constancy, it would not move her? She knows it all; and if she is not an *incorrigible*, she loves me, or regards me with a feeling next to love. I don't believe that any woman was ever courted more passionately than she has been by me. As Rousseau said of Madame d'Houptot (forgive the allusion) my heart has found a tongue in speaking to her, and I have talked to her the divine language of love. Yet she says, she is insensible to it. Am I to believe her or you ? You—for I wish it to madness, now that I am like to be free, and to have it in my power to say to her without a possibility of suspicion 'Sarah, will you be mine ? ' When I sometimes think of the time I first saw the sweet apparition, August 16, 1820, and that possibly she may be my bride before that day two years, it makes me dizzy with incredible joy and love of her. Write soon.

## *Letter V*

MY DEAR FRIEND,

I read your answer this morning with gratitude. I have felt somewhat easier since. It showed your interest in my vexations, and also that you know nothing worse than I do. I cannot describe the weakness of mind to which she has reduced me. This state of suspense is like hanging in the air by a single thread that exhausts all your strength to keep hold of it ; and yet if that fails you, you have nothing in the world else left to trust to. I am come back to Edinburgh about this cursed business, and Mrs.—— is coming from Montrose next week. How will it end, I can't say; and don't care, except as it regards the other affair. I should, I confess, like to have it in my power to make her the offer direct and unequivocal, to see how she'd receive it. It would be worth something at any rate to see her superfine airs upon the occasion ; and if she should take it into her head to turn round her sweet neck, drop her eye-lids, and say 'Yes, I will be yours !'—why then, 'treason domestic, foreign levy, nothing could touch me further.' By Heaven ! I doat on her. The truth is, I never had any pleasure, like love, with anyone but her. Then how can I bear to part with her ? Do you know I like to think of her best in her morning-gown and mob-cap—it is so she has oftenest come into my room and enchanted me ! She was once ill, pale, and had lost all her freshness. I only adored her the more for it, and fell in love with the decay of her beauty. I could devour the little witch. If she had a plague-spot on her, I could touch the infection : if she was in a burning fever, I could kiss her, and drink death as I have drank life from her lips. When I press her hand, I enjoy perfect happiness and contentment of soul. It is not what she says or what she does—it is herself that I love. To be with her is to be at peace. I have no other wish or desire. The air about her is serene, blissful ; and he who breathes it is like one of the gods ! So that I can but have her with me always, I care for nothing more. I never could tire of her sweetness ! I feel that I could grow to her, body and soul ? My heart, my heart is hers.

## *Letter VI*

[*Written in May.*]

Dear P——,

What have I suffered since I parted with you! A raging fire is in my heart and in my brain that never quits me. The steam-boat (which I foolishly ventured on board) seems a prison-house, a sort of spectre-ship, moving on through an infernal lake, without wind or tide, by some necromantic power—the splashing of the waves, the noise of the engine gives me no rest, night or day—no tree, no natural object varies the scene—but the abyss is before me, and all my peace lies weltering in it! I feel the eternity of punishment in this life; for I see no end of my woes. The people about me are ill, uncomfortable, wretched enough, many of them—but to-morrow or next day, they reach the place of their destination, and all will be new and delightful. To me it will be the same. I can neither escape from her, nor from myself. All is endurable where there is a limit; but I have nothing but the blackness and the fiendishness of scorn around me—mocked by her (the false one) in whom I placed my hope, and who hardens herself against me!—I believe you thought me quite gay, vain, insolent, half mad, the night I left the house—no tongue can tell the heaviness of heart I felt at that moment. No footsteps ever fell more slow, more sad than mine; for every step bore me farther from her, with whom my soul and every thought lingered. I had parted with her in anger, and each had spoken words of high disdain, not soon to be forgiven. Should I ever behold her again? Where go to live and die far from her? In her sight there was Elysium; her smile was heaven ; her voice was enchantment ; the air of love waved round her, breathing balm into my heart ; for a little while I had sat with the gods at their golden tables, I had tasted of all earth's bliss, 'both living and loving !' But now Paradise barred its doors against me ; I was driven from her presence, where rosy blushes and delicious sighs and all soft wishes dwelt, the outcast of nature and the scoff of love ! I thought of the time when I was a little happy careless child, of my father's house, of my early lessons, of my brother's picture of me when a boy, of all that had since happened to me, and of the waste of years to come—I stopped, faltered, and was going to turn back once more to make a longer truce with wretchedness, and patch up a hollow league with love, when the recollection of her words—'I always told you I had no affection for you'—steeled my resolution, and I determined to proceed. You see by this she always hated me, and only played with my credulity till she could find some one to supply the place of her unalterable attachment to *the little image.* * * *

I am a little, a very little better to-day. Would it were quietly over ; and that this misshapen form (made to be mocked) were hid out of the sight of cold, sullen eyes ! The people about me even take notice of my dumb despair, and pity me. What is to be done ? I cannot forget *her* ; and I can find no other like what *she seemed*. I should wish you to call, if you can make an excuse, and see whether or no she is quite marble—whether I may go back again at my return, and whether she will see me and talk to me sometimes as an old friend. Suppose you were to call on M—— from me, and ask him what his impression is that I ought to do. But do as you think best. Pardon, pardon.

*P.S.*—I send this from Scarborough, where the vessel stops for a few minutes. I scarcely know what I should have done, but for this relief to my feelings.

## *Letter VII*

My Dear Friend,

The important step is taken, and I am virtually a free man. * * * What had I better do in these circumstances ? I dare not write to her, I dare not write to her father, or else I would. She has shot me through with poisoned arrows, and I think another 'winged wound' would finish me. It is a pleasant sort of balm (as you express it) she has left in my heart ! One thing I agree with you in, it will remain there for ever; but yet not very long. It festers, and consumes me. If it were not for my little boy, whose face I see struck blank at the news, looking through the world for pity and meeting with contempt instead, I should soon, I fear, settle the question by my death. That recollection is the only thought that brings my wandering reason to an anchor ; that stirs the smallest interest in me ; or gives me fortitude to bear up against what I am doomed to feel for the *ungrateful*. Otherwise I am dead to everything but the sense of what I have lost. She was my life—it is gone from me, and I am grown spectral ! If I find myself in a place I am acquainted with, it reminds me of her, of the way in which I thought of her,

> And carved on every tree
> The soft, the fair, the inexpressive she !

If it is a place that is new to me, it is desolate, barren of all interest ; for nothing touches me but what has a reference to her. If the clock strikes, the sound jars me ; a million of hours will not bring back peace to my breast. The light startles me ; the darkness terrifies me. I seem falling into a pit, without a hand to help me. She has deceived me, and the earth fails from under my feet; no object in nature is substantial, real, but false and hollow, like her faith on which I built my trust. She came (I knew not how) and sat by my side and was folded in my arms, a vision of love and joy, as if she had dropped from the Heavens to bless me by some especial dispensation of a favouring Providence, and make me amends for all; and now without any fault of mine but too much fondness, she has vanished from me, and I am left to perish. My heart is torn out of me, with every feeling for which I wished to live. The whole is like a dream, an effect of enchantment; it torments me, and it drives me mad. I lie down with it; I rise up with it; and see no chance of repose. I grasp at a shadow, I try to undo the past, and weep with rage and pity over my own weakness and misery. I spared her again and again (fool that I was) thinking what she allowed from me was love, friendship, sweetness, not wantonness. How could I doubt it, looking in her face, and hearing her words, like sighs breathed from the gentlest of all bosoms? I had hopes, I had prospects to come, the flattery of something like fame, a pleasure in writing, health even would have come back with her smile—she has blighted all, turned all to poison and childish tears. Yet the barbed arrow is in my heart—I can neither endure it, nor draw it out; for with it flows my life's-blood. I had conversed too long with abstracted truth to trust myself with the immortal thoughts of love. *That S. L. might have been mine, and now never can*—these are the two sole propositions that for ever stare me in the face, and look ghastly in at my poor brain. I am in some sense proud that I can feel this dreadful passion—it gives me a kind of rank in the kingdom of love—but I could have wished it had been for an object that at least could have understood its value and pitied its excess. You say her not coming to the door when you went is a proof—yes, that her complement is at present full! That is the reason she doesn't want me there, lest I should discover the new affair—wretch that I am! Another has possession of her, oh Hell! I'm satisfied of it from her manner, which had a wanton insolence in it. Well might I run wild when I received no letters from her. I foresaw, I felt my fate. The gates of Paradise were once open to me too, and I blushed to enter but with the golden keys of love! I would die; but her lover—my love of her—ought not to die. When I am dead, who will love her as I have done? If she should be in misfortune, who will comfort her? when she is old, who will look in her face, and bless her? Would there be any harm in calling upon M——, to know confidentially if he thinks it worth my while to make her an offer the instant it is in my power? Let me have an answer, and save me, if possible, *for* her and *from* myself.

## *Letter VIII*

My Dear Friend,

Your letter raised me for a moment from the depth of despair; but not hearing from you yesterday or to-day (as I hoped) I have had a relapse. You say I want to get rid of her. I hope you are more right in your conjectures about her than in this about me. Oh no! believe it, I love her as I do my own soul; my very heart is wedded to her (be she what she may) and I would not hesitate a moment between her and 'an angel from Heaven.' I grant all you say about my self-tormenting folly; but has it been without cause? Has she not refused me again and again with a mixture of scorn and resentment, after going the utmost lengths with a man for whom she now disclaims all affection; and what security can I have for her reserve with others, who will not be restrained by feelings of delicacy towards her, and whom she has probably preferred to me for their want of it. '*She can make no more confidences*'—these words ring for ever in my ears, and will be my death-watch. They can have but one meaning, be sure of it—she always expressed herself with the exactest propriety. That was one of the things for which I loved her—shall I live to hate her for it? My poor fond heart, that brooded over her and the remains of her affections as my only hope of comfort upon earth, cannot brook this new degradation. Who is there so low as me? Who is there besides (I ask) after the homage I have paid her and the caresses she has lavished on me, so vile, so abhorrent to love, to whom such an indignity could have happened? When

I think of this (and I think of nothing else) it stifles me. I am pent up in burning, fruitless desires, which can find no vent or object. Am I not hated, repulsed, derided by her whom alone I love or ever did love ? I cannot stay in any place, and seek in vain for relief from the sense of her contempt and her ingratitude. I can settle to nothing ; what is the use of all I have done ? Is it not that very circumstance (my thinking beyond my strength, my feelings more than I need about so many things) that has withered me up, and made me a thing for Love to shrink from and wonder at ? Who could ever feel that peace from the touch of her dear hand that I have done ; and is it not torn from me for ever ? My state is this, that I shall never lie down again at night nor rise up in the morning in peace, nor ever behold my little boy's face with pleasure while I live—unless I am restored to her favour. Instead of that delicious feeling I had when she was heavenly-kind to me, and my heart softened and melted in its own tenderness and her sweetness, I am now inclosed in a dungeon of despair. The sky is marble to my thoughts ; nature is dead around me, as hope is within me ; no object can give me one gleam of satisfaction now, nor the prospect of it in time to come. I wander by the sea-side ; and the eternal ocean and lasting despair and her face are before me. Slighted by her, on whom my heart by its last fibre hung, where shall I turn ? I wake with her by my side, not as my sweet bedfellow, but as the corpse of my love, without a heart in her bosom, cold, insensible, or struggling from me ; and the worm gnaws me, and the sting of unrequited love, and the canker of a hopeless, endless sorrow. I have lost the taste of my food by feverish anxiety ; and my favourite beverage, which used to refresh me when I got up, has no moisture in it. Oh ! cold, solitary, sepulchral breakfasts, compared with those which I promised myself with her ; or which I made when she had been standing an hour by my side, my guardian-angel, my wife, my sister, my sweet friend, my Eve, my all ; and had blest me with her seraph kisses ! Ah ! what I suffer at present only shows what I have enjoyed. But 'the girl is a good girl, if there is goodness in human nature.' I thank you for those words ; and I will fall down and worship you, if you can prove them true : and I would not do much less for him that proves her a demon. She is one or the other, that's certain ; but I fear the worst. Do let me know if anything has passed : suspense is my greatest punishment. I am going into the country to see if I can work a little in the three weeks I have yet to say here. Write on the receipt of this, and believe me your unspeakably obliged friend.

## *To Edinburgh*

'Stony-hearted' Edinburgh! What art thou to me? The dust of thy streets mingles with my tears and blinds me. City of palaces, or of tombs—a quarry, rather than the habitation of men! Art thou like London, that populous hive, with its sunburnt, well-baked, brick-built houses—its public edifices, its theatres, its bridges, its squares, its ladies, and its pomp, its throng of wealth, its outstretched magnitude, and its mighty heart that never lies still? Thy cold grey walls reflect back the leaden melancholy of the soul. The square, hard-edged, unyielding faces of thy inhabitants have no sympathy to impart. What is it to me that I look along the level line of thy tenantless streets, and meet perhaps a lawyer like a grasshopper chirping and skipping, or the daughter of a Highland laird, haughty, fair, and freckled? Or why should I look down your boasted Princes Street, with the beetle-browed Castle on one side, and the Calton Hill with its proud monument at the further end, and the ridgy steep of Salisbury Crag, cut off abruptly by Nature's boldest hand, and Arthur's Seat overlooking all, like a lioness watching her cubs? Or shall I turn to the far-off Pentland Hills, with Craig-Crook nestling beneath them, where lives the prince of critics and the king of men? Or cast my eye unsated over the Firth of Forth, that from my window of an evening (as I read of AMY and her love) glitters like a broad golden mirror in the sun, and kisses the winding shores of kingly Fife ? Oh no ! But to thee, to thee I turn, North Berwick-Law, with thy blue cone rising out of summer seas ; for thou art the beacon of my banished thoughts, and dost point my way to her, who is my heart's true home. The air is too thin for me, that hast not the breath of Love in it ; that is not embalmed with her sighs !

## *A Thought*

I am not mad, but my heart is so ; and raves within me, fierce and untameable, like a panther in its den, and tries to get loose to its lost mate, and fawn on her hand, and bend lowly at her feet.

## *Another*

Oh ! thou dumb heart, lonely, sad, shut up in prison-house of this rude form, that hast never found a fellow but for an instant, and in very mockery of thy misery, speak, find bleeding words to express thy thoughts, break thy dungeon-gloom, or die pronouncing thy Infelice's name !

## *Another*

Within my heart is lurking suspicion, and base fear, and shame and hate ; but above all, tyrannous love sits throned, crowned with her graces, silent and in tears.

## *Letter IX*

My Dear P——

You have been very kind to me in this business; but I fear even your indulgence for my infirmities is beginning to fail. To what a state am I reduced, and for what? For fancying a little artful vixen to be an angel and a saint, because she affected to look like one, to hide her rank thoughts and deadly purposes. Has she not murdered me under the mask of the tenderest friendship? And why? Because I have loved her with unutterable love, and sought to make her my wife. You say it is my own 'outrageous conduct' that has estranged her: nay, I have been *too gentle* with her. I ask you first in candour whether the ambiguity of her behaviour with respect to me, sitting and fondling a man (circumstanced as I was) sometimes for half a day together, and then declaring she had no love for him beyond common regard, and professing never to marry, was not enough to excite my suspicions, which the different exposures from the conversations below-stairs were not calculated to allay? I ask you what you yourself would have felt or done, if loving her as I did, you had heard what I did, time after time? Did not her mother own to one of the grossest charges (which I shall not repeat)—and is such indelicacy to be reconciled with her pretended character (that character with which I fell in love, and to which I *made love*) without supposing her to be the greatest hypocrite in the world? My unpardonable offence has been that I took her at her word, and was willing to believe her the precise little puritanical person she set up for. After exciting her wayward desires by the fondest embraces and the purest kisses, as if she had been 'made my wedded wife yestreen', or was to become so to-morrow (for that was always my feeling with respect to her)—I did not proceed to gratify them, or to follow up my advantage by any action which should declare 'I think you a common adventurer, and will see whether you are so or not?' Yet anyone but a credulous fool like me would have made the experiment, with whatever violence to himself, as a matter of life and death; for I had every reason to distrust appearances. Her conduct has been of a piece from the beginning. In the midst of her closest and falsest endearments, she has always (with one or two exceptions) disclaimed the natural inference to be drawn from them, and made a verbal reservation, by which she might lead me on in a Fool's Paradise, and make me the tool of her levity, her avarice, and her love of intrigue as long as she liked, and dismiss me whenever it suited her. This, you see, she has done, because my intentions grew serious, and if complied with, would deprive her of *the pleasures of a single life*! Offer marriage to this 'tradesman's daughter, who has as nice a sense of honour as anyone can have'; and like Lady Bellaston in *Tom Jones*, she *cuts* you immediately in a fit of abhorrence and alarm. Yet she seemed to be of a different mind formerly, when struggling from me in the height of our first intimacy, she exclaimed 'However I might agree to my own ruin, I never will consent to bring disgrace upon my family!' That I should have spared the traitress after expressions like this astonishes me when I look back upon it. Yet, if it were all to do over again, I know I should act just the same part. Such is her power over me! I cannot run the least risk of offending her—I love her so. When I look in her face, I cannot doubt her truth! Wretched being that I am! I have thrown away my heart and soul upon an unfeeling girl ; and my life (that might have been so happy, had she been what I thought her) will soon follow either voluntarily, or by the force of grief, remorse, and disappointment. I cannot get rid of the reflection for an instant, nor even seek relief from its galling pressure. Ah ! what a heart she has lost ! All the love and affection of my whole life were centered in her, who alone, I thought, of all women had found out my true character, and knew how to value my tenderness. Alas ! alas ! that this, the only hope, joy, or comfort I ever had, should turn to a mockery, and hang like an ugly film over the remainder of my days !—I was at Roslin Castle yesterday. It lies low in a rude, but sheltered valley, hid from the vulgar gaze, and powerfully reminds one of the old song. The straggling fragments of the russet ruins, suspended smiling and graceful in the air as if they would linger out another century to please the curious beholder, the green larch-trees trembling between with the blue sky and white silver clouds, the wild mountain plants starting out here and there, the date of the year on an old low door-way, but still more, the beds of flowers in orderly decay, that seem to have no hand to tend them, but keep up a sort of traditional remembrance of civilization in former ages, present altogether a delightful and amiable subject for contemplation. The exquisite beauty of the scene, with the thought of what I should feel, should I ever be restored to her, and have to lead her through such places as my adored, my angel-wife, almost drove me beside myself. For this picture, this ecstatic vision, what have I of late instead as the image of the reality ? Demoniacal possessions. I see the young witch seated in another's lap, twining her serpent arms round him, her eye glancing and her cheeks on fire—why does not the hideous thought choke me ? Or why do I not go and find out the truth at once ? The moonlight streams over the silver waters: the bark is in the bay that might waft me to her, almost with a wish. The mountain-breeze sighs out her name: old ocean with a world of tears murmurs back my woes! Does not my heart yearn to be with her; and shall I not follow its bidding? No, I must wait till I am free; and then I will take my Freedom (a glad prize) and lay it at her feet and tell her my proud love of her that would not brook a rival in her dishonour, and that would have her all or none, and gain her or lose myself forever!—

You see by this letter the way I am in, and I hope you will excuse it as the picture of a half-disordered mind. The least respite from my uneasiness (such as I had yesterday) only brings the contrary reflection back upon me, like a flood; and by letting me see the happiness I have lost, makes me feel, by contrast, more acutely what I am doomed to bear.

## *Letter X*

Dear Friend,

Here I am at St. Bees once more, amid the scenes which I greeted in their barrenness in winter; but which have now put on their full green attire that shows luxuriant to the eye, but speaks a tale of sadness to this heart widowed of its last, its dearest, its only hope? Oh! lovely Bees-Inn! here I composed a volume of law-cases, here I wrote my enamoured follies to her, thinking her human, and that 'all below was not the fiend's'—here I got two cold, sullen answers from the little witch, and here I was——and I was damned. I thought the revisiting the old haunts would have soothed me for a time, but it only brings back the sense of what I have suffered for her and of her unkindness the more strongly, till I cannot endure the recollection. I eye the Heavens in dumb despair, or vent my sorrows in the desert air. 'To the winds, to the waves, to the rocks I complain'—you may suppose with what effect! I fear I shall be obliged to return. I am tossed about (backwards and forwards) by my passion, so as to become ridiculous. I can now understand how it is that mad people never remain in the same place—they are moving on for ever, *from themselves*!

Do you know, you would have been delighted with the effect of the Northern twilight on this romantic country as I rode along last night? The hills and groves and herds of cattle were seen reposing in the grey dawn of midnight, as in moonlight without shadow. The whole wide canopy of Heaven shed its reflex light upon them, like a pure crystal mirror. No sharp points, no petty details, no hard contrasts—every object was seen softened yet distinct, in its simple outline and natural tones, transparent with an inward light, breathing its own mild lustre. The landscape altogether was like an airy piece of mosaic-work, or like one of Poussin's broad massy landscapes, or Titian's lovely pastoral scenes. Is it not so, that poets see nature, veiled to the sight, but revealed to the soul in visionary grace and grandeur! I confess the sight touched me; and might have removed all sadness except mine. So (I thought) the light of her celestial face once shone into my soul, and wrapped me in a heavenly trance. The sense I have of beauty raises me for a moment above myself, but depresses me the more afterwards, when I recollect how it is thrown away in vain admiration, and that it only makes me more susceptible of pain from the mortifications I meet with. Would I had never seen her! I might then not indeed have been happy, but at least I might have passed my life in peace, and sunk into forgetfulness without a pang. The noble scenery in this country mixes with my passion, and refines, but does not relieve it. I was at Stirling Castle not long ago. It gave me no pleasure. The declivity seemed to me abrupt, not sublime; for in truth I did not shrink back from it with terror. The weather-beaten towers were stiff and formal: the air was damp and chill: the river winded its dull, slimy way like a snake along the marshy grounds: and the dim misty tops of Ben Ledi, and the lovely Highlands (woven fantastically of thin air) mocked my embraces and tempted my longing eyes like her, the sole queen and mistress of my thoughts! I never found my contemplations on this subject so subtilised and at the same time so desponding as on that occasion. I wept myself almost blind, and I gazed at the broad golden sunset through my tears that fell in showers. As I trod the green mountain turf, oh! how I wished to be laid beneath it—in one grave with her—that I might sleep with her in that cold bed, my hand in hers, and my heart for ever still—while worms should taste her sweet body, that I had never tasted! There was a time when I could bear solitude; but it is too much for me at present. Now I am no sooner left to myself than I am lost in infinite space, and look around me in vain for support or comfort. She was my stay, my hope: without her hand to cling to, I stagger like an infant on the edge of a precipice. The universe without her is one wide, hollow abyss, in which my harassed thoughts can find no resting-place. I must break off here; for the *hysterica passio* comes upon me, and threatens to unhinge my reason.

## *Letter XI*

My Dear and Good Friend,

I am afraid I trouble you with my querulous epistles, but this is probably the last. To-morrow or the next day decides my fate with respect to the divorce, when I expect to be a free man. In vain! Was it not for her and to lay my freedom at her feet, that I consented to this step which has cost me infinite perplexity, and now to be discarded for the first pretender that came in her way! If so, I hardly think I can survive it. You who have been a favourite with women, do not know what it is to be deprived of one's only hope, and to have it turned to shame and disappointment. There is nothing in the world left that can afford me one drop of comfort —this I feel more and more. Everything is to me a mockery of pleasure, like her love. The breeze does not cool me: the blue sky does not cheer me. I gaze only on her face averted from me—alas! the only face that ever was turned fondly to me! And why am I thus treated? Because I wanted her to be mine forever in love or friendship, and did not push my gross familiarities as far as I might. 'Why can you not go on as we have done, and say nothing about the word, *forever*?' Was it not plain from this that she even then meditated an escape from me to some less sentimental lover? 'Do you allow anyone else to do so?' I said to her once, as I was toying with her. 'No, not now!' was her answer; that is, because there was nobody else in the house to take freedoms with her. I was very well as a stop-gap, but I was to be nothing more. While the coast was clear, I had it all my own way: but the instant

C—— came, she flung herself at his head in a most bare-faced way, ran breathless up stairs before him, blushed when his foot was heard, watched for him in the passage, and was sure to be in close conference with him when he went down again. It was then my mad proceedings commenced. No wonder. Had I not reason to be jealous of every appearance of familiarity with others, knowing how easy she had been with me at first, and that she only grew shy when I did not take further liberties? What has her character to rest upon but her attachment to me, which she now denies, not modestly, but impudently? Will you yourself say that if she had all along no particular regard for me, she will not do as much or more with other more likely men? 'She has had', she says, 'enough of my conversation'—so it could not be that! Ah! my friend, it was not to be supposed I should ever meet even with the outward demonstrations of regard from any woman but a common trader in the endearments of love! I have tasted the sweets of the well practised illusion, and now feel the bitterness of knowing what a bliss I am deprived of, and must ever be deprived of. Intolerable conviction! Yet I might, I believe, have won her by other methods; but some demon held my hand. How indeed could I offer her the least insult when I worshipped her very footsteps; and even now pay her divine honours from my inmost heart, whenever I think of her, abased and brutalized as I have been by that Circean cup of kisses, of enchantments, of which I have drunk! I am choked, withered, dried up with chagrin, remorse, despair, from which I have not a moment's respite, day or night. I have always some horrid dream about her, and wake wondering what is the matter that 'she is no longer the same to me as ever?' I thought at least we should always remain dear friends, if nothing more—did she not talk of coming to live with me only the day before I left her in the winter? But 'she's gone, I am abused, and my revenge must be to *love* her!'—Yet she knows that one line, one word would save me, the cruel, heartless destroyer! I see nothing for it but madness, unless Friday brings a change, or unless she is willing to let me go back. You must know I wrote to her to that purpose, but it was a very quiet, sobeı letter, begging pardon, and professing reform for the future, and all that. What effect it will have, I know not. I was forced to get out of the way of her answer, till Friday came.

Ever yours.

## *To S.L.*

My dear Miss L——,

*Evil to them that evil think*, is an old saying: and I have found it a true one. I have ruined myself by my unjust suspicions of you. Your sweet friendship was the balm of my life; and I have lost it, I fear for ever, by one fault and folly after another. What would I give to be restored to the place in your esteem, which, you assured me, I held only a few months ago! Yet I was not contented, but did all I could to torment myself and harass you by endless doubts and jealousy. Can you not forget and forgive the past, and judge of me by my conduct in future? Can you not take all my follies in the lump, and say like a good, generous girl, 'Well, I'll think no more of them!' In a word, may I come back, and try to behave better? A line to say so would be an additional favour to so many already received by

Your obliged friend,
And sincere well-wisher.

## *Letter XII to C.P.*

I have no answer from her. I'm mad. I wish you to call on M—— in confidence, to say I intend to make her an offer of my hand, and that I will write to her father to that effect the instant I am free, and ask him whether he thinks it will be to any purpose, and what he would advise me to do.

## *Unaltered Love*

Love Is not love that alteration finds :
Oh no ! it is an ever-fixed mark,
That looks on tempests and is never shaken.

Shall I not love her for herself alone, in spite of fickleness and folly ? To love her for her regard to me, is not to love her, but myself. She has robbed me of herself : shall she also rob me of my love of her ? Did I not live on her smile ? Is it less sweet because it is withdrawn from me ? Did I not adore her every grace ? Does she bend less enchantingly, because she has turned from me to another ? Is my love then in the power of fortune, or of her caprice ? No, I will have it lasting as it is pure ; and I will make a Goddess of her, and build a temple to her in my heart, and worship her on indestructible altars, and raise statues to her : and my homage shall be unblemished as her unrivalled symmetry of form ; and when that fails, the memory of it shall survive ; and my bosom shall be proof to scorn, as her's has been to pity ; and I will pursue her with an unrelenting love, and sue to be her slave, and tend her steps without notice and without reward ; and serve her living, and mourn for her when dead. And thus my love will have shewn itself superior to her hate ; and I shall triumph and then die. This is my idea of the only true and heroic love ! Such is mine for her.

## *Perfect Love*

Perfect love has this advantage in it, that it leaves the possessor of it nothing farther to desire. There is one object (at least) in which the soul finds absolute content, for which it seeks to live, or dares to die. The heart as it were filled up the moulds of the imagination. The truth of passion keeps pace with and outvies the extravagance of mere language. There are no words so fine, no flattery so soft, that there is not a sentiment beyond them, that it is impossible to express, at the bottom of the heart where true love is. What idle sounds the common phrases, *adorable creature*, *angel*, *divinity*, are ! What a proud reflection it is to have a feeling answering to all these, rooted in the breast, unalterable, unutterable, to which all other feelings are light and vain ! Perfect love reposes on the object of its choice, like the halcyon on the wave ; and the air of heaven is around it.

# *From C.P. Esq.*

*London, July 4th,* 1822.

I have seen M——! Now my dear H——, let me entreat and adjure you to take what I have to tell you, *for what it is worth*—neither for less, nor more. In the first place, I have learned nothing decisive from him. This, as you will at once see, is, as far as it goes, good. I am either to hear from him, or see him again in a day or two; but I thought you would like to know what passed, inconclusive as it was—so I write without delay, and in great haste to save a post. I found him frank, and even friendly in his manner to me, and in his views respecting you. I think that he is sincerely sorry for your situation; and he feels that the person who has placed you in that situation is not much less awkwardly situated herself; and he professes that he would willingly do what he can for the good of both. But he sees great difficulties attending the affair—which he frankly professes to consider as an altogether unfortunate one. With respect to the marriage, he seems to see the most formidable objections to it, on both sides; but yet he by no means decidedly says that it cannot, or that it ought not to take place. These, mind you, are his own feelings on the subject; but the most important point I learn from him is this, that he is not prepared to use his influence either way—that the rest of the family are of the same way of feeling; and that, in fact, the thing must and does entirely rest with herself. To learn this was, as you see, gaining a great point.—When I then endeavoured to ascertain whether he knew anything decisive as to what are her views on the subject, I found that he did not. He has an opinion on the subject, and he didn't scruple to tell me what it was; but he has no positive knowledge. In short, he believes, from what he learns from herself (and he had purposely seen her on the subject, in consequence of my application to him) that she is at present indisposed to the marriage; but he is not prepared to say positively that she will not consent to it. Now, all this, coming from him in the most frank and unaffected manner, and without any appearance of cant, caution, or reserve, I take to be most important as it respects your views, whatever they may be; and certainly much more favourable to them (I confess it) than I was prepared to expect, supposing them to remain as they were. In fact, as I said before, the affair rests entirely with herself. They are none of them disposed either to further the marriage, or throw any insurmountable obstacles in the way of it; and what is more important than all, they are evidently by no means *certain* that *she* may not, at some future period, consent to it; or they would, for her sake as well as their own, let you know as much flatly, and put an end to the affair at once.

Seeing in how frank and straightforward a manner he received what I had to say to him and replied to it, I proceeded to ask him what were *his* views, and what were likely to be *hers* (in case she did not consent) as to whether you should return to live in the house?—but I added, without waiting for his answer, that if she intended to persist in treating you as she had done for some time past, it would be worse than madness for you to think of returning. I added that, in case you did return, all you would expect from her would be that she would treat you with civility and kindness—that she would continue to evince that friendly feeling towards you, that she had done for a great length of time, etc. To this, he said, he could really give no decisive reply, but that he should be most happy if, by any intervention of his, he could conduce to your comfort: but he seemed to think that for you to return on any express understanding that she should behave to you in any particular manner, would be to place her in a most awkward situation. He went somewhat at length into this point, and talked very reasonably about it; the result, however, was that he would not throw any obstacles in the way of your return, or of her treating you as a friend, etc., nor did it appear that he believed she would refuse to do so. And, finally, we parted on the understanding that he would see them on the subject, and ascertain what could be done for the comfort of all parties; though he was of opinion that if you could make up your mind to break off the acquaintance altogether, it would be the best plan of all. I am to hear from him again in a day or two.—Well, what do you say to all this? Can you turn it to anything but good—comparative good? If you would know what *I* say to it, it is this:—She is still to be won by wise and prudent conduct on your part; she was always to have been won by such;—and if she is lost, it has been (not, as you sometimes suppose, because you have not carried that unwise, may I not say *unworthy*? conduct still farther, but) because you gave way to it at all. Of course I use the terms 'wise' and 'prudent' with reference to your object. Whether the pursuit of that object is wise, only yourself can judge. I say she has all along been to be won, and she is still to be won; and all that stands in the way of your views at this moment is your past conduct. They are all of them, every soul, frightened at you; they have *seen* enough of you to make them so; and they have doubtless heard ten times more than they have seen, or than anyone else has seen. They are all of them, including M—— (and particularly she herself) frightened out of her wits, as to what might be your treatment of her if she were yours; and they dare not trust you—they will not trust you, at present. I do not say that they will trust you, or rather that *she* will, for it all depends on her, when you have gone through a probation, but I am sure that she will not trust you till you have. You will, I hope, not be angry with me when I say that she would be a fool if she did. If she were to accept you at present, and without knowing more of you, even *I* should begin to suspect that she had an unworthy motive for doing it. Let me not forget to mention what is perhaps as important a point as any, as it regards the marriage. I of course stated to M—— that when you are free, you are prepared to make her a formal offer of your hand; but I begged him if he was certain that such an offer would be refused, to tell me so plainly at once, that I might endeavour, in that case, to dissuade you from subjecting yourself to the pain of such a refusal. *He would not tell me that he was certain.* He said his opinion was that she would not accept your offer, but still he seemed to think there would be no harm in making it!—One word more, and a very important one. He once, and without my referring in the slightest manner to that part of the subject spoke of her as a *good girl*, and *likely to make any man an excellent wife*! Do you think if she were a bad girl (and if she were, he must know her to be so) he would have dared to do this, under these circumstances?—And once, in speaking of *his* not being a fit person to set his face against 'marrying for love', he added 'I did so myself, and out of that house; and I have had reason to rejoice at it ever since.' And mind (for I anticipate your cursed suspicions) I'm certain, at least, if manner can entitle one to be certain of anything, that he said all this spontaneously, and without any understood motive; and I'm certain, too, that he knows you to be a person that it would not do to play any tricks of this kind with. I believe—(and all this would never have entered my thoughts, but that I know it will enter yours), I believe that even if they thought (as you have sometimes supposed they do) that she needs whitewashing, or making an honest woman of, *you* would be the last person they would think of using for such a purpose, for they know (as well as I do) that you couldn't fail to find out the trick in a month, and would turn her into the street the next moment, though she were twenty times your wife—and that, as to the consequences of doing so, you would laugh at them, even if you couldn't escape from them—I shall lose the post if I say more.

Believe me,

Ever truly your friend,

C. P.

## *Letter XIII*

My Dear P——,

You have saved my life. If I do not keep friends with her now, I deserve to be hanged, drawn, and quartered. She is an angel from Heaven, and you cannot pretend I ever said a word to the contrary! The little rogue must have liked me from the first, or she never could have stood all these hurricanes without slipping her cable. What could she find in me? 'I have mistook my person all this while,' etc. Do you know I saw a picture, the very pattern of her, the other day, at Dalkeith Palace (Hope finding Fortune in the Sea), just before this blessed news came, and the resemblance drove me almost out of my senses. Such delicacy, suchfulness, such perfect softness, such buoyancy, such grace! If it is not the very image of her, I am no judge.—You have the face to doubt my making the best husband in the world; you might as well doubt it if I was married to one of the Houris of Paradise. She is a saint, an angel, a love. If she deceives me again, she kills me. But I will have such a kiss when I get back, as shall last me twenty years. May God bless her for not utterly disowning and destroying me! What an exquisite little creature it is, and how she holds out to the last in her system of consistent contradictions! Since I wrote to you about making a formal proposal, I have had her face constantly before me, looking so like some faultless marble statue, as cold, as fixed and graceful as ever statue did; the expression (nothing was ever like *that*!) seemed to say, 'I wish I could love you better than I do, but still I will be yours.' No, I'll never believe again that she will not be mine; for I think she was made on purpose for me. If there's anyone else that understands that turn of her head as I do, I'll give her up without scruple. I have made up my mind to this, never to dream of another woman, while she even thinks it worth her while to *refuse to have me*. You see, I am not hard to please, after all. Did M—— know of the intimacy that had subsisted between us? Or did you hint at it? I think it would be a *clencher*, if he did. How ought I to behave when I go back? Advise a fool, who had nearly lost a goddess by his folly. The thing was, I could not think it possible she would ever like *me*. Her taste is singular, but not the worse for that. I'd rather have her love, or liking (call it what you will) than empires. I deserve to call her mine; for nothing else *can* atone for what I've gone through for her. I hope your next letter will not reverse all, and then I shall be happy till I see her, one of the blest when I do see her, if she looks like my own beautiful love. I may perhaps write a line when I come to my right wits.—Farewell at present, and thank you a thousand times for what you have done for your poor friend.

P.S.—I like what M—— said about her sister, much. There are good people in the world: I begin to see it, and believe it.

## *Letter The Last*

DEAR P——,

To-morrow is the decisive day that makes me or mars me. I will let you know the result by a line added to this. Yet what signifies it, since either way I have little hope there, 'whence alone my hope cometh?' You must know I am strangely in the dumps at this present writing. My reception with her is doubtful, and my fate is then certain. The hearing of your happiness has, I own, made me thoughtful. It is just what I proposed to her to do—to have crossed the Alps with me, to sail on sunny seas, to bask in Italian skies, to have visited Vevai and the rocks of Meillerie, and to have repeated to her on the spot the story of Julia and St. Preux, and to have shewn her all that my heart had stored up for her—but on my forehead alone is written—*Rejected*! Yet I too could have adored as fervently, and loved as tenderly as others, had I been permitted. You are going abroad, you say, happy in making happy. Where shall I be? In the grave, I hope, or else in her arms. To me, alas! there is no sweetness out of her sight, and that sweetness has turned to bitterness, I fear; that gentleness to sullen scorn! Still I hope for the best. If she will but *have* me, I'll make her *love* me: and I think her not giving a positive answer looks like it, and also shews that there is no one else. Her holding out to the last also, I think, proves that she was never to have been gained but with honour. She's a strange, almost inscrutable girl: but if I once win her consent, I shall kill her with kindness. —Will you let me have a sight of *somebody* before you go ? I should be most proud. I was in hopes to have got away by the steamboat to-morrow, but owing to the business not coming on till then, I cannot ; and may not be in town for another week, unless I come by the Mail, which I am strongly tempted to do. In the latter case I shall be *there*, and visible on Saturday evening. Will you look in and see, about eight o'clock ? I wish much to see you and her and J. H. and my little boy once more ; and then, if she is not what she once was to me, I care not if I die that instant. I will conclude here till to-morrow, as I am getting into my old melancholy.—

It is all over, and I am my own man, and yours ever—

# LIBER AMORIS

## *PART III*

## *Addressed to J. S. K.*

My Dear K——,

It is all over, and I know my fate. I told you I would send you word, if anything decisive happened; but an impenetrable mystery hung over the affair till lately. It is at last (by the merest accident in the world) dissipated; and I keep my promise, both for your satisfaction, and for the ease of my own mind.

You remember the morning when I said 'I will go and repose my sorrows at the foot of Ben Lomond'—and when from Dumbarton Bridge its giant-shadow, clad in air and sunshine, appeared in view. We had a pleasant day's walk. We passed Smollett's monument on the road (somehow these poets touch one in reflection more than most military heroes)—talked of old times; you repeated Logan's beautiful verses to the cuckoo*, which I wanted

* Sweet bird, thy bower is ever green,
Thy sky is ever clear;
Thou hast no sorrow in thy song,
No winter in thy year.

to compare with Wordsworth's, but my courage failed me; you then told me some passages of an early attachment which was suddenly broken off; we considered together which was the most to be pitied, a disappointment in love where the attachment was mutual or one where there has been no return, and we both agreed, I think, that the former was best to be endured, and that to have the consciousness of it a companion for life was the least evil of the two, as there was a secret sweetness that took off the bitterness and the sting of regret, and 'the memory of what once had been' atoned, in some measure, and at intervals, for what 'never more could be.' In the other case, there was nothing to look back to with tender satisfaction, no redeeming trait, not even a possibility of turning it to good. It left behind it not cherished sighs, but stifled pangs. The galling sense of it did not bring moisture into the eyes, but dried up the heart ever after. One had been my fate, the other had been yours!—

You startled me every now and then from my reverie by the robust voice, in which you asked the country people (by no means prodigal of their answers)—'If there was any trout-fishing in those streams?'—and our dinner at Luss set us up for the rest of our day's march. The sky now became overcast; but this, I think, added to the effect of the scene. The road to Tarbet is superb. It is on the very verge of the lake—hard, level, rocky, with low stone bridges constantly flung across it, and fringed with birch trees, just then budding into spring, behind which, as through a slight veil, you saw the huge shadowy form of Ben Lomond. It lifts its enormous but graceful bulk direct from the edge of the water without any projecting lowlands, and has in this respect much the advantage of Skiddaw. Loch Lomond comes upon you by degrees as you advance, unfolding and then withdrawing its conscious beauties like an accomplished coquet. You are struck with the point of a rock, the arch of a bridge, the Highland huts (like the first rude habitations of men) dug out of the soil, built of turf, and covered with brown heather, a sheep-cote, some straggling cattle feeding half-way down a

*So they begin. It was the month of May; the cuckoo sang shrouded in some woody copse; the showers fell between whiles; my friend repeated the lines with native enthusiasm in a clear manly voice, still resonant of youth and hope. Mr. Wordsworth will excuse me, if in these circumstances I declined entering the field with his profounder metaphysical strain, and kept my preference to myself.

precipice; but as you advance farther on, the view expands into the perfection of lake scenery. It is nothing (or your eye is caught by nothing) but water, earth, and sky. Ben Lomond waves to the right, in its simple majesty, cloud-capt or bare, and descending to a point at the head of the lake, shews the Trossachs beyond, tumbling about their blue ridges like woods waving; to the left is the Cobler, whose top is like a castle shattered in pieces and nodding to its ruin; and at your side rise the shapes of round pastoral hills, green, fleeced with herds, and retiring into mountainous bays and upland valleys, where solitude and peace might make their lasting home, if peace were to be found in solitude! That it was not always so, I was a sufficient proof; for there was one image that alone haunted me in the midst of all this sublimity and beauty, and turned it to a mockery and a dream!

The snow on the mountain would not let us ascend; and being weary of waiting and of being visited by the guide every two hours to let us know that the weather would not do, we returned, you homewards, and I to London:

Italiam, Italiam!

You know the anxious expectations with which I set out:—now hear the result.

As the vessel sailed up the Thames, the air thickened with the consciousness of being near her, and I 'heaved her name pantingly forth.' As I approached the house, I could not help thinking of the lines:

How near am I to a happiness,
That earth exceeds not! Not another like it.
The treasures of the deep are not so precious
As are the conceal'd comforts of a man
Lock'd up in woman's love. I scent the air
Of blessings when I come but near the house.
What a delicious breath true love sends forth!
The violet-beds not sweeter. Now for a welcome

Able to draw men's envies upon man :
A kiss now that will hang upon my lip,
As sweet as morning dew upon a rose,
And full as long !

I saw her, but I saw at the first glance that there was something amiss. It was with much difficulty and after several pressing entreaties that she was prevailed on to come up into the room, and when she did, she stood at the door, cold, distant, averse ; and when at length she was persuaded by my repeated remonstrances to come and take my hand, and I offered to touch her lips, she turned her head and shrunk from my embraces, as if quite alienated or mortally offended. I asked what it could mean ? What had I done in her absence to have incurred her displeasure ? Why had she not written to me ? I could get only short, sullen, disconnected answers, as if there was something labouring in her mind which she either could not or would not impart. I hardly knew how to bear this first reception after so long an absence, and so different from the one my sentiments towards her merited ; but I thought it possible it might be prudery (as I had returned without having actually accomplished what I went about) or that she had taken offence at something in my letters. She saw how much I was hurt. I asked her 'if she was altered since I went away ?'—'No.' 'If there was anyone else who had been so fortunate as to gain her favourable opinion ?'—'No, there was no one else.' 'What was it then ? Was it anything in my letters ? Or had I displeased her by letting Mr. P—— know she wrote to me ?'—'No, not at all ; but she did not apprehend my last letter required any answer, or she would have replied to it.' All this appeared to me very unsatisfactory and evasive ; but I could get no more from her, and was obliged to let her go with a heavy, foreboding heart. I however found that C—— was gone, and no one else had been there, of whom I had cause to be jealous.—'Should I see her on the morrow?'—'She believed so, but she could not promise.' The next morning she did not appear with the breakfast as usual. At this I grew somewhat uneasy. The little Bonaparte, however, was placed in its old position on the mantelpiece, which I considered as a sort of recognition of old times. I saw her once or twice casually; nothing particular happened till the next day, which was Sunday. I took occasion to go into the parlour for the newspaper, which she gave me with a gracious smile, and seemed tolerably frank and cordial. This of course acted as a spell upon me. I walked out with my little boy, intending to go and dine out at one or two places, but I found that I still contrived to bend my steps towards her, and I went back to take tea at home. While we were out I talked to William about Sarah, saying that she too was unhappy, and asking him to make it up with her. He said, if she was unhappy, he would not bear her malice any more. When she came up with the tea-things, I said to her 'William has something to say to you—I believe he wants to be friends.' On which he said in his abrupt, hearty manner 'Sarah, I'm sorry if I ever said anything to vex you'—so they shook hands, and she said, smiling affably, 'Then I'll think no more of it!' I added 'I see you've brought me back my little Bonaparte'—She answered with tremulous softness 'I told you I'd keep it safe for you!' as if her pride and pleasure in doing so had been equal, and she had, as it were, thought of nothing during my absence but how to greet me with this proof of her fidelity on my return. I cannot describe her manner. Her words are few and simple; but you can have no idea of the exquisite, unstudied, irresistible graces with which she accompanies them, unless you can suppose a Greek statue to smile, move, and speak. Those lines in Tibullus seem to have been written on purpose for her:

Quicquid agit quoquo vestigia vertit,
Componit furtim, subsequiturque decor.

Or what do you think of those in a modern play, which might actually have been composed with an eye to this little trifler :

See with what a waving air she goes
Along the corridor. How like a fawn !
Yet statelier. No sound (however soft)
Nor gentlest echo telleth when she treads,
But every motion of her shape doth seem
Hallowed by silence. So did Hebe grow
Among the gods a paragon ! Away, I'm grown
The very fool of love !

The truth is, I never saw anything like her, nor I never shall again. How then do I console myself for the loss of her ? Shall I tell you, but you will not mention it again ? I am foolish enough to believe that she and I, in spite of everything, shall be sitting together over a sea-coal fire, a comfortable good old couple, twenty years hence ! But to my narrative.

I was delighted with the alteration in her manner, and said, referring to the bust :

'You know it is not mine, but yours ; I gave it you ; nay, I have given you all—my heart, and whatever I possess, is yours !' She seemed good-humouredly to decline this *carte blanche* offer, and waved, like a thing of enchantment, out of the room. False calm !—Deceitful smiles !—Short interval of peace, followed by lasting woe ! I sought an interview with her that same evening. I could not get her to come any farther than the door. 'She was busy—she could hear what I had to say there.' 'Why do you seem to avoid me as you do ? Not one five minutes' conversation, for the sake of old acquaintance ? Well, then, for the sake of *the little image* !' The appeal seemed to have lost its efficacy ; the charm was broken ; she remained immovable. 'Well, then I must come to you, if you will not run away.' I went and sat down in a chair near the door, and took her hand, and talked to her for three-quarters of an hour; and she listened patiently, thoughtfully, and seemed a good deal affected by what I said. I told her how much I had felt, how much I had suffered for her in my absence, and how I had been hurt by her sudden silence, for which I knew not how to account. I could have done nothing to offend her while I was away; and my letters were, I hoped, tender and respectful. I had had but one thought ever present with me; her image never quitted my side, alone or in company, to delight or distract me. Without her I could have no peace, nor ever should again, unless she would behave to me as she had done formerly. There was no abatement of my regard to her; why was she so changed? I said to her 'Ah, Sarah, when I think that it is only a year ago that you were everything to me I could wish, and that now you seem lost to me for ever, the month of May (the name of which ought to be a signal for joy and hope) strikes chill to my heart. How different is this meeting from that delicious parting, when you seemed never weary of repeating the proofs of your regard and tenderness, and it was with difficulty we tore ourselves asunder at last! I am ten thousand times fonder of you than I was then, and ten thousand times more unhappy.' 'You have no reason to be so; my feelings towards you are the same as they ever were.' I told her 'She was my all of hope or comfort: my passion for her grew stronger every time I saw her.' She answered 'She was sorry for it for *that* she never could return.' I said something about looking ill: she said in her pretty, mincing, emphatic way, 'I despise looks!' So, thought I, it is not that; and she says there's no one else; it must be some strange air she gives herself, in consequence of the approaching change in my circumstances. She has been probably advised not to give up till all is fairly over, and then she will be my own sweet girl again. All this time she was standing just outside the door, my hand in hers (would that they could have grown together !) ; she was dressed in a loose morning-gown, her hair curled beautifully ; she stood with her profile to me, and looked down the whole time. No expression was ever more soft or perfect. Her whole attitude, her whole form, was dignity and betwitching grace. I said to her 'You look like a queen, my love, adorned with your own graces !' I grew idolatrous, and would have kneeled to her. She made a movement, as if she was displeased. I tried to draw her towards me. She wouldn't. I then got up, and offered to kiss her at parting. I found she obstinately refused. This stung me to the quick. It was the first time in her life she had ever done so. There must be some new bar between us to produce these continued denials ; and she had not even esteem enough left to tell me so. I followed her half-way downstairs, but to no purpose, and returned into my room, confirmed in my most dreadful surmises. I could bear it no longer. I gave way to all the fury of disappointed hope and jealous passion. I was made the dupe of trick and cunning, killed with cold, sullen scorn ; and, after all the agony I had suffered, could obtain no explanation why I was subjected to it. I was still to be tantalized, tortured, made the cruel sport of one for whom I would have sacrificed all. I tore the locket which contained her hair (and which I used to wear continually in my bosom, as the precious token of her dear regard) from my neck, and trampled it in pieces. I then dashed the little Bonaparte on the ground, and stamped upon it, as one of her instruments of mockery. I could not stay in the room ; I could not leave it ; my rage, my despair were uncontrollable. I shrieked curses on her name, and on her false love ; and the scream I uttered (so pitiful and so piercing was it, that the sound of it terrified me), instantly brought the whole house, father, mother, lodgers and all, into the room. They thought I was destroying her and myself. I had gone into the bedroom, merely to hide away from myself, and as I came out of it, raging mad with the new sense of present shame and lasting misery, Mrs. F—— said 'She's in there! He has got her in there!' thinking the cries had proceeded from her, and that I had been offering her violence. 'Oh! no', I said, 'She's in no danger from me; I am not the person'; and tried to burst from this scene of degradation. The mother endeavoured to stop me, and said 'For God's sake, don't go out, Mr.——! for God's sake, don't!' Her father, who was not, I believe, in the secret, and was therefore justly scandalised at such outrageous conduct, said angrily 'Let him go! Why should he stay?' I however sprang downstairs, and as they called out to me 'What is it?—What has she done to you?' I answered 'She has murdered me!—She has detroyed me for ever!—She has doomed my soul to perdition!' I rushed out of the house, thinking to quit it for ever; but I was no sooner in the street, than the desolation and the darkness became greater, more intolerable; and the eddying violence of my passion drove me back to the source, from whence it sprung. This unexpected explosion, with the conjectures to which it would give rise, could not be very agreeable to the *precieuse* or her family; and when I went back, the father was waiting at the door, as if anticipating this sudden turn of my feelings, with no friendly aspect. I said 'I have to beg pardon, Sir; but my mad fit is over, and I wish to say a few words to you in private.' He seemed to hesitate, but some uneasy forebodings on his own account, probably, prevailed over his resentment; or, perhaps (as philosophers have a desire to know the cause of thunder) it was a natural curiosity to know what circumstances of provocation had given rise to such an extraordinary scene of confusion.

When we reached my room, I requested him to be seated. I said 'It is true, Sir, I have lost my peace of mind for ever, but at present I am quite calm and collected, and I wish to explain to you why I have behaved in so extravagant a way, and to ask for your advice and intercession.' He appeared satisfied, and I went on. I had no chance either of exculpating myself, or of probing the question to the bottom, but by stating the naked truth, and therefore I said at once 'Sarah told me, Sir (and I never shall forget the way in which she told me, fixing her dove's eyes upon me, and looking a thousand tender reproaches for the loss of that good opinion, which she held dearer than all the world) she told me, Sir, that as you one day passed the door, which stood ajar, you saw her in an attitude which a good deal startled you; I mean sitting in my lap, with her arms round my neck, and mine twined round her in the fondest manner. What I wished to ask was, whether this was actually the case, or whether it was a mere invention of her own, to enhance the sense of my obligations to her; for I begin to doubt everything?' 'Indeed, it was so; and very much surprised and hurt I was to see it.' 'Well then, Sir, I can only say, that as you saw her sitting then, so she had been sitting for the last year and a half, almost every day of her life, by the hour together; and you may judge yourself, knowing what a nice modest-looking girl she is, whether, after having been admitted to such intimacy with so sweet a creature, and for so long a time, it is not enough to make any one frantic to be received by her as I have been since my return, without any provocation given or cause assigned for it.' The old man answered very seriously, and, as I think, sincerely, 'What you now tell me, Sir, mortifies and shocks me as much as it can do yourself. I had no idea such a thing was possible. I was much pained at what I saw; but I thought it an accident, and that it would never happen again.' 'It was a constant habit; it has happened a hundred times since, and a thousand before. I lived on her caresses as my daily food, nor can I live without them.' So I told him the whole story, 'what conjurations, and what mighty magic I won his daughter with', to be anything but *mine for life*. Nothing could well exceed his astonishment and apparent mortification. 'What I had said,' he owned, 'had left a weight upon his mind that he should not easily get rid of.' I told him 'For myself, I never could recover the blow I had received, I thought, however, for her own sake, she ought to alter her present behaviour. Her marked neglect and dislike, so far from justifying, left her former intimacies without excuse; for nothing could reconcile them to propriety, or even a pretence to common decency, but either love or friendship so strong and pure that it could put on the guise of love. She was certainly a singular girl. Did she think it right and becoming to be free with strangers, and strange to old friends?' I frankly declared 'I did not see how it was in human nature for anyone who was not rendered callous to such familiarities by bestowing them indiscriminately on every one, to grant the extreme and continued indulgences she had done to me, without either liking the man at first or coming to like him in the end in spite of herself. When my addresses had nothing, and could have nothing honourable in them, she gave them every encouragement; when I wished to make them honourable, she treated them with the utmost contempt. The terms we had been all along on were such as if she had been to be my bride next day. It was only when I wished her actually to become so, to ensure her own character and my happiness, that she shrunk back with precipitation and panic-fear. There seemed to me something wrong in all this; a want both of common propriety, and I might say of natural feeling ; yet, with all her faults, I loved her, and ever should beyond any other human being. I had drank in the poison of her sweetness too long ever to be cured of it ; and though I might find it to be poison in the end, it was still in my veins. My only ambition was to be permitted to live with her, and to die in her arms. Be she what she would, treat me how she would, I felt that my soul was wedded to hers ; and were she a mere lost creature, I would try to snatch her from perdition, and marry her to-morrow if she would have me. That was the question—' Would she have me, or would she not ? ' He said he could not tell ; but should not attempt to put any constraint upon her inclinations, one way or other. I acquiesced, and added, that ' I had brought all this upon myself, by acting contrary to the suggestions of a friend, Mr.——, who had desired me to take no notice whether she came near me or kept away, whether she smiled or frowned, was kind or contemptuous—" all you have to do is to wait patiently for a month till you are your own man, as you will be in all probability ; then make her an offer of your hand, and if she refuses, there's an end to the matter." ' Mr. L. said ' Well, Sir, and I don't think you can follow a better advice ! ' I took this as at least a sort of negative encouragement, and so we parted.

## *To the Same (in continuation)*

My Dear Friend,

The next day I felt almost as sailors must do after a violent storm over-night, that has subsided towards day-break. The morning was a dull and stupid calm, and I found she was unwell, in consequence of what had happened. In the evening I grew more uneasy, and determined on going into the country for a week or two. I gathered up the fragments of the locket of her hair, and the little bronze statue, which were strewed about the floor, kissed them, folded them up in a sheet of paper, and sent them to her, with these lines written in pencil on the outside :—'*Pieces of a broken heart, to be kept in remembrance of the unhappy. Farewell.*' No notice was taken ; nor did I expect any. The following morning I requested Betsy to pack up my box for me, as I should go out of town the next day, and at the same time wrote a note to her sister to say, I should take it as a favour if she would please to accept of the enclosed copies of *The Vicar of Wakefield*, *The Man of Feeling*, and *Nature and Art*, in lieu of three volumes of my own writings, which I had given her on different occasions, in the course of our acquaintance. I was piqued, in fact, that she should have these to show as proofs of my weakness, and as if I thought the way to win her was by plaguing her with my own performances. She sent me word back that the books I had sent were of no use to her, and that I should have those I wished for in the afternoon ; but that she could not before, as she had lent them to her sister, Mrs. M——. I said 'Very well' ; but observed (laughing) to Betsy

'It's a bad rule to give and take; so, if Sarah won't have these books, you must; they are very pretty ones, I assure you.' She curtsied and took them, according to the family custom. In the afternoon, when I came back to tea, I found the little girl on her knees, busy in packing up my things, and a large paper parcel on the table, which I could not at first tell what to make of. On opening it, however, I soon found what it was. It contained a number of volumes which I had given her at different times (among others, a little Prayer-Book, bound in crimson velvet, with green silk linings; she kissed it twenty times when she received it, and said it was the prettiest present in the world, and that she would shew it to her aunt, who would be proud of it)—and all these she had returned together. Her name in the title-page was cut out of them all. I doubted at the instant whether she had done this before or after I had sent for them back, and I have doubted of it since; but there is no occasion to suppose her *ugly all over with hypocrisy*. Poor little thing! She has enough to answer for, as it is. I asked Betsy if she could carry a message for me, and she said '*Yes*'. 'Will you tell your sister, then, that I did not want all these books; and give my love to her, and say that I shall be obliged if she will still keep these that I have sent back, and tell her that it is only those of my own writing that I think unworthy of her.' What do you think the little imp made answer? She raised herself on the other side of the table where she stood, as if inspired by the genius of the place, and said 'AND THOSE ARE THE ONES THAT SHE PRIZES THE MOST!' If there were ever words spoken that could revive the dead, those were the words. Let me kiss them, and forget that my ears have heard aught else! I said, 'Are you sure of that?' and she said, 'Yes, quite sure.' I told her, 'If I could be, I should be very different from what I was.' And I became so that instant, for these casual words carried assurance to my heart of her esteem—that once implied, I had proofs enough of her fondness. Oh! how I felt at that moment! Restored to love, hope, and joy, by a breath which I had caught by the merest accident, and which I might have pined in absence and mute despair for want of hearing! I did not know how to contain myself; I was childish, wanton, drunk with pleasure. I gave Betsy a twenty-shilling note which I happened to have in my hand, and on her asking 'What's this for, Sir?' I said 'It's for you. Don't you think it worth that to be made happy? You once made me very wretched by some words I heard you drop, and now you have made me as happy; and all I wish you is, when you grow up, that you may find some one to love you as well as I do your sister, and that you may love better than she does me!' I continued in this state of delirium or dotage all that day and the next, talked incessantly, laughed at everything, and was so extravagant, nobody could tell what was the matter with me. I murmured her name; I blest her; I folded her to my heart in delicious fondness; I called her by my own name; I worshipped her: I was mad for her. I told P—— I should laugh in her face, if ever she pretended not to like me again. Her mother came in and said, she hoped I should excuse Sarah's coming up. 'Oh, Ma'am,' I said, 'I have no wish to see her; I feel her at my heart; she does not hate me after all, and I wish for nothing. Let her come when she will, she is to me welcomer than light, than life; but let it be in her own sweet time, and at her own dear pleasure.' Betsy also told me she was 'so glad to get the books back.' I, however, sobered and wavered (by degrees) from seeing nothing of her, day after day; and in less than a week I was devoted to the Infernal Gods. I could hold out no longer than the Monday evening following. I sent a message to her; she returned an ambiguous answer; but she came up. Pity me, my friend, for the shame of this recital. Pity me for the pain of having ever had to make it! If the spirits of mortal creatures, purified by faith and hope, can (according to the highest assurances) ever, during thousands of years of smooth-rolling eternity and balmy, sainted repose, forget the pain, the toil, the anguish, the helplessness, and the despair they have suffered here, in this frail being, then may I forget that withering hour, and her, that fair, pale form that entered, my inhuman betrayer, and my only earthly love! She said 'Did you wish to speak to me, Sir!' I said, 'Yes, may I not speak to you? I wanted to see you and be friends.' I rose up, offered her an arm-chair which stood facing, bowed on it, and knelt to her adoring. She said (going) 'If that's all, I have nothing to say.' I replied 'Why do you treat me thus? What have I done to become thus hateful to you?' *Answer*: 'I always told you I had no affection for you.' You may suppose this was a blow, after the imaginary honey-moon in which I had passed the preceding week. I was stunned by it; my heart sunk within me. I contrived to say 'Nay, my dear girl, not always neither; for did you not once (if I might presume to look back to those happy, happy times), when you were sitting on my knee as usual, embracing and embraced, and I asked if you could not love me at last, did you not make answer, in the softest tones that ever man heard: "*I could easily say so, whether I did or not; you should judge by my actions!*" Was I to blame in taking you at your word, when every hope I had depended on your sincerity? And did you not say since I came back "*Your feelings to me were the same as ever?*" Why then is your behaviour so different?' S. 'Is it nothing, your exposing me to the whole house in the way you did the other evening?' H. 'Nay, that was the consequence of your cruel reception of me, not the cause of it. I had better have gone away last year, as I proposed to do, unless you would give some pledge of your fidelity; but it was your own offer that I should remain. "Why should I go?" you said, "Why could we not go on the same as we had done, and say nothing about the word *forever*?"' S. 'And how did you behave when you returned?' H. 'That was all forgiven when we last parted, and your last words were "I should find you the same as ever" when I came home? Did you not that very day enchant and madden me over again by the purest kisses and embraces, and did I not go from you (as I said) adoring, confiding, with every assurance of mutual esteem and friendship?' S. 'Yes, and in your absence I found that you had told my aunt what had passed between us.' H. 'It was to induce her to extort your real sentiments from you, that you might no longer make a secret of your true regard for me, which your actions (but not your words) confessed.' S. 'I own I have been guilty of improprieties, which you have gone and repeated, not only in the house, but out of it; so that it has come to my ears from various quarters, as if I was a light character. And I am determined in future to be guided by the advice of my relations, and particularly of my aunt, whom I consider as my best friend, and keep every lodger at a proper distance.' You will find hereafter that her favourite lodger, whom she visits daily, had left the house; so that she might easily make and keep this vow of extraordinary self-denial. Precious little dissembler! Yet her aunt, her best friend, says 'No, Sir, no; Sarah's no hypocrite!' which I was fool enough to believe; and yet my great and unpardonable offence is to have entertained passing doubts on this delicate point. I said, Whatever errors I had committed, arose from my anxiety to have everything explained to her honour: my conduct shewed that I had that at heart, and that I built on the purity of her character as on a rock. My esteem for her amounted to adoration. 'She did not want adoration.' It was only when anything happened to imply that I had been mistaken, that I committed any extravagance, because I could not bear to think her short of perfection. 'She was far from perfection,' she replied, with an air and manner (oh, my God!) as near it as possible. 'How could she accuse me of a want of regard to her? It was but the other day, Sarah,' I said to her, 'when that little circumstance of the books happened, and I fancied the expressions your sister dropped proved the sincerity of all your kindness to me—you don't know how my heart melted within me at the thought, that after all, I might be dear to you. New hopes sprung up in my heart, and I felt as Adam must have done when his Eve was created for him!' 'She had heard enough of that sort of conversation' (moving towards the door). This, I own, was the unkindest cut of all. I had, in that case, no hopes whatever. I felt that I had expended words in vain, and that the conversation below-stairs (which I told you of when I saw you) had spoiled her taste for mine. If the allusion had been classical I should have been to blame; but it was scriptural, it was a sort of religious courtship, and Miss L. is religious!

> At once he took his Muse and dipt her
> Right in the middle of the Scripture.

It would not do—the lady could make neither head nor tail of it. This is a poor attempt at levity. Alas! I am sad enough. 'Would she go and leave me so? If it was only my own behaviour, I still did not doubt of success. I knew the sincerity of my love, and she would be convinced of it in time. If that was all, I did not care: but tell me true, is there not a new attachment that is the real cause of your estrangement? Tell me, my sweet friend, and before you tell me, give me your hand (nay, both hands) that I may have something to support me under the dreadful conviction.' She let me take her hands in mine, saying ‘ She supposed there could be no objection to that ’—as if she acted on the suggestions of others, instead of following her own will —but still avoided giving me any answer. I conjured her to tell me the worst and kill me on the spot. Anything was better than my present state. I said ‘ Is it Mr. C—— ? ’ She smiled, and said with gay indifference, ‘ Mr. C—— was here a very short time.’ ‘ Well, then, was it Mr.——? ’ She hesitated, and then replied faintly ‘ No.’ This was a mere trick to mislead ; one of the profoundnesses of Satan, in which she is an adept. ‘ But,’ she added hastily, ‘ she could make no more confidences.’ ‘ Then,’ said I, ‘ you have something to communicate.’ ‘ No ; but she had once mentioned a thing of the sort, which I had hinted to her mother, though it signified little.’ All this while I was in tortures. Every word, every half-denial, stabbed me. ‘ Had she any tie ? ’ ‘ No, I have no tie ! ’ ‘ You are not going to be married soon ? ’ ‘ I don’t intend ever to marry at all ! ’ ‘ Can’t you be friends with me as of old ? ’ ‘ She could give no promises.’ ‘ Would she make her own terms ? ’ ‘ She would make none.’—‘ I was sadly afraid the *little image* was dethroned from her heart, as I had dashed it to the ground the other night.’ ‘ She was neither desperate nor violent.’ I did not answer : ‘ But deliberate and deadly ’—though I might ; and so she vanished in this running fight of question and answer, in spite of my vain efforts to detain her. The cockatrice, I said, mocks me : so she has always done. The thought was a dagger to me. My head reeled, my heart recoiled within me. I was stung with scorpions ; my flesh crawled ; I was choked with rage ; her scorn scorched me like flames ; her air (her heavenly air) withdrawn from me, stifled me, and left me gasping for breath and being. It was a fable. She started up in her own likeness, a serpent in place of a woman. She had fascinated, she had stung me, and had returned to her proper shape, gliding from me after inflicting the mortal wound, and instilling deadly poison into every pore; but her form lost none of its original brightness by the change of character, but was all glittering, beauteous, voluptuous grace. Seed of the serpent or of the woman, she was divine! I felt that she was a witch, and had bewitched me. Fate had enclosed me round about. *I* was transformed too, no longer human (any more than she, to whom I had knit myself) my feelings were marble; my blood was of molten lead; my thoughts on fire. I was taken out of myself, wrapt into another sphere, far from the light of day, of hope, of love. I had no natural affection left; she had slain me, but no other thing had power over me. Her arms embraced another; but her mock-embrace, the phantom of her love, still bound me, and I had not a wish to escape. So I felt then, and so perhaps shall feel till I grow old and die, nor have any desire that my years should last longer than they are linked in the chain of those amorous folds, or than her enchantments steep my soul in oblivion of all other things! I started to find myself alone—for ever alone, without a creature to love me. I looked round the room for help; I saw the tables, the chairs, the place where she stood or sat, empty, deserted, dead. I could not stay where I was; I had no one to go to but to the parent-mischief, the preternatural hag, that had 'drugged this posset' of her daughter's charms and falsehood for me, and I went down and (such was my weakness and helplessness) sat with her for an hour, and talked with her of her daughter, and the sweet days we had passed together, and said I thought her a good girl, and believed that if there was no rival, she still had a regard for me at the bottom of her heart; and how I liked her all the better for her coy, maiden airs: and I received the assurance over and over that there was no one else;

and that Sarah (they all knew) never staid five minutes with any other lodger, while with me she would stay by the hour together, in spite of all her father could say to her (what were her motives, was best known to herself!); and while we were talking of her, she came bounding into the room, smiling with smothered delight at the consummation of my folly and her own art; and I asked her mother whether she thought she looked as if she hated me, and I took her wrinkled, withered, cadaverous, clammy hand at parting, and kissed it. Faugh!

I will make an end of this story; there is something in it discordant to honest ears. I left the house the next day, and returned to Scotland in a state so near to phrenzy, that I take it the shades sometimes ran into one another. R—— met me the day after I arrived, and will tell you the way I was in. I was like a person in a high fever; only mine was in the mind instead of the body. It had the same irritating, uncomfortable effect on the by-standers. I was incapable of any application, and I don't know what I should have done, had it not been for the kindness of ——. I came to see you, to 'bestow some of my tediousness upon you', but you were gone from home. Everything went on well as to the law business; and as it approached to a conclusion, I wrote to my good friend P—— to go to M——, who had married her sister, and ask him if it would be worth my while to make her a formal offer, as soon as I was free, as, with the least encouragement, I was ready to throw myself at her feet; and to know, in case of refusal, whether I might go back there and be treated as an old friend. Not a word of answer could be got from her on either point, notwithsandting every importunity and intreaty; but it was the opinion of M.—— that I might go and try my fortune. I did so with joy, with something like confidence. I thought her giving no positive answer implied a chance, at least, of the reversion of her favour, in case I behaved well. All was false, hollow insidious. The first night after I got home I slept on down. In Scotland, the flint had been my pillow. But now I slept under the same roof with her. What softness, what balmy repose in the very thought! I saw her that same day and shook hands with her, and told her how glad I was to see her; and she was kind and comfortable, though still cold and distant. Her manner was altered from what it was last time. She still absented herself from the room, but was mild and affable when she did come. She was pale, dejected, evidently uneasy about something, and had been ill. I thought it was perhaps her reluctance to yield to my wishes, her pity for what I suffered; and that in the struggle between both, she did not know what to do. How I worshipped her at these moments! We had a long interview the third day, and I thought all was doing well. I found her sitting at work in the window-seat of the front parlour; and on my asking if I might come in, she made no objection. I sat down by her; she let me take her hand; I talked to her of indifferent things, and of old times. I asked her if she would put some new frills on my shirts?—'With the greatest pleasure.' If she could get *the little image* mended? 'It was broken in three pieces, and the sword was gone, but she would try.' I then asked her to make up a plaid silk which I had given her in the winter, and which she said would make a pretty summer gown. I so longed to see her in it!—'She had little time to spare, but perhaps might!' Think what I felt, talking peaceably, kindly, tenderly with my love—not passionately, not violently. I tried to take pattern by her patient meekness, as I thought it, and to subdue my desires to her will. I then sued to her, but respectfully, to be admitted to her friendship—she must know I was as true a friend as ever woman had—or if there was a bar to our intimacy from a dearer attachment, to let me know it frankly, as I shewed her all my heart. She drew out her handkerchief and wiped her eyes 'of tears which sacred pity had engendered there.' Was it so or not? I cannot tell. But so she stood (while I pleaded my cause to her with all the earnestness, and fondness in the world) with the tears trickling from her eye-lashes, her head stooping, her attitude fixed, with the finest expression that ever was seen of mixed regret, pity, and stubborn resolution; but without speaking a word, without altering a feature. It was like a petrification of a human face in the softest moment of passion. 'Ah!' I said, 'how you look! I have prayed again and again while I was away from you, in the agony of my spirit, that I might but live to see you look so again, and then breath my last!' I entreated her to give me some explanation. In vain! At length she said she must go, and disappeared like a spirit. That week she did all the little trifling favours I had asked of her. The frills were put on, and she sent up to know if I wanted any more done. She got the Bonaparte mended. This was like healing old wounds indeed! How? As follows, for thereby hangs the conclusion of my tale. Listen.

I had sent a message one evening to speak to her about some special affairs of the house, and received no answer. I waited an hour expecting her, and then went out in great vexation at my disappointment. I complained to her mother a day or two after, saying I thought it so unlike Sarah's usual propriety of behaviour, that she must mean it as a mark of disrespect. Mrs. L—— said 'La, Sir, you're always fancying things! Why, she was dressing to go out, and she was only going to get the little image you're both so fond of mended; and it's to be done this evening. She has been to two or three places to see about it, before she could get anyone to undertake it.' My heart, my poor fond heart, almost melted within me at this news. I answered 'Ah, Madam, that's always the way with the dear creature. I am finding fault with her and thinking the hardest things of her; and at that very time she's doing something to shew the most delicate attention and that she has no greater satisfaction than in gratifying my wishes!' On this we had some farther talk, and I took nearly the whole of the lodgings at a hundred guineas a year, that (as I said) she might have a little leisure to sit at her needle of an evening, or to read if she chose, or to walk out when it was fine. She was not in good health, and it would do her good to be less confined. I would be the drudge and she should no longer be the slave. I asked nothing in return. To see her happy, to make her so, was to be so myself.—This was agreed to. I went over to Blackheath that evening, delighted as I could be after all I had suffered, and lay the whole of the next morning on the heath under the open sky, dreaming of my earthly goddess. This was Sunday. That evening I returned, for I could hardly bear to be for a moment out of the house where she was, and the next morning she tapped at the door—it was opened—it was she—she hesitated and then came forward; she had got the little image in her hand, I took it, and blest her from my heart. She said 'They have been obliged to put some new pieces to it.' I said 'I didn't care how it was done, so that I had it restored to me safe, by her.' I thanked her and begged to shake hands with her. She did so, and as I held the only hand in the world that I never wished to let go, I looked up in her face, and said 'Have pity on me, have pity on me, and save me if you can!' Not a word of answer, but she looked full in my eyes, as much as to say 'Well, I'll think of it; and if I can, I will save you!' We talked about the expense of repairing the figure. 'Was the man waiting!'—

'No, she had fetched it on Saturday evening.' I said I'd give her the money in the course of the day, and then shook hands with her again in token of reconciliation; and she went waving out of the room, but at the door turned round and looked full at me, as she did the first time she beguiled me of my heart. This was the last.

All that day I longed to go downstairs to ask her and her mother to set out with me for Scotland on Wednesday, and on Saturday I would make her my wife. Something withheld me. In the evening, however, I could not rest without seeing her, and I said to her younger sister 'Betsy, if Sarah will come up now, I'll pay her what she laid out for me the other day.'—'My sister's gone out, Sir' was the answer. What again? thought I, that's somewhat sudden. I told P—— her sitting in the window-seat of the front parlour boded me no good. It was not in her old character. She did not use to know there were doors or windows in the house—and now she goes out three times in a week. It is to meet some one, I'll lay my life on't. 'Where is she gone?'—'To my grandmother's, Sir.' 'Where does your grandmother live now?'—'At Somers' Town.' I immediately set out to Somers' Town. I passed one or two streets, and at last turned up King Street, thinking it most likely she would return that way home. I passed a house in King Street where I had once lived, and had not proceeded many paces, ruminating on chance and change and old times, when I saw her coming towards me. I felt a strange pang at the sight, but I thought her alone. Some people before me moved on, and I saw another person with her. *The murder was out.* It was a tall, rather well-looking young man, but I did not at first recollect him. We passed at the crossing of the street without speaking. Will you believe it, after all that had passed between us for two years, after what had passed in the last half-year, after what had passed that very morning, she went by me without even changing countenance, without expressing the slightest emotion, without betraying either shame or pity or remorse or any other feeling that any other human being but herself must have shown in the same situation. She had no time to prepare for acting a part, to suppress her feelings—the truth is, she has not one natural feeling in her bosom to suppress. I turned and looked—they also turned and looked—and as if by mutual consent, we both retrod our steps and passed again, in the same way. I went home. I was stifled. I could not stay in the house, walked into the street and met them coming towards home. As soon as he had left her at the door (I fancy she had prevailed with him to accompany her, dreading some violence) I returned, went upstairs, and requested an interview. Tell her, I said, I'm in excellent temper and good spirits, but I must see her! She came smiling, and I said 'Come in, my dear girl, and sit down, and tell me all about it, how it is and who it is.'—'What', she said, 'do you mean Mr. C—— ?' 'Oh', said I, 'Then it is he! Ah! you rogue, I always suspected there was something between you, but you know you denied it lustily: why did you not tell me all about it at the time, instead of letting me suffer as I have done? But, however, no reproaches. I only wish it may all end happily and honourably for you, and I am satisfied. But', I said, 'you know you used to tell me, you despised looks.'—'She didn't think Mr. C—— was so particularly handsome.' 'No, but he's very well to pass, and a well-grown youth into the bargain.' Pshaw! let me put an end to the fulsome detail. I found he had lived over the way, that he had been lured thence, no doubt, almost a year before, that they had first spoken in the street, and that he had never once hinted at marriage, and had gone away, because (as he said) they were too much together, and that it was better for her to meet him occasionally out of doors. 'There could be no harm in them walking together.' 'No, but you may go somewhere afterwards.'—'One must trust to one's principle for that.' Consummate hypocrite? * * * I told her Mr. M——, who had married her sister, did not wish to leave the house. I, who would have married her, did not wish to leave it. I told her I hoped I should not live to see her come to shame, after all my love of her; but put her on her guard as well as I could, and said, after the lengths she had permitted herself with me, I could not help being alarmed at the influence of one over her, whom she could hardly herself suppose to have a tenth part of my esteem for her!! She made no answer to this, but thanked me coldly for my good advice, and rose to go. I begged her to sit a few minutes, that I might try to recollect if there was anything else I wished to say to her, perhaps for the last time; and then, not finding anything, I bade her goodnight, and asked for a farewell kiss. Do you know she refused; so little does she understand what is due to friendship, or love, or honour! We parted friends, however, and I felt deep grief, but no enmity against her. I thought C—— had pressed his suit after I went, and had prevailed. There was no harm in that—a little fickleness or so, a little over-pretension to unalterable attachment—but that was all. She liked him better than me—it was my hard hap, but I must bear it. I went out to roam the desert streets, when, turning a corner, whom should I meet but her very lover? I went up to him and asked for a minutes' conversation on a subject that was highly interesting to me and I believed not indifferent to him: and in the course of four hours' talk, it came out that for three months previous to my quitting London for Scotland, she had been playing the same game with him as with me—that he breakfasted first, and enjoyed an hour of her society, and then I took my turn, so that we never jostled; and this explained why, when he came back sometimes and passed my door, as she was sitting in my lap, she coloured violently, thinking if her lover looked in what a *denouement* there would be. He could not help again and again expressing his astonishment at finding that our intimacy had continued unimpaired up to so late a period after he came, and when they were on the most intimate footing. She used to deny positively to him that there was anything between us, just as she used to assure me with impenetrable effrontery that 'Mr. C—— was nothing to her, but merely a lodger.' All this while she kept up the farce of her romantic attachment to her old lover, vowed that she never could alter in that respect, let me go to Scotland on the solemn and repeated assurance that there was no new flame, that there was no bar between us but this shadowy love—I leave her on this understanding, she becomes more fond or more intimate with her new lover; he quitting the house (whether tired out or not, I can't say)—in revenge she ceases to write to me, keeps me in wretched suspense, treats me like something loathsome to her when I return to enquire the cause, denies it with scorn and impudence, destroys me and shows no pity, no desire to soothe or shorten the pangs she has occasioned by her wantonness and hypocrisy, and wishes to linger the affair on to the last moment, going out to keep an appointment with another while she pretends to be obliging me in the tenderest point (which C—— himself said was too much). . . What do you think of all this? Shall I tell you my opinion? But I must try to do it in another letter.

## *To the Same (in conclusion)*

I did not sleep a wink all that night; nor did I know till the next day the full meaning of what had happened to me. With the morning's light, conviction glared in upon me that I had not only lost her for ever—but every feeling I had ever had towards her—respect, tenderness, pity—all but my fatal passion, was gone. The whole was a mockery, a frightful illusion. I had embraced the false Florimel instead of the true; or was like the man in the Arabian Nights who had married a *goul*. How different was the idea I once had of her! Was this she,

> Who had been beguiled—she who was made
> Within a gentle bosom to be laid—
> To bless and to be blessed—to be heart-bare
> To one who found his bettered likeness there—
> To think for ever with him, like a bride—
> To haunt his eye, like taste personified—
> To double his delight, to share his sorrow,
> And like a morning beam, wake to him every morrow?

I saw her pale, cold form glide silent by me, dead to shame as to pity. Still I seemed to clasp this piece of witchcraft to my bosom; this lifeless image, which was all that was left of my love, was the only thing to which my sad heart clung. Were she dead, should I not wish to gaze once more upon her pallid features? She is dead to me; but what she once was to me, can never die! The agony, the conflict of hope and fear, of adoration and jealousy is over; or it would, ere long, have ended with my life. I am no more lifted now to Heaven, and then plunged in the abyss; but I seem to have been thrown from the top of a precipice, and to lie groveling, stunned, and stupified. I am melancholy, lonesome, and weaker than a child. The worst is, I have no prospect of any alteration for the better: she has cut off all possibility of a reconcilement at any future period. Were she even to return to her former pretended fondness and endearments, I could have no pleasure, no confidence in them. I can scarce make out the contradiction to myself. I strive to think she always was what I now know she is; but I have great difficulty in it, and can hardly believe but she still *is* what she so long *seemed*. Poor thing! I am afraid she is little better off herself; nor do I see what is to become of her, unless she throws off the mask at once, and *runs a-muck* at infamy. She is exposed and laid bare to all those whose opinion she set a value upon. Yet she held her head very high, and must feel (if she feels anything) proportionably mortified.—A more complete experiment on character was never made. If I had not met her lover immediately after I parted with her, it would have been nothing. I might have supposed she had changed her mind in my absence, and had given him the preference as soon as she felt it, and even shewn her delicacy in declining any farther intimacy with me. But it comes out that she had gone on in the most forward and familiar way with both at once—(she could not change her mind in passing from one room to another)—told both the same bare-faced and unblushing falsehoods, like the commonest creature; received presents from me to the very last, and wished to keep up the game still longer, either to gratify her humour, her avarice, or her vanity in playing with my passion, or to have me as a *dernier resort*, in case of accidents. Again, it would have been nothing, if she had not come up with her demure, well-composed, wheedling looks that morning, and then met me in the evening in a situation, which (she believed) might kill me on the spot, with no more feeling than a common courtesan shews, who *bilks* a customer, and passes him, leering up at her bully, the moment after. If there had been the frailty of passion, it would have been excusable ; but it is evident she is a practised, callous jilt, a regular lodging-house decoy, played off by her mother upon the lodgers, one after another, applying them to her different purposes, laughing at them in turns, and herself the probable dupe and victim of some favourite gallant in the end. I know all this ; but what do I gain by it, unless I could find some one with her shape and air, to supply the place of that lovely apparition ? That a professed wanton should come and sit on a man's knee, and put her arms round his neck, and caress him, and seem fond of him, means nothing, proves nothing, no one concludes anything from it ; but that a pretty, reserved, modest, delicate-looking girl should do this, from the first hour to the last of your being in the house without intending anything by it, is new, and, I think, worth explaining. It was, I confess, out of my calculation, and may be out of that of others. Her unmoved indifference and self-possession all the while, shew that it is her constant practice. Her look even, if closely examined, bears this interpretation. It is that of studied hypocrisy or startled guilt, rather than of refined sensibility or conscious innocence. 'She defied anyone to read her thoughts ?' she once told me. 'Do they then require concealing ?' I impudently asked her. The command over herself is surprising. She never once betrays herself by any momentary forgetfulness, by any appearance of triumph or superiority to the person who is her dupe, by any levity of manner in the plenitude of her success ; it is one faultless, undeviating, consistent, consummate piece of acting. Were she a saint on earth, she could not seem more like one. Her hypocritical high-flown pretensions, indeed, make her the worse ; but still the ascendancy of her will, her determined perseverance in what she undertakes to do, has something admirable in it, approaching to the heroic. She is certainly an extraordinary girl! Her retired manner, and invariable propriety of behaviour made me think it next to impossible she could grant the same favours indiscriminately to everyone that she did to me. Yet this now appears to be the fact. She must have done the very same with C——, invited him into the house to carry on a closer intrigue with her, and then commenced the double game with both together. She always ‘ despised looks ’. This was a favourite phrase with her, and one of the hooks which she baited for me. Nothing could win her but a man's behaviour and sentiments. Besides, she could never like another—she was a martyr to disappointed affection—and friendship was all she could even extend to any other man. All the time, she was making signals, playing off her pretty person, and having occasional interviews in the street with this very man, whom she could only have taken so sudden and violent a liking to from his looks, his personal appearance, and what she probably conjectured of his circumstances. Her sister had married a counsellor—the Miss F——'s, who kept the house before, had done so too—and so would she. ‘ There was a precedent for it.’ Yet if she was so desperately enamoured of this new acquaintance, if he had displaced *the little image* from her breast, if he was become her *second* ‘ unalterable attachment ’ (which I would have given my life to have been) why continue the same unwarrantable familiarities with me to the last, and promise that they should be renewed on my return (if I had not unfortunately stumbled upon the truth to her aunt) and yet keep up the same refined cant about her old attachment all the time, as if it was that which stood in the way of my pretensions, and not her faithlessness to it? ‘ If one swerves from one, one shall swerve from another ’—was her excuse for not returning my regard. Yet that which I thought a prophecy, was I suspect a history. She had swerved twice from her vowed engagements, first to me, and then from me to another. If she made a fool of me, what did she make of her lover? I fancy he has put that question to himself. I said nothing to him about the amount of the presents; which is another damning circumstance, that might have opened my eyes long before; but they were shut by my fond affection, which 'turned all to favour and to prettiness.' She cannot be supposed to have kept up an appearance of old regard to me, from a fear of hurting my feelings by her desertion; for she not only shewed herself indifferent to, but evidently triumphed in my sufferings, and heaped every kind of insult and indignity upon them. I must have incurred her contempt and resentment by my mistaken delicacy at different times; and her manner, when I have hinted at becoming a reformed man in this respect, convinces me of it. 'She hated it!' She always hated whatever she liked most. She 'hated Mr. C——'s red slippers', when he first came! One more count finishes the indictment. She not only discovered the most hardened indifference to the feelings of others; she has not shewn the least regard to her own character, or shame when she was detected. When found out, she seemed to say 'Well, what if I am? I have played the game as long as I could; and if I could keep it up no longer, it was not for want of good will!' Her colouring once or twice is the only sign of grace she has exhibited. Such is the creature on whom I had thrown away my heart and soul—one who was incapable of feeling the commonest emotions of human nature, as they regarded herself or anyone else. 'She had no feelings with respect to herself' she often said. She, in fact, knows what she is, and recoils from the good opinion or sympathy of others, which she feels to be founded on a deception ; so that my overweening opinion of her must have appeared like irony, or direct insult. My seeing her in the street has gone a good way to satisfy me. Her manner there explains her manner in-doors to be conscious and overdone ; and besides, she looks but indifferently. She is diminutive in stature, and her measured step and timid air do not suit these public airings. I am afraid she will soon grow common to my imagination, as well as worthless in herself. Her image seems fast ' going into the wastes of time ', like a weed that the wave bears farther and farther from me. Alas ! thou poor hapless weed, when I entirely lose sight of thee, and for ever, no flower will ever bloom on earth to glad my heart again !

*THE END*

# DRAMATIC CRITICISMS

# *Contents*

# *On Actors and Acting I*

Players are 'the abstracts and brief chronicles of the time'; the motley representatives of human nature. They are the only honest hypocrites. Their life is a voluntary dream; a studied madness. The height of their ambition is to be *beside themselves*. To-day kings, to-morrow beggars, it is only when they are themselves, that they are nothing. Made up of mimic laughter and tears, passing from the extremes of joy or woe at the prompter's call, they wear the livery of other men's fortunes; their very thoughts are not their own. They are, as it were, train-bearers in the pageant of life, and hold a glass up to humanity, frailer than itself. We see ourselves at second-hand in them: they shew us all that we are, all that we wish to be, and all that we dread to be. The stage is an epitome, a bettered likeness of the world, with the dull part left out: and, indeed, with this omission, it is nearly big enough to hold all the rest. What brings the resemblance nearer is, that, as *they* imitate us, we, in our turn, imitate them. How many fine gentlemen do we owe to the stage? How many romantic lovers are mere Romeos in masquerade? How many soft bosoms have heaved with Juliet's sighs? They teach us when to laugh and when to weep, when to love and when to hate, upon principle and with a good grace! Wherever there is a playhouse, the world will go on not amiss. The stage not only refines the manners, but it is the best teacher of morals, for it is the truest and most intelligible picture of life. It stamps the image of virtue on the mind by first softening the rude materials of which it is composed, by a sense of pleasure. It regulates the passions by giving a loose to the imagination. It points out the selfish and depraved to our detestation, the amiable and generous to our admiration; and if it clothes the more seductive vices with the borrowed graces of wit and fancy, even those graces operate as a diversion to the coarser poison of experience and bad example, and often prevent or carry off the infection by inoculating the mind with a certain taste and elegance. To shew how little we agree with the common declamations against the immoral tendency of the stage on this score, we will hazard a conjecture, that the acting of the Beggar's Opera a certain number of nights every year since it was first brought out, has done more towards putting down the practice of highway robbery, than all the gibbets that ever were erected. A person, after seeing this piece, is too deeply imbued with a sense of humanity, is in too good humour with himself and the rest of the world, to set about cutting throats or rifling pockets. Whatever makes a jest of vice, leaves it too much a matter of indifference for any one in his senses to rush desperately on his ruin for its sake. We suspect that just the contrary effect must be produced by the representation of George Barnwell, which is too much in the style of the Ordinary's sermon to meet with any better success. The mind, in such cases, instead of being deterred by the alarming consequences held out to it, revolts against the denunciation of them as an insult offered to its free-will, and, in a spirit of defiance, returns a practical answer to them, by daring the worst that can happen. The most striking lesson ever read to levity and licentiousness, is in the last act of the Inconstant, where young Mirabel is preserved by the fidelity of his mistress, Orinda, in the disguise of a page, from the hands of assassins, into whose power he has been allured by the temptations of vice and beauty.

There never was a rake who did not become in imagination a reformed man, during the representation of the last trying scenes of this admirable comedy.

If the stage is useful as a school of instruction, it is no less so as a source of amusement. It is the source of the greatest enjoyment at the time, and a never-failing fund of agreeable reflection afterwards. The merits of a new play, or of a new actor, are always among the first topics of polite conversation. One way in which public exhibitions contribute to refine and humanise mankind, is by supplying them with ideas and subjects of conversation and interest in common. The progress of civilization is in proportion to the number of commonplaces current in society. For instance, if we meet with a stranger at an inn or in a stage-coach, who knows nothing but his own affairs, his shop, his customers, his farm, his pigs, his poultry, we can carry on no conversation with him on these local and personal matters: the only way is to let him have all the talk to himself. But if he has fortunately ever seen Mr. Liston act, this is an immediate topic of mutual conversation, and we agree together the rest of the evening in discussing the merits of that inimitable actor, with the same satisfaction as in talking over the affairs of the most intimate friend.

If the stage thus introduces us familiarly to our contemporaries, it also brings us acquainted with former times. It is an interesting revival of past ages, manners, opinions, dresses, persons, and actions,—whether it carries us back to the wars of York and Lancaster, or half way back to the heroic times of Greece and Rome, in some translation from the French, or quite back to the age of Charles II in the scenes of Congreve and of Etherege (the gay Sir George!)—happy age, when kings and nobles led purely ornamental lives; when the utmost stretch of a morning's study went no further than the choice of a sword-knot, or the adjustment of a side-curl; when the soul spoke out in all the pleasing eloquence of dress; and beaux and belles, enamoured of themselves in one another's follies, fluttered like gilded butterflies in giddy mazes through the walks of St. James's Park!

A good company of comedians, a Theatre-Royal judiciously managed, is your true Herald's College; the only Antiquarian Society, that is worth a rush. It is for this reason that there is such an air of romance about players, and that it is pleasanter to see them, even in their own persons, than any of the three learned professions. We feel more respect for John Kemble in a plain coat, than for the Lord Chancellor on the woolsack. He is surrounded, to our eyes, with a greater number of imposing recollections: he is a more reverend piece of formality; a more complicated tissue of costume. We do not know whether to look upon this accomplished actor as Pierre or King John or Coriolanus or Cato or Leontes or the Stranger. But we see him in a stately hieroglyphic of humanity; a living monument of departed greatness, a sombre comment on the rise and fall of kings. We look after him till he is out of sight, as we listen to a story of one of Ossian's heroes, to 'a tale of other times!'

One of the most affecting things we know is to see a favourite actor take leave of the stage. We were present not long ago when Mr. Bannister quitted it. We do not wonder that his feelings were overpowered on the occasion: ours were nearly so too. We remembered him, in the first heyday of our youthful spirits, in the *Prize,* in which he played so delightfully with that fine old croaker Suett, and Madame Storace,—in the farce of *My Grandmother,* in the *Son–in–Law,* in *Autolycus,* and in *Scrub,* in which our satisfaction was at its height. At that time, King and Parsons, and Dodd, and Quick, and Edwin were in the full vigour of their reputation, who are now all gone.

We still feel the vivid delight with which we used to see their names in the play-bills, as we went along to the Theatre. Bannister was one of the last of these that remained ; and we parted with him as we should with one of our oldest and best friends. The most pleasant feature in the profession of a player, and which, indeed, is peculiar to it, is that we not only admire the talents of those who adorn it, but we contract a personal intimacy with them. There is no class of society whom so many persons regard with affection as actors. We greet them on the stage ; we like to meet them in the streets ; they almost always recall to us pleasant associations ; and we feel our gratitude excited, without the uneasiness of a sense of obligation. The very gaiety and popularity, however, which surround the life of a favourite performer, make the retiring from it a very serious business. It glances a mortifying reflection on the shortness of human life, and the vanity of human pleasures. Something reminds us, that ' all the world's a stage, and all the men and women merely players '.

# *On Actors and Acting II*

It has been considered as the misfortune of first-rate talents for the stage, that they leave no record behind them except that of vague rumour, and that the genius of a great actor perishes with him, 'leaving the world no copy'. This is a misfortune, or at lease an unpleasant circumstance, to actors; but it is, perhaps, an advantage to the stage. It leaves an opening to originality. The stage is always beginning anew; the candidates for theatrical reputation are always setting out afresh unencumbered by the affectation of the faults or excellences of their predecessors. In this respect, we should imagine that the average quantity of dramatic talent remains more nearly the same than that in any other walk of art. In no other instance do the complaints of the degeneracy of the moderns seem so unfounded as in this; and Colley Cibber's account of the regular decline of the stage, from the time of Shakespeare to that of Charles II, and from the time of Charles II to the beginning of George II, appears quite ridiculous. The stage is a place where genius is sure to come upon its legs, in a generation or two at farthest. In the other arts (as painting and poetry), it has been contended that what has been well done already, by giving rise to endless vapid imitations, is an obstacle to what might be done well hereafter: that the models or *chef-d'oeuvres* of art, where they are accumulated, choke up the path to excellence; and that the works of genius, where they can be rendered permanent and handed down from age to age, not only prevent, but render superfluous, future productions of the same kind. We have not, neither do we want, two Shakespeares, two Miltons, two Raphaels, any more than we require two suns in the same sphere. Even Miss O'Neill stands a little in the way of our recollections of Mrs. Siddons. But Mr. Kean is an excellent substitute for the memory of Garrick, whom we never saw. When an author dies, it is no matter, for his works remain. When a great actor dies, there is a void produced in society, a gap which requires to be filled up. Who does not go to see Kean? Who, if Garrick were alive, would go to see him? At least one or the other must have quitted the stage. We have seen what a ferment has been excited among our living artists by the exhibition of the works of the old Masters at the British Gallery. What would the actors say to it, if, by any spell or power of necromancy, all the celebrated actors, for the last hundred years, could be made to appear again on the boards of Covent Garden and Drury-Lane, for the last time, in all their most brilliant parts? What a rich treat to the town, what a feast for the critics, to go and see Betterton, and Booth, and Wilks, and Sandford, and Nokes, and Leigh, and Penkethman, and Bullock and Estcourt, and Dogget, and Mrs. Barry, and Mrs. Montfort, and Mrs. Oldfield, and Mrs. Bracegirdle, and Mrs. Cibber, and Cibber himself, the prince of coxcombs, and Macklin, and Quin, and Rich, and Mrs. Clive, and Mrs. Pritchard, and Mrs. Abington, and Weston, and Shuter, and Garrick, and all the rest of those who 'gladdened life, and whose deaths eclipsed the gaiety of nations'! We should certainly be there. We should buy a ticket for the season. We should enjoy *our hundred days* again. We should not lose a single night. We would not, for a great deal, be absent from Betterton's Hamlet or his Brutus, or from Booth's Cato, as it was first acted to the contending applause of Whigs and Tories. We should be in the first row when Mrs. Barry (who was kept by Lord Rochester, and with whom Otway was in love) played Monimia or Belvidera ; and we suppose we should go to see Mrs. Bracegirdle (with whom all the world was in love) in all her parts. We should then know exactly whether Penkethman's manner of picking a chicken, and Bullock's mode of devouring asparagus, answered to the ingenious account of them in the Tatler ; and whether Dogget was equal to Dowton—whether Mrs. Montfort[1] or Mrs. Abington was the finest lady—whether Wilks or Cibber was the best Sir Harry Wildair—whether Macklin was really ' the Jew that Shakespeare drew ', and whether Garrick was, upon the whole, so great an actor as the world have made him out ! Many people have a strong desire to pry into the secrets of futurity : for our own parts, we should be satisfied if we had the power to recall the dead, and live the past over again as often as we pleased ! Players, after all, have little reason to complain of their hard-earned, short-lived popularity. One thunder of applause from pit, boxes, and gallery, is equal to a whole immortality of posthumous fame : and when we hear an actor, whose modesty is equal to his

[1]The following lively description of this actress is given by Cibber in his Apology :—

' What found most employment for her whole various excellence at once, was the part of Melantha, in Marriage-à-la-mode. Melantha is as finished an impertinent as ever fluttered in a drawing-room, and seems to contain the most complete system of female foppery that could possibly be crowded into the tortured form of a fine lady. Her language, dress, motion, manners, soul, and body, are in a continual hurry to be something more than is necessary or commendable. And though I doubt it will be a vain labour to offer you a just likeness of Mrs. Montfort's action, yet the fantastic impression is still so strong in my memory, that I cannot help saying something, though fantastically, about it. The first ridiculous airs that break from her are upon a gallant never seen before, who delivers her a letter from her father, recommending him to her good graces as an honourable lover. Here now, one would think she might naturally shew a little of the sex's decent reserve, though never so slightly covered ! No, sir ; not a tittle of it ; modesty is the virtue of a poor-soul'd country gentlewoman : she is too

merit, declare, that he would like to see a dog wag his tail in approbation, what must he feel when he sees the whole house in a roar! Besides, Fame, as if their reputation had been entrusted to her alone, has been particularly careful of the renown of her theatrical favourites: she forgets one by one, and year by year, those who have been great lawyers, great statesmen, and great warriors in their day; but the name of Garrick still survives with the works of Reynolds and of Johnson.

Actors have been accused, as a profession, of being extravagant and dissipated. While they are said to be so as a piece of common cant, they are likely to continue so. But there is a sentence in Shakespeare which should be stuck as a label in the mouths of our beadles and whippers-in of morality: 'The web of our life is of a mingled yarn, good and ill together: our virtues would be proud if our faults whipped them not: and our vices would despair if they were not cherished by our virtues'. With respect to the extravagance of actors, as a traditional character, it is not to be wondered at. They live from hand to mouth: they plunge from want into

much a court-lady, to be under so vulgar a confusion: she reads the letter, therefore, with a careless, dropping lip, and an erected brow, humming it hastily over, as if she were impatient to outgo her father's commands, by making a complete conquest of him at once; and that the letter might not embarrass her attack, crack! she crumbles it at once into her palm, and pours upon him her whole artillery of airs, eyes, and motion; down goes her dainty, diving body to the ground, as if she were sinking under the conscious load of her own attractions; then launches into a flood of fine language and compliment, still playing her chest forward in fifty falls and risings, like a swan upon waving water; and, to complete her impertinence, she is so rapidly fond of her own wit, that she will not give her lover leave to praise it: Silent assenting bows, and vain endeavours to speak, are all the share of the conversation he is admitted to, which, at last he is relieved from, by her engagement to half a score visits, which she *swims* from him to make, with a promise to return in a twinkling'.—*The Life of Colley Cibber p.* 138.

luxury ; they have no means of making money *breed*, and all professions that do not live by turning money into money, or have not a certainty of accumulating it in the end by parsimony, spend it. Uncertain of the future, they make sure of the present moment. This is not unwise. Chilled with poverty, steeped in contempt, they sometimes pass into the sunshine of fortune, and are lifted to the very pinnacle of public favour ; yet even there cannot calculate on the continuance of success, but are, 'like the giddy sailor on the mast, ready with every blast to topple down into the fatal bowels of the deep !' Besides, if the young enthusiast, who is smitten with the stage, and with the public as a mistress, were naturally a close *hunks*, he would become or remain a city clerk, instead of turning player. Again, with respect to the habit of convivial indulgence, an actor, to be a good one, must have a great spirit of enjoyment in himself, strong impulses, strong passions, and a strong sense of pleasure : for it is his business to imitate the passions, and to communicate pleasure to others. A man of genius is not a machine. The neglected actor may be excused if he drinks oblivion of his disappointments ; the successful one, if he quaffs the applause of the world, and enjoys the friendship of those who are the friends of the favourites of fortune, in draughts of nectar. There is no path so steep as that of fame : no labour so hard as the pursuit of excellence. The intellectual excitement, inseparable from those professions which call forth all our sensibility to pleasure and pain, requires some corresponding physical excitement to support our failure, and not a little to allay the ferment of the spirits attendant on success. If there is any tendency to dissipation beyond this in the profession of a player, it is owing to the prejudices entertained against them, to that spirit of bigotry which in a neighbouring country would deny actors Christian burial after their death, and to that cant of criticism, which, in our own, slurs over their characters, while living, with a half-witted jest.

A London engagement is generally considered by actors as the *ne plus ultra* of their ambition, as 'a consummation devoutly to be wished', as the great prize in the lottery of their professional life. But this appears to us, who are not in the secret, to be rather the prose termination of their adventurous career: it is the provincial commencement that is the poetical and truly enviable part of it. After that, they have comparatively little to hope or fear. 'The wine of life is drunk, and but the lees remain'. In London, they become gentlemen, and the King's servants: but it is the romantic mixture of the hero and the vagabond that constitutes the essence of the player's life. It is the transition from their real to their assumed characters, from the contempt of the world to the applause of the multitude, that gives its zest to the latter, and raises them as much above common humanity at night, as in the daytime they are depressed below it. 'Hurried from fierce extremes, by contrast made more fierce',—it is rags and a flock-bed which give their splendour to a plume of feathers and a throne. We should suppose, that if the most admired actor on the London stage were brought to confession on this point, he would acknowledge that all the applause he had received from 'brilliant and overflowing audiences', was nothing to the light-headed intoxication of unlooked-for success in a barn. In town, actors are criticised: in country-places, they are wondered at, or hooted at: it is of little consequence which, so that the interval is not too long between. For ourselves, we own that the description of the strolling player in Gil Blas, soaking his dry crusts in the well by the road-side, presents to us a perfect picture of human felicity.

# *Preface*

It is observed by Mr. Pope, that 'If ever any author deserved the name of an *original*, it was Shakespeare. Homer himself drew not his art so immediately from the fountains of nature; it proceeded through Ægyptian strainers and channels, and came to him not without some tincture of the learning, or some cast of the models, of those before him. The poetry of Shakespeare was inspiration: indeed, he is not so much an imitator, as an instrument of nature; and it is not so just to say that he speaks from her, as that she speaks through him.

'His *characters* are so much nature herself, that it is a sort of injury to call them by so distant a name as copies of her. Those of other poets have a constant resemblance, which shows that they received them from one another, and were but multipliers of the same image: each picture, like a mock-rainbow, is but the reflection of a reflection. But every single character in Shakespeare, is as much an individual, as those in life itself; it is as impossible to find any two alike; and such, as from their relation or affinity in any respect appear most to be twins, will, upon comparison, be found remarkably distinct. To this life and variety of character, we must add the wonderful preservation of it; which is such throughout his plays, that had all the speeches been printed without the very names of the persons, I believe one might have applied them with certainty to every speaker.'

The object of the volume here offered to the public, is to illustrate these remarks in a more particular manner by a reference to each play. A gentleman of the name of Mason, the author of a Treatise on Ornamental Gardening (not Mason the poet), began a work of a similar kind about forty years ago, but he only lived to finish a parallel between the characters of Macbeth and Richard III which is an exceedingly ingenious piece of analytical criticism. Richardson's Essays include but a few of Shakespeare's principal characters. The only work which seemed to supersede the necessity of an attempt like the present was Schlegel's very admirable Lectures on the Drama, which give by far the best account of the plays of Shakespeare that has hitherto appeared. The only circumstances in which it was thought not impossible to improve on the manner in which the German critic has executed this part of his design, were in avoiding an appearance of mysticism in his style, not very attractive to the English reader, and in bringing illustrations from particular passages of the plays themselves, of which Schlegel's work, from the extensiveness of his plan, did not admit. We will at the same time confess, that some little jealousy of the character of the national understanding was not without its share in producing the following undertaking, for 'we were piqued' that it should be reserved for a foreign critic to give 'reasons for the faith which we English have in Shakespeare.' Certainly, no writer among ourselves has shown either the same enthusiastic admiration of his genius, or the same philosophical acuteness in pointing out his characteristic excellences. As we have pretty well exhausted all we had to say upon this subject in the body of the work, we shall here transcribe Schlegel's general account of Shakespeare, which is in the following words:

'Never, perhaps, was there so comprehensive a talent for the delineation of character as Shakespeare's. It not only grasps the diversities of rank, sex, and age, down to the dawnings of infancy;

not only do the king and the beggar, the hero and the pickpocket, the sage and the idiot, speak and act with equal truth; not only does he transport himself to distant ages and foreign nations, and pourtray in the most accurate manner, with only a few apparent violations of costume, the spirit of the ancient Romans, of the French in their wars with the English, of the English themselves during a great part of their history, of the Southern Europeans (in the serious part of many comedies) the cultivated society of that time, and the former rude and barbarous state of the North; his human characters have not only such depth and precision that they cannot be arranged under classes, and are inexhaustible, even in conception:—no—this Prometheus not merely forms men, he opens the gates of the magical world of spirits; calls up the midnight ghost; exhibits before us his witches amidst their unhallowed mysteries; peoples the air with sportive fairies and sylphs:—and these beings, existing only in imagination, possess such truth and consistency, that even when deformed monsters like Caliban, he extorts the conviction, that if there should be such beings, they would so conduct themselves. In a word, as he carries with him the most fruitful and daring fancy into the kingdom of nature—on the other hand, he carries nature into the regions of fancy, lying beyond the confines of reality. We are lost in astonishment at seeing the extraordinary, the wonderful, and the unheard of, in such intimate nearness.

'If Shakespeare deserves our admiration for his characters, he is equally deserving of it for his exhibition of passion, taking this word in its widest signification, as including every mental condition, every tone from indifference or familiar mirth to the wildest rage and despair. He gives us the history of minds; he lays open to us, in a single word, a whole series of preceding conditions. His passions do not at first stand displayed to us in all their height, as is the case with so many tragic poets, who, in the language of Lessing, are thorough masters of the legal style of love. He paints, in a most inimitable manner, the gradual progress from the first origin. "He gives", as Lessing says, "a living picture of all the most minute and secret artifices by which a feeling steals into our souls; of all the imperceptible advantages which it there gains; of all the stratagems by which every other passion is made subservient to it, till it becomes the sole tyrant of our desires and our aversions." Of all poets, perhaps, he alone has pourtrayed the mental diseases—melancholy, delirium, lunacy,—with such inexpressible, and, in every respect, definite truth, that the physician may enrich his observations from them in the same manner as from real cases.

'And yet Johnson has objected to Shakespeare, that his pathos is not always natural and free from affectation. There are, it is true, passages, though, comparatively speaking, very few, where his poetry exceeds the bounds of true dialogue, where a too soaring imagination, a too luxuriant wit, rendered the complete dramatic forgetfulness of himself impossible. With this exception, the censure originates only in a fanciless way of thinking, to which everything appears unnatural that does not suit its own tame insipidity. Hence, an idea has been formed of simple and natural pathos, which consists in exclamations destitute of imagery, and nowise elevated above every-day life. But energetical passions electrify the whole of the mental powers, and will, consequently, in highly favoured natures, express themselves in an ingenious and figurative manner. It has been often remarked, that indignation gives wit; and, as despair occasionally breaks out into laughter, it may sometimes also give vent to itself in antithetical comparisons.

'Besides, the rights of the poetical form have not

been duly weighed. Shakespeare, who was always sure of his object, to move in a sufficiently powerful manner when he wished to do so, has occasionally, by indulging in a freer play, purposely moderated the impressions when too painful, and immediately introduced a musical alleviation of our sympathy. He had not those rude ideas of his art which many moderns seem to have, as if the poet, like the clown in the proverb, must strike twice on the same place. An ancient rhetorician delivered a caution against dwelling too long on the excitation of pity; for nothing, he said, dries so soon as tears; and Shakespeare acted conformably to this ingenious maxim, without knowing it.

'The objection, that Shakespeare wounds our feelings by the open display of the most disgusting moral odiousness, harrows up the mind unmercifully, and tortures even our senses by the exhibition of the most insupportable and hateful spectacles, is one of much greater importance. He has never, in fact, varnished over wild and blood-thirsty passions with a pleasing exterior,—never clothed crime and want of principle with a false show of greatness of soul; and in that respect he is every way deserving of praise. Twice he has pourtrayed downright villains; and the masterly way in which he has contrived to elude impressions of too painful a nature, may be seen in Iago and Richard the Third. The constant reference to a petty and puny race must cripple the boldness of the poet. Fortunately for his art, Shakespeare lived in an age extremely susceptible of noble and tender impressions, but which had still enough of the firmness inherited from a vigorous olden time not to shrink back with dismay from every strong and violent picture. We have lived to see tragedies of which the catastrophe consists in the swoon of an enamoured princess. If Shakespeare falls occasionally into the opposite extreme, it is a noble error, originating in the fulness of a gigantic strength : and yet this tragical Titan, who storms the heavens, and threatens to tear the world from off its hinges ; who, more terrible than Æschylus, makes our hair stand on end, and congeals our blood with horror, possessed, at the same time, the insinuating loveliness of the sweetest poetry. He plays with love like a child ; and his songs are breathed out like melting sighs. He unites in his genius the utmost elevation and the utmost depth ; and the most foreign, and even apparently irreconcilable properties subsist in him peaceably together. The world of spirits and nature have laid all their treasures at his feet. In strength a demi-god, in profundity of view a prophet, in all-seeing wisdom a protecting spirit of a higher order, he lowers himself to mortals, as if unconscious of his superiority : and is as open and unassuming as a child.

'Shakespeare's comic talent is equally wonderful with that which he has shown in the pathetic and tragic : it stands on an equal elevation, and possesses equal extent and profundity. All that I before wished was, not to admit that the former preponderated. He is highly inventive in comic situations and motives. It will be hardly possible to show whence he has taken any of them ; whereas, in the serious part of his drama, he has generally laid hold of something already known. His comic characters are equally true, various, and profound, with his serious. So little is he disposed to caricature, that we may rather say many of his traits are almost too nice and delicate for the stage, that they can only be properly seized by a great actor, and fully understood by a very acute audience. Not only has he delineated many kinds of folly ; he has also contrived to exhibit mere stupidity in a most diverting and entertaining manner.' Vol. ii, p. 145.

We have the rather availed ourselves of this

testimony of a foreign critic in behalf of Shakespeare, because our own countryman, Dr. Johnson, has not been so favourable to him. It may be said of Shakespeare, that 'those who are not for him are against him': for indifference is here the height of injustice. We may sometimes, in order 'to do a great right, do a little wrong'. An overstrained enthusiasm is more pardonable with respect to Shakespeare than the want of it; for our admiration cannot easily surpass his genius. We have a high respect for Dr. Johnson's character and understanding, mixed with something like personal attachment: but he was neither a poet nor a judge of poetry. He might in one sense be a judge of poetry as it falls within the limits and rules of prose, but not as it is poetry. Least of all was he qualified to be a judge of Shakespeare, who 'alone is high fantastical'. Let those who have a prejudice against Johnson read Boswell's Life of him: as those whom he has prejudiced against Shakespeare should read his *Irene*. We do not say that a man to be a critic must necessarily be a poet; but to be a good critic, he ought not to be a bad poet. Such poetry as a man deliberately writes, such, and such only will he like. Dr. Johnson's Preface to his edition of Shakespeare looks like a laborious attempt to bury the characteristic merits of his author under a load of cumbrous phraseology, and to weigh his excellences and defects in equal scales, stuffed full of 'swelling figures and sonorous epithets'. Nor could it well be otherwise; Dr. Johnson's general powers of reasoning overlaid his critical susceptibility. All his ideas were cast in a given mould, in a set form: they were made out by rule and system, by climax, inference, and antithesis:—Shakespeare's were the reverse. Johnson's understanding dealt only in round numbers: the fractions were lost upon him. He reduced everything to the common standard of conventional propriety; and the most exquisite refinement or sublimity produced an effect on his mind, only as they could be translated into the language of measured prose. To him an excess of beauty was a fault ; for it appeared to him like an excrescence ; and his imagination was dazzled by the blaze of light. His writings neither shone with the beams of native genius, nor reflected them. The shifting shapes of fancy, the rainbow hues of things, made no impression on him : he seized only on the permanent and tangible. He had no idea of natural objects but ' such as he could measure with a two-foot rule, or tell upon ten fingers ' , he judged of human nature in the same way, by mood and figure : he saw only the definite, the positive, and the practical, the average forms of things, not their striking differences —their classes, not their degrees. He was a man of strong common sense and practical wisdom, rather than of genius or feeling. He retained the regular, habitual impressions of actual objects, but he could not follow the rapid flights of fancy or the strong movements of passion. That is, he was to the poet what the painter of still life is to the painter of history. Common sense sympathizes with the impressions of things on ordinary minds in ordinary circumstances : genius catches the glancing combinations presented to the eye of fancy, under the influence of passion. It is the province of the didactic reasoner to take cognizance of those results of human nature which are constantly repeated and always the same, which follow one another in regular succession, which are acted upon by large classes of men, and embodied in received customs, laws, language, and institutions ; and it was in arranging, comparing, and arguing on these kind of general results, that Johnson's excellence lay. But he could not quit his hold of the commonplace and mechanical, and apply the general rule to the particular exception, or show how the nature of man was modified by the workings of passion, or the infinite fluctuations of thought and accident. Hence he could judge neither of the heights nor depths of poetry. Nor is this all ; for being conscious of great powers in himself, and those powers of an adverse tendency to those of his author, he would be for setting up a foreign jurisdiction over poetry, and making criticism a kind of Procrustes' bed of genius, where he might cut down imagination to matter-of-fact, regulate the passions according to reason, and translate the whole into logical diagrams and rhetorical declamation. Thus he says of Shakespeare's characters, in contradiction to what Pope had observed, and to what every one else feels, that each character is a species, instead of being an individual. He in fact found the general species or *didactic* form in Shakespeare's characters, which was all he sought or cared for ; he did not find the individual traits, or the *dramatic* distinctions which Shakespeare has engrafted on this general nature, because he felt no interest in them. Shakespeare's bold and happy flights of imagination were equally thrown away upon our author. He was not only without any particular fineness of organic sensibility, alive to all the 'mighty world of ear and eye', which is necessary to the painter or musician, but without that intenseness of passion, which, seeking to exaggerate whatever excites the feelings of pleasure or power in the mind, and moulding the impressions of natural objects according to the impulses of imagination, produces a genius and a taste for poetry. According to Dr. Johnson, a mountain is sublime, or a rose is beautiful ; for that their name and definition imply. But he would no more be able to give the description of Dover cliff in *Lear*, or the description of flowers in *The Winter's Tale*, than to describe the objects of a sixth sense ; nor do we think he would have any very profound feeling of the beauty of the passages here referred to. A stately common-place, such as Congreve's description of a ruin in *The Mourning Bride*, would have answered Johnson's purpose just as well, or better than the first; and an indiscriminate profusion of scents and hues would have interfered less with the ordinary routine of his imagination than Perdita's lines, which seem enamoured of their own sweetness—

> Daffodils
> That come before the swallow dares, and take
> The winds of March with beauty; violets dim,
> But sweeter than the lids of Juno's eyes,
> Or Cytherea's breath.—

No one who does not feel the passion which these objects inspire can go along with the imagination which seeks to express that passion and the uneasy sense of delight accompanying it by something still more beautiful, and no one can feel this passionate love of nature without quick natural sensibility. To a mere literal and formal apprehension, the inimitably characteristic epithet, 'violets *dim*', must seem to imply a defect, rather than a beauty; and to any one, not feeling the full force of that epithet, which suggests an image like 'the sleepy eye of love', the allusion to 'the lids of Juno's eyes' must appear extravagant and unmeaning. Shakespeare's fancy lent words and images to the most refined sensibility to nature, struggling for expression: his descriptions are identical with the things themselves, seen through the fine medium of passion: strip them of that connexion, and try them by ordinary conceptions and ordinary rules, and they are as grotesque and barbarous as you please!—By thus lowering Shakespeare's genius to the standard of common-place invention, it was easy to show that his faults were as great as his beauties; for the excellence, which consists merely in a conformity to rules, is counterbalanced by the technical violation of them. Another circumstance which led to Dr. Johnson's indiscriminate praise or censure of Shakespeare, is the very structure of his style. Johnson wrote a kind of rhyming prose, in which he was as much compelled to finish the different clauses of his sentences, and to balance one period against another, as the writer of heroic verse is to keep to lines of ten syllables with similar terminations. He no sooner acknowledges the merits of his author in one line than the periodical revolution in his style carries the weight of his opinion completely over to the side of objection, thus keeping up a perpetual alternation of perfections and absurdities. We do not otherwise know how to account for such assertions as the following: 'In his tragic scenes, there is always something wanting, but his comedy often surpasses expectation or desire. His comedy pleases by the thoughts and the language, and his tragedy, for the greater part, by incident and action. His tragedy seems to be skill, his comedy to be instinct,' Yet after saying that 'his tragedy was skill', he affirms in the next page, 'His declamations or set speeches are commonly cold and weak, *for his power was the power of nature*: when he endeavoured, like other tragic writers, to catch opportunities of amplification, and instead of inquiring what the occasion demanded, to show how much his stores of knowledge could supply, he seldom escapes without the pity or resentment of his reader.' Poor Shakespeare! Between the charges here brought against him, of want of nature in the first instance, and of want of skill in the second, he could hardly escape being condemned. And again, 'But the admirers of this great poet have most reason to complain when he approaches nearest to his highest excellence, and seems fully resolved to sink them in dejection, or mollify them with tender emotions by the fall of greatness, the danger of innocence, or the crosses of love. What he does best, he soon ceases to do. He no sooner begins to move than he counteracts himself; and terror and pity, as they are rising in the mind, are checked and blasted by sudden frigidity.' In all this, our critic seems more bent on maintaining the equilibrium of his style than the consistency or truth of his opinions.—If Dr. Johnson's opinion was right, the following observations on Shakespeare's plays must be greatly exaggerated, if not ridiculous. If he was wrong, what has been said may perhaps account for his being so, without detracting from his ability and judgement in other things.

It is proper to add, that the account of the *Midsummer Night's Dream* has appeared in another work.

April 15th, 1817

## *Cymbeline*

Cymbeline is one of the most delightful of Shakespeare's historical plays. It may be considered as a dramatic romance, in which the most striking parts of the story are thrown into the form of a dialogue, and the intermediate circumstances are explained by the different speakers, as occasion renders it necessary. The action is less concentrated in consequence; but the interest becomes more aerial and refined from the principle of perspective introduced into the subject by the imaginary changes of scene as well as by the length of time it occupies. The reading of this play is like going a journey with some uncertain object at the end of it, and in which the suspense is kept up and heightened by the long intervals between each action. Though the events are scattered over such an extent of surface, and relate to such a variety of characters, yet the links which bind the different interests of the story together are never entirely broken. The most straggling and seemingly casual incidents are contrived in such a manner as to lead at last to the most complete development of the catastrophe. The ease and conscious unconcern with which this is effected only makes the skill more wonderful. The business of the plot evidently thickens in the last act: the story moves forward with increasing rapidity at every step; its various ramifications are drawn from the most distant points to the same centre; the principal characters are brought together, and placed in very critical situations; and the fate of almost every person in the drama is made to depend on the solution of a single circumstance—the answer of Iachimo to the question of Imogen respecting the obtaining of the ring from Posthumus. Dr. Johnson is of opinion that Shakespeare was generally inattentive to the winding up of his plots. We think the contrary is true; and we might cite in proof of this remark not only the present play, but the conclusion of *Lear*, of *Romeo and Juliet*, of *Macbeth*, of *Othello*, even of *Hamlet*, and of other plays of less moment, in which the last act is crowded with decisive events brought about by natural and striking means.

The pathos in *Cymbeline* is not violent or tragical, but of the most pleasing and amiable kind. A certain tender gloom o'erspreads the whole. Posthumus is the ostensible hero of the piece, but its greatest charm is the character of Imogen. Posthumus is only interesting from the interest she takes in him, and she is only interesting herself from her tenderness and constancy to her husband. It is the peculiar characteristic of Shakespeare's heroines, that they seem to exist only in their attachment to others. They are pure abstractions of the affections. We think as little of their persons as they do themselves, because we are let into the secrets of their hearts, which are more important. We are too much interested in their affairs to stop to look at their faces, except by stealth and at intervals. No one ever hit the true perfection of the female character, the sense of weakness leaning on the strength of its affections for support, so well as Shakespeare—no one ever so well painted natural tenderness free from affectation and disguise—no one else ever so well showed how delicacy and timidity, when driven to extremity, grow romantic and extravagant; for the romance of his heroines (in which they abound) is only an excess of the habitual prejudices of their sex, scrupulous of being false to their vows, truant to their affections, and taught by the force of feeling when to forgo the forms of propriety for the essence of it. His women were in this respect exquisite logicians; for there is nothing so logical as passion. They knew their own minds exactly; and only followed up a favourite idea, which they had sworn to with their tongues, and which was engraven on their hearts, into its untoward consequences. They were the prettiest little set of martyrs and confessors on record.—Cibber, in speaking of the early English stage, accounts for the want of prominence and theatrical display in Shakespeare's female characters from the circumstance, that women in those days were not allowed to play the parts of women, which made it necessary to keep them a good deal in the background. Does not this state of manners itself, which prevented their exhibiting themselves in public, and confined them to the relations and charities of domestic life, afford a truer explanation of the matter? His women are certainly very unlike stage-heroines; the reverse of tragedy-queens.

We have almost as great an affection for Imogen as she had for Posthumus; and she deserves it better. Of all Shakespeare's women she is perhaps the most tender and the most artless. Her incredulity in the opening scene with Iachimo, as to her husband's infidelity, is much the same as Desdemona's backwardness to believe Othello's jealousy. Her answer to the most distressing part of the picture is only, 'My lord, I fear, has forgot Britain.' Her readiness to pardon Iachimo's false imputations and his designs against herself, is a good lesson to prudes; and may show that where there is real attachment to virtue, it has no need to bolster itself up with an outrageous or affected antipathy to vice. The scene in which Pisanio gives Imogen his master's letter, accusing her of incontinency on the treacherous suggestions of Iachimo, is as touching as it is possible for any thing to be:

*Pisanio.* What cheer, Madam ?
*Imogen.* False to his bed ! What is it to be false ?
To lie in watch there, and to think on him ?
To weep 'twixt clock and clock ? If sleep charge nature,
To break it with a fearful dream of him,
And cry myself awake ? That's false to's bed, is it ?
*Pisanio.* Alas, good lady !
*Imogen.* I false ? thy conscience witness, Iachimo,
Thou didst accuse him of incontinency,
Thou then look'dst like a villain : now methinks,
Thy favour's good enough. Some jay of Italy,
Whose mother was her painting, hath betrayed him :
Poor I am stale, a garment out of fashion,
And for I am richer than to hang by th' walls,
I must be ript ; to pieces with me. Oh,
Men's vows are women's traitors. All good seeming,
By thy revolt, oh husband, shall be thought
Put on for villany : not born where't grows,
But worn a bait for ladies.
*Pisanio.* Good madam, hear me—
*Imogen.* Talk thy tongue weary, speak :
I have heard I am a strumpet, and mine ear,
Therein false struck, can take no greater wound,
Nor tent to bottom that.—

When Pisanio, who had been charged to kill his mistress, puts her in a way to live, she says :

Why, good fellow,
What shall I do the while ? Where bide ? How live ?
Or in my life what comfort, when I am
Dead to my husband ?

Yet when he advises her to disguise herself in boy's clothes, and suggests 'a course pretty and full in view', by which she may 'happily be near the residence of Posthumus', she exclaims :

Oh, for such means,
Though peril to my modesty, not death on 't,
I would adventure.

And when Pisanio, enlarging on the consequences, tells her she must change

——Fear and niceness,
The handmaids of all women, or more truly,
Woman its pretty self, into a waggish courage,
Ready in gibes, quick answer'd, saucy, and
As quarrellous as the weasel——

she interrupts him hastily:

Nay, be brief;
I see into thy end, and am almost
A man already.

In her journey thus disguised to Milford Haven, she loses her guide and her way; and unbosoming her complaints, says beautifully:

——My dear Lord,
Thou art one of the false ones; now I think on thee,
My hunger's gone; but even before, I was
At point to sink for food.

She afterwards finds, as she thinks, the dead body of Posthumus, and engages herself as a foot-boy to serve a Roman officer, when she has done all due obsequies to him whom she calls her former master:

——And when
With wild wood-leaves and weeds I ha' strew'd his grave,
And on it said a century of pray'rs,
Such as I can, twice o'er, I'll weep and sigh,
And leaving so his service, follow you,
So please you entertain me.

Now this is the very religion of love. She all along relies little on her personal charms, which she fears may have been eclipsed by some painted jay of Italy; she relies on her merit, and her merit is in the depth of her love, her truth and constancy. Our admiration of her beauty is excited with as little consciousness as possible on her part. There are two delicious descriptions given of her, one when she is asleep, and one when she is supposed dead. Arviragus thus addresses her:

——With fairest flowers,
While summer lasts, and I live here, Fidele,
I'll sweeten thy sad grave ; thou shalt not lack
The flow'r that's like thy face, pale primrose, nor
The azur'd hare-bell, like thy veins, no, nor
The leaf of eglantine, which not to slander,
Out-sweeten'd not thy breath.

The yellow Iachimo gives another thus, when he steals into her bed-chamber :

——Cytherea,
How bravely thou becom'st thy bed ! Fresh lily,
And whiter than the sheets ! That I might touch—
But kiss, one kiss—'Tis her breathing that
Perfumes the chamber thus : the flame o' th' taper
Bows toward her, and would under-peep her lids,
To see th' enclosed lights now canopied
Under the windows, white and azure, laced
With blue of Heav'ns own tinct—on her left breast
A mole cinque-spotted, like the crimson drops
I' the bottom of a cowslip.

There is a moral sense in the proud beauty of this last image, a rich surfeit of the fancy,—as that well-known passage beginning, ' Me of my lawful pleasure she restrained, and prayed me oft forbearance ', sets a keener edge upon it by the inimitable picture of modesty and self-denial.

The character of Cloten, the conceited, booby lord, and rejected lover of Imogen, though not very agreeable in itself, and at present obsolete, is drawn with great humour and knowledge of character. The description which Imogen gives of his unwelcome addresses to her—' Whose love-suit hath been to me as fearful as a siege '—is enough to cure the most ridiculous lover of his folly. It is remarkable that though Cloten makes so poor a figure in love, he is described as assuming an air of consequence as the Queen's son in a council of state, and with all the absurdity of his person and manners, is not without shrewdness in his observations. So true is it that folly is as often owing to a want of proper sentiments as to a want of understanding! The exclamation of the ancient critic, 'O Menander and Nature, which of you copied from the other?' would not be misapplied to Shakespeare.

The other characters in this play are represented with great truth and accuracy, and as it happens in most of the author's works, there is not only the utmost keeping in each separate character; but in the casting of the different parts, and their relation to one another, there is an affinity and harmony, like what we may observe in the gradations of colour in a picture. The striking and powerful contrasts in which Shakespeare abounds could not escape observation; but the use he makes of the principle of analogy to reconcile the greatest diversities of character and to maintain a continuity of feeling throughout, has not been sufficiently attended to. In *Cymbeline*, for instance, the principal interest arises out of the unalterable fidelity of Imogen to her husband under the most trying circumstances. Now the other parts of the picture are filled up with subordinate examples of the same feeling, variously modified by different situations, and applied to the purposes of virtue or vice. The plot is aided by the amorous importunities of Cloten, by the tragical determination of Iachimo to conceal the defeat of his project by a daring imposture: the faithful attachment of Pisanio to his mistress is an affecting accompaniment to the whole; the obstinate adherence to his purpose in Bellarius, who keeps the fate of the young princes so long a secret in resentment for the ungrateful return to his former services, the incorrigible wickedness of the Queen, and even the blind uxorious confidence of Cymbeline, are all so many lines of the same story, tending to the same point. The effect of this coincidence is rather felt than observed; and as the impression exists unconsciously in the mind of the reader, so it probably arose in the same manner in the mind of the author, not from design, but from the force of natural association, a particular train of feeling suggesting different inflections of the same predominant principle, melting into, and strengthening one another, like chords in music.

The characters of Bellarius, Guiderius, and Arviragus, and the romantic scenes in which they appear, are a fine relief to the intrigues and artificial refinements of the court from which they are banished. Nothing can surpass the wildness and simplicity of the descriptions of the mountain life they lead. They follow the business of huntsmen, not of shepherds; and this is in keeping with the spirit of adventure and uncertainty in the rest of the story, and with the scenes in which they are afterwards called on to act. How admirably the youthful fire and impatience to emerge from their obscurity in the young princes is opposed to the cooler calculations and prudent resignation of their more experienced counsellor! How well the disadvantages of knowledge and of ignorance, of solitude and society, are placed against each other!

*Guiderius.* Out of your proof you speak: we poor unfledg'd
Have never wing'd from view o' th' nest; nor know not
What air's from home. Haply this life is best,
If quiet life is best; sweeter to you
That have a sharper known; well corresponding
With your stiff age: but unto us it is
A cell of ignorance; travelling a-bed,
A prison for a debtor, that not dares
To stride a limit.

*Arviragus.* What should we speak of
When we are old as you? When we shall hear
The rain and wind beat dark December! How,
In this our pinching cave, shall we discourse
The freezing hours away? We have seen nothing.
We are beastly; subtle as the fox for prey,
Like warlike as the wolf for what we eat:
Our valour is to chase what flies; our cage
We make a quire, as doth the prison's bird,
And sing our bondage freely.

The answer of Bellarius to this expostulation is hardly satisfactory; for nothing can be an answer to hope, or the passion of the mind for unknown good, but experience.—The forest of Arden in *As You Like It* can alone compare with the mountain scenes in *Cymbeline*: yet how different the contemplative quiet of the one from the enterprising boldness and precarious mode of subsistence in the other! Shakespeare not only lets us into the minds of his characters, but gives a tone and colour to the scenes he describes from the feelings of their imaginary inhabitants. He at the same time preserves the utmost propriety of action and passion, and gives all their local accompaniments. If he was equal to the greatest things, he was not above an attention to the smallest. Thus the gallant sportsmen in *Cymbeline* have to encounter the abrupt declivities of hill and valley: Touchstone and Audrey jog along a level path. The deer in *Cymbeline* are only regarded as objects of prey, 'The game's a-foot', &c.—with Jaques they are fine subjects to moralize upon at leisure, 'under the shade of melancholy boughs.'

We cannot take leave of this play, which is a favourite with us, without noticing some occasional touches of natural piety and morality. We may allude here to the opening of the scene in which Bellarius instructs the young princes to pay their orisons to heaven:

> ——See, Boys! this gate
> Instructs you how t' adore the Heav'ns; and bows you
> To morning's holy office.
> *Guiderius.* Hail, Heav'n!
> *Arviragus.* Hail, Heav'n!
> *Bellarius.* Now for our mountain-sport, up to yon hill.

What a grace and unaffected spirit of piety breathes in this passage! In like manner, one of the brothers says to the other, when about to perform the funeral rites to Fidele:

> Nay, Cadwall, we must lay his head to the east;
> My Father hath a reason for't.

Shakespeare's morality is introduced in the same simple, unobtrusive manner. Imogen will not let her companions stay away from the chase to attend her when sick, and gives her reason for it :

> Stick to your journal course ; *the breach of custom*
> *Is breach of all* !

When the Queen attempts to disguise her motives for procuring the poison from Cornelius, by saying she means to try its effects on ' creatures not worth the hanging ', his answer conveys at once a tacit reproof of her hypocrisy, and a useful lesson of humanity :

> ——Your Highness
> Shall from this practice but make hard your heart.

# *Macbeth*

The poet's eye in a fine frenzy rolling
Doth glance from heaven to earth, from earth to heaven ;
And as imagination bodies forth
The forms of things unknown, the poet's pen
Turns them to shape, and gives to airy nothing
A local habitation and a name.

*Macbeth* and *Lear, Othello* and *Hamlet,* are usually reckoned Shakespeare's four principal tragedies. *Lear* stands first for the profound intensity of the passion ; *Macbeth* for the wildness of the imagination and the rapidity of the action ; *Othello* for the progressive interest and powerful alternations of feeling ; *Hamlet* for the refined development of thought and sentiment. If the force of genius shown in each of these works is astonishing, their variety is not less so. They are like different creations of the same mind, not one of which has the slightest reference to the rest. This distinctness and originality is indeed the necessary consequence of truth and nature. Shakespeare's genius alone appeared to possess the resources of nature. He is ' your only *tragedy-maker* '. His plays have the force of things upon the mind. What he represents is brought home to the bosom as a part of our experience, implanted in the memory as if we had known the places, persons, and things of which he treats. *Macbeth* is like a record of a preternatural and tragical event. It has the rugged severity of an old chronicle with all that the imagination of the poet can engraft upon traditional belief. The castle of Macbeth, round which ' the air smells wooingly ', and where ' the temple-haunting martlet builds', has a real subsistence in the mind; the Weird Sisters meet us in person on 'the blasted heath'; the 'air-drawn dagger' moves slowly before our eyes; the 'gracious Duncan', the 'blood-boltered Banquo' stand before us; all that passed through the mind of Macbeth passes, without the loss of a tittle, through ours. All that could actually take place, and all that is only possible to be conceived, what was said and what was done, the workings of passion, the spells of magic, are brought before us with the same absolute truth and vividness.—Shakespeare excelled in the openings of his plays: that of Macbeth is the most striking of any. The wildness of the scenery, the sudden shifting of the situations and characters, the bustle, the expectations excited, are equally extraordinary. From the first entrance of the Witches and the description of them when they meet Macbeth:

> ——What are these
> So wither'd and so wild in their attire,
> That look not like the inhabitants of th' earth
> And yet are on't?

the mind is prepared for all that follows.

This tragedy is alike distinguished for the lofty imagination it displays, and for the tumultuous vehemence of the action; and the one is made the moving principle of the other. The overwhelming pressure of preternatural agency urges on the tide of human passion with redoubled force. Macbeth himself appears driven along by the violence of his fate like a vessel drifting before a storm: he reels to and fro like a drunken man; he staggers under the weight of his own purposes and the suggestions of others; he stands at bay with his situation; and from the superstitious awe and breathless suspense into which the communications of the Weird Sisters throw him, is hurried on with daring impatience to verify their predictions, and with impious and bloody hand to tear aside the veil, which hides the uncertainty of the future. He is not equal to the struggle with fate and conscience. He now ' bends up each corporal instrument to the terrible feat '; at other times his heart misgives him, and he is cowed and abashed by his success. ' The deed, no less than the attempt, confounds him '. His mind is assailed by the stings of remorse, and full of ' preternatural solicitings '. His speeches and soliloquies are dark riddles on human life, baffling solution, and entangling him in their labyrinths. In thought he is absent and perplexed, sudden and desperate in act, from a distrust of his own resolution. His energy springs from the anxiety and agitation of his mind. His blindly rushing forward on the objects of his ambition and revenge, or his recoiling from them, equally betrays the harassed state of his feelings.—This part of his character is admirably set off by being brought in connexion with that of Lady Macbeth, whose obdurate strength of will and masculine firmness give her the ascendancy over her husband's faltering virtue. She at once seizes on the opportunity that offers for the accomplishment of all their wished-for greatness, and never flinches from her object till all is over. The magnitude of her resolution almost covers the magnitude of her guilt. She is a great bad woman, whom we hate, but whom we fear more than we hate. She does not excite our loathing and abhorrence like Regan and Goneril. She is only wicked to gain a great end; and is perhaps more distinguished by her commanding presence of mind and inexorable self-will, which do not suffer her to be diverted from a bad purpose, when once formed, by weak and womanly regrets, than by the hardness of her heart or want of natural affections. The impression which her lofty determination of character makes on the mind of Macbeth is well described where he exclaims:

——Bring forth men children only;
For thy undaunted mettle should compose
Nothing but males!

Nor do the pains she is at to 'screw his courage to the sticking-place', the reproach to him, not to be 'lost so poorly in himself', the assurance that 'a little water clears them of this deed', show anything but her greater consistency in depravity. Her strong-nerved ambition furnishes ribs of steel to 'the sides of his intent'; and she is herself wound up to the execution of her baneful project with the same unshrinking fortitude in crime, that in other circumstances she would probably have shown patience in suffering. The deliberate sacrifice of all other considerations to the gaining 'for their future days and nights sole sovereign sway and masterdom', by the murder of Duncan, is gorgeously expressed in her invocation on hearing of 'his fatal entrance under her battlements':

——Come all you spirits
That tend on mortal thoughts, unsex me here:
And fill me, from the crown to th' toe, top-full
Of direst cruelty; make thick my blood,
Stop up the access and passage to remorse,
That no compunctious visitings of nature
Shake my fell purpose, nor keep peace between
The effect and it. Come to my woman's breasts,
And take my milk for gall, you murthering ministers,
Wherever in your sightless substances
You wait on nature's mischief. Come, thick night!
And pall thee in the dunnest smoke of hell,
That my keen knife see not the wound it makes,
Nor heav'n peep through the blanket of the dark,
To cry, hold, hold!—

When she first hears that 'Duncan comes there to sleep' she is so overcome by the news, which is beyond her utmost expectations, that she answers the messenger, 'Thou'rt mad to say it': and on receiving her husband's account of the predictions of the Witches, conscious of his instability of purpose, and that her presence is necessary to goad him on to the consummation of his promised greatness, she exclaims :

> ——Hie thee hither,
> That I may pour my spirits in thine ear,
> And chastise with the valour of my tongue
> All that impedes thee from the golden round,
> Which fate and metaphysical aid doth seem
> To have thee crowned withal.

This swelling exultation and keen spirit of triumph, this uncontrollable eagerness of anticipation, which seems to dilate her form and take possession of all her faculties, this solid, substantial flesh-and-blood display of passion, exhibit a striking contrast to the cold, abstracted, gratuitous, servile malignity of the Witches, who are equally instrumental in urging Macbeth to his fate for the mere love of mischief, and from a disinterested delight in deformity and cruelty. They are hags of mischief, obscene panders to iniquity, malicious from their impotence of enjoyment, enamoured of destruction, because they are themselves unreal, abortive, half-existences, and who become sublime from their exemption from all human sympathies and contempt for all human affairs, as Lady Macbeth does by the force of passion ! Her fault seems to have been an excess of that strong principle of self-interest and family aggrandizement, not amenable to the common feelings of compassion and justice, which is so marked a feature in barbarous nations and times. A passing reflection of this kind, on the resemblance of the sleeping king to her father, alone prevents her from slaying Duncan with her own hand.

In speaking of the character of Lady Macbeth, we ought not to pass over Mrs. Siddon's manner of acting that part. We can conceive of nothing grander. It was something above nature. It seemed almost as if a being of a superior order had dropped from a higher sphere to awe the world with the majesty of her appearance. Power was seated on her brow, passion emanated from her breast as from a shrine; she was tragedy personified. In coming on in the sleeping-scene, her eyes were open, but their sense was shut. She was like a person bewildered and unconscious of what she did. Her lips moved involuntarily—all her gestures were involuntary and mechanical. She glided on and off the stage like an apparition. To have seen her in that character was an event in every one's life, not to be forgotten.

The dramatic beauty of the character of Duncan, which excites the respect and pity even of his murderers, has been often pointed out. It forms a picture of itself. An instance of the author's power of giving a striking effect to a common reflection, by the manner of introducing it, occurs in a speech of Duncan, complaining of his having been deceived in his opinion of the Thane of Cawdor, at the very moment that he is expressing the most unbounded confidence in the loyalty and services of Macbeth.

> There is no art
> To find the mind's construction in the face:
> He was a gentleman, on whom I built
> An absolute trust.
> O worthiest cousin, [*addressing himself to Macbeth*]
> The sin of my ingratitude e'en now
> Was great upon me, &c.

Another passage to show that Shakespeare lost sight of nothing that could in any way give relief or heightening to his subject, is the conversation which takes place between Banquo and Fleance immediately before the murder-scene of Duncan.

> *Banquo.* How goes the night, boy?
> *Fleance.* The moon is down: I have not heard the clock.
> *Banquo.* And she goes down at twelve.
> *Fleance.* I take 't, 'tis later, Sir.
> *Banquo.* Hold, take my sword. There's husbandry in heav'n,
> Their candles are all out.—

A heavy summons lies like lead upon me,
And yet I would not sleep : Merciful Powers,
Restrain in me the cursed thoughts that nature
Gives way to in repose.

In like manner, a fine idea is given of the gloomy coming on of evening, just as Banquo is going to be assassinated.

Light thickens and the crow
Makes wing to the rooky wood.
* * *
Now spurs the lated traveller apace
To gain the timely inn.

*Macbeth* (generally speaking) is done upon a stronger and more systematic principle of contrast than any other of Shakespeare's plays. It moves upon the verge of an abyss, and is a constant struggle between life and death. The action is desperate and the reaction is dreadful. It is a huddling together of fierce extremes, a war of opposite natures which of them shall destroy the other. There is nothing but what has a violent end or violent beginnings. The lights and shades are laid on with a determined hand ; the transitions from triumph to despair, from the height of terror to the repose of death, are sudden and startling ; every passion brings in its fellow-contrary, and the thoughts pitch and jostle against each other as in the dark. The whole play is an unruly chaos of strange and forbidden things, where the ground rocks under our feet. Shakespeare's genius here took its full swing, and trod upon the furthest bounds of nature and passion. This circumstance will account for the abruptness and violent antitheses of the style, the throes and labour which run through the expression, and from defects will turn them into beauties. ' So far and foul a day I have not seen ', &c. ' Such welcome and unwelcome news together '. ' Men's lives are like the flowers in their caps, dying or ere they sicken '. ' Look like the innocent flower, but be the serpent under it'. The scene before the castle-gate follows the appearance of the Witches on the heath, and is followed by a midnight murder. Duncan is cut off betimes by treason leagued with witchcraft, and Macduff is ripped untimely from his mother's womb to avenge his death. Macbeth, after the death of Banquo, wishes for his presence in extravagant terms, 'To him and all we thirst', and when his ghost appears, cries out, 'Avaunt and quit my sight', and being gone, he is 'himself again'. Macbeth resolves to get rid of Macduff, that 'he may sleep in spite of thunder'; and cheers his wife on the doubtful intelligence of Banquo's taking-off with the encouragement—'Then be thou jocund: ere the bat has flown his cloistered flight; ere to black Hecate's summons the shard-born beetle has rung night's yawning peal, there shall be done—a deed of dreadful note'. In Lady Macbeth's speech, 'Had he not resembled my father as he slept, I had done 't', there is murder and filial piety together, and in urging him to fulfill his vengeance against the defenceless king, her thoughts spare the blood neither of infants nor old age. The description of the Witches is full of the same contradictory principle; they 'rejoice when good kings bleed'; they are neither of the earth nor the air, but both; 'they should be women, but their beards forbid it'; they take all the pains possible to lead Macbeth on to the height of his ambition, only to betray him in deeper consequence, and after showing him all the pomp of their art, discover their malignant delight in his disappointed hopes, by that bitter taunt, 'Why stands Macbeth thus amazedly?' We might multiply such instances everywhere.

The leading features in the character of Macbeth are striking enough, and they form what may be thought at first only a bold, rude, Gothic outline. By comparing it with other characters of the same author we shall perceive the absolute truth and identity which is observed in the midst of the giddy whirl and rapid career of events. Macbeth in Shakespeare no more loses his identity of character in the fluctuations of fortune or the storm of passion, than Macbeth in himself would have lost the identity of his person. Thus he is as distinct a being from Richard III as it is possible to imagine, though these two characters in common hands, and indeed in the hands of any other poet, would have been a repetition of the same general idea, more or less exaggerated. For both are tyrants, usurpers, murderers, both aspiring and ambitious, both courageous, cruel, treacherous. But Richard is cruel from nature and constitution. Macbeth becomes so from accidental circumstances. Richard is from his birth deformed in body and mind, and naturally incapable of good. Macbeth is full of 'the milk of human kindness', is frank, sociable, generous. He is tempted to the commission of guilt by golden opportunities, by the instigations of his wife, and by prophetic warnings. Fate and metaphysical aid conspire against his virtue and his loyalty. Richard, on the contrary, needs no prompter, but wades through a series of crimes to the height of his ambition from the ungovernable violence of his temper and a reckless love of mischief. He is never gay but in the prospect or in the success of his villanies: Macbeth is full of horror at the thoughts of the murder of Duncan, which he is with difficulty prevailed on to commit, and of remorse after its perpetration. Richard has no mixture of common humanity in his composition, no regard to kindred or posterity, he owns no fellowship with others, he is 'himself alone'. Macbeth is not destitute of feelings of sympathy, is accessible to pity, is even made in some measure the dupe of his uxoriousness, ranks the loss of friends, of the cordial love of his followers, and of his good name, among the causes which have made him weary of life, and regrets that he has ever seized the crown by unjust means, since he cannot transmit it to his own posterity:

> For Banquo's issue have I 'fil'd my mind—
> For them the gracious Duncan have I murther'd,
> To make them kings, the seed of Banquo kings.

In the agitation of his thoughts, he envies those whom he has sent to peace. 'Duncan is in his grave; after life's fitful fever he sleeps well'. It is true, he becomes more callous as he plunges deeper in guilt, 'direness is thus rendered familiar to his slaughterous thoughts', and he in the end anticipates his wife in the boldness and bloodiness of his enterprises, while she, for want of the same stimulus of action, is 'troubled with thick-coming fancies that rob her of her rest', goes mad and dies. Macbeth endeavours to escape from reflection on his crimes by repelling their consequences, and banishes remorse for the past by the meditation of future mischief. This is not the principle of Richard's cruelty, which resembles the wanton malice of a fiend as much as the frailty of human passion. Macbeth is goaded on to acts of violence and retaliation by necessity; to Richard, blood is a pastime.—There are other decisive differences inherent in the two characters. Richard may be regarded as a man of the world, a plotting, hardened knave, wholly regardless of everything but his own ends, and the means to secure them.—Not so Macbeth. The superstitions of the age, the rude state of society, the local scenery and customs, all give a wildness and imaginary grandeur to his character. From the strangeness of the events that surround him, he is full of amazement and fear; and stands in doubt between the world of reality and the world of fancy. He sees sights not shown to mortal eye, and hears unearthly music. All is tumult and disorder within and without his mind; his purposes recoil upon himself, are broken and disjointed; he is the double thrall of his passions and his evil destiny. Richard is not a character either of imagination or pathos, but of pure self-will. There is no conflict of opposite feelings in his breast. The apparitions which he sees only haunt him in his sleep; nor does he live like Macbeth in a waking dream. Macbeth has considerable energy and manliness of character; but then he is 'subject to all the skyey influences'. He is sure of nothing but the present moment. Richard in the busy turbulence of his projects never loses his self-possession, and makes use of every circumstance that happens as an instrument of his long-reaching designs. In his last extremity we can only regard him as a wild beast taken in the toils: we never entirely lose our concern for Macbeth; and he calls back all our sympathy by that fine close of thoughtful melancholy:

> My way of life is fallen into the sear,
> The yellow leaf; and that which should accompany old age,
> As honour, troops of friends, I must not look to have;
> But in their stead, curses not loud but deep,
> Mouth-honour, breath, which the poor heart
> Would fain deny and dare not.

We can conceive a common actor to play Richard tolerably well; we can conceive no one to play Macbeth properly, or to look like a man that had encountered the Weird Sisters. All the actors that we have ever seen, appear as if they had encountered them on the boards of Covent Garden or Drury Lane, but not on the heath at Fores, and as if they did not believe what they had seen. The Witches of *Macbeth* indeed are ridiculous on the modern stage, and we doubt if the furies of Aeschylus would be more respected. The progress of manners and knowledge has an influence on the stage, and will in time perhaps destroy both tragedy and comedy. Filch's picking pockets, in the *Beggars' Opera*, is not so good a jest as it used to be: by the force of the police and of philosophy, Lillo's murders and the ghosts in Shakespeare will become obsolete. At last there will be nothing left, good nor bad, to be desired or dreaded, on the theatre or in real life. A question has been started with respect to the originality of Shakespeare's Witches, which has been well answered by Mr. Lamb in his notes to the *Specimens of Early Dramatic Poetry* :

'Though some resemblance may be traced between the charms in *Macbeth* and the incantations in this play (the *Witch* of Middleton), which is supposed to have preceded it, this coincidence will not detract much from the originality of Shakespeare. His Witches are distinguished from the Witches of Middleton by essential differences. These are creatures to whom man or woman plotting some dire mischief might resort for occasional consultation. Those originate deeds of blood, and begin bad impulses to men. From the moment that their eyes first meet with Macbeth's, he is spellbound. That meeting sways his destiny. He can never break the fascination. These Witches can hurt the body; those have power over the soul.—Hecate in Middleton has a son, a low buffoon; the hags of Shakespeare have neither child of their own, nor seem to be descended from any parent. They are foul anomalies, of whom we know not whence they are sprung, nor whether they have beginning or ending. As they are without human passions, so they seem to be without human relations. They come with thunder and lightning, and vanish to airy music. This is all we know of them.—Except Hecate, they have no names, which heightens their mysteriousness. The names, and some of the properties which Middleton has given to his hags, excite smiles, The Weird Sisters are serious things. Their presence cannot co-exist with mirth. But, in a lesser degree, the Witches of Middleton are fine creations. Their power too is, in some measure, over the mind. They raise jars, jealousies, strifes, *like a thick scurf o'er life*'.

# *Julius Caesar*

Julius Caesar was one of three principal plays by different authors, pitched upon by the celebrated Earl of Halifax to be brought out in a splendid manner by subscription, in the year 1707. The other two were the *King and No King* of Fletcher, and Dryden's *Maiden Queen*. There perhaps might be political reasons for this selection, as far as regards our author. Otherwise, Shakespeare's *Julius Caesar* is not equal, as a whole, to either of his other plays taken from the Roman history. It is inferior in interest to *Coriolanus*, and both in interest and power to *Antony and Cleopatra* It, however, abounds in admirable and affecting passages, and is remarkable for the profound knowledge of character, in which Shakespeare could scarcely fail. If there is any exception to this remark, it is in the hero of the piece himself. We do not much admire the representation here given of Julius Caesar, nor do we think it answers to the portrait given of him in his Commentaries. He makes several vapouring and rather pedantic speeches, and does nothing. Indeed, he has nothing to do. So far, the fault of the character might be the fault of the plot.

The spirit with which the poet has entered at once into the manners of the common people, and the jealousies and heartburnings of the different factions, is shown in the first scene, when Flavius and Marullus, tribunes of the people, and some citizens of Rome, appear upon the stage.

*Flavius*. Thou art a cobbler, art thou ?
*Cobbler*. Truly, Sir, *all* that I live by, is the *awl* : I meddle with

no tradesman's matters, nor woman's matters, but *with-al*, I am indeed, Sir, a surgeon to old shoes; when they are in great danger, I recover them.

*Flavius*. But wherefore art not in thy shop to-day? Why dost thou lead these men about the streets?

*Cobbler*. Truly, Sir, to wear out their shoes, to get myself into more work. But indeed, Sir, we make holiday to see Caesar, rejoice in his triumph.

To this specimen of quaint low humour immediately follows that unexpected and animated burst of indignant eloquence, put into the mouth of one of the angry tribunes.

*Marullus*. Wherefore rejoice!—What conquest brings he home?
What tributaries follow him to Rome,
To grace in captive-bonds his chariot-wheels?
Oh you hard hearts, you cruel men of Rome!
Knew you not Pompey? Many a time and oft
Have you climb'd up to walls and battlements,
To towers and windows, yea, to chimney-tops,
Your infants in your arms, and there have sat
The live-long day with patient expectation,
To see great Pompey pass the streets of Rome:
And when you saw his chariot but appear,
Have you not made an universal shout,
That Tiber trembled underneath his banks
To hear the replication of your sounds,
Made in his concave shores?
And do you now put on your best attire?
And do you now cull out an holiday?
And do you now strew flowers in his way
That comes in triumph over Pompey's blood?
Begone——
Run to your houses, fall upon your knees,
Pray to the Gods to intermit the plague,
That needs must light on this ingratitude.

The well-known dialogue between Brutus and Cassius, in which the latter breaks the design of the conspiracy to the former, and partly gains him over to it, is a noble piece of high-minded declamation. Cassius's insisting on the pretended effeminacy of

Caesar's character, and his description of their swimming across the Tiber together, 'once upon a raw and gusty day', are among the finest strokes in it. But perhaps the whole is not equal to the short scene which follows when Caesar enters with his train.

*Brutus*. The games are done, and Caesar is returning.
*Cassius*. As they pass by, pluck Casca by the sleeve,
And he will, after his sour fashion, tell you
What has proceeded worthy note to day.
*Brutus*. I will do so ; but look you, Cassius—
The angry spot doth glow on Caesar's brow,
And all the rest look like a chidden train.
Calphurnia's cheek is pale ; and Cicero
Looks with such ferret and such fiery eyes,
As we have seen him in the Capitol,
Being crost in conference by some senators.
*Cassius*. Casca will tell us what the matter is.
*Caesar*. Antonius—
*Antony*. Caesar ?
*Caesar*. Let me have men about me that are fat,
Sleek-headed men, and such as sleep a-nights :
Yond Cassius has a lean and hungry look,
He thinks too much ; such men are dangerous.
*Antony*. Fear him not, Caesar, he's not dangerous :
He is a noble Roman, and well given.
*Caesar*. Would he were fatter ; but I fear him not :
Yet if my name were liable to fear,
I do not know the man I should avoid
So soon as that spare Cassius. He reads much ;
He is a great observer ; and he looks
Quite through the deeds of men. He loves no plays,
As thou dost, Antony ; he hears no music :
Seldom he smiles, and smiles in such a sort,
As if he mock'd himself, and scorn'd his spirit,
That could be mov'd to smile at any thing.
Such men as he be never at heart's ease,
Whilst they behold a greater than themselves ;
And therefore are they very dangerous.
I rather tell thee what is to be fear'd
Than what I fear ; for always I am Caesar.
Come on my right hand, for this ear is deaf,
And tell me truly what thou think'st of him.

We know hardly any passage more expressive

of the genius of Shakespeare than this. It is as if he had been actually present, had known the different characters and what they thought of one another, and had taken down what he heard and saw, their looks, words, and gestures, just as they happened.

The character of Mark Antony is further speculated upon where the conspirators deliberate whether he shall fall with Caesar. Brutus is against it :

And for Mark Antony, think not of him :
For he can do no more than Caesar's arm,
When Caesar's head is off.
*Cassius*. Yet do I fear him :
For in th' ingrafted love he bears to Caesar—
*Brutus*. Alas, good Cassius, do not think of him :
If he love Caesar, all that he can do
Is to himself, take thought, and die for Caesar :
And that were much, he should ; for he is giv'n
To sports, to wildness, and much company.
*Trebonius*. There is no fear in him ; let him not die :
For he will live, and laugh at this hereafter.

They were in the wrong ; and Cassius was right.

The honest manliness of Brutus is, however, sufficient to find out the unfitness of Cicero to be included in their enterprise, from his affected egotism and literary vanity.

O, name him not : let us not break with him ;
For he will never follow any thing,
That other men begin.

His scepticism as to prodigies and his moralizing on the weather—' This disturbed sky is not to walk in '—are in the same spirit of refined imbecility.

Shakespeare has in this play and elsewhere shown the same penetration into political character and the springs of public events as into those of everyday life. For instance, the whole design to liberate their country fails from the generous temper and overweening confidence of Brutus in the goodness of their cause and the assistance of others. Thus it has always been. Those who mean well themselves think well of others, and fall a prey to their security. That humanity and sincerity which dispose men to resist injustice and tyranny render them unfit to cope with the cunning and power of those who are opposed to them. The friends of liberty trust to the professions of others because they are themselves sincere, and endeavour to secure the public good with the least possible hurt to its enemies, who have no regard to anything but their own unprincipled ends, and stick at nothing to accomplish them. Cassius was better cut out for a conspirator. His heart prompted his head. His habitual jealousy made him fear the worst that might happen, and his irritability of temper added to his inveteracy of purpose, and sharpened his patriotism. The mixed nature of his motives made him fitter to contend with bad men. The vices are never so well employed as in combating one another. Tyranny and servility are to be dealt with after their own fashion: otherwise, they will triumph over those who spare them, and finally pronounce their funeral panegyric, as Antony did that of Brutus.

> All the conspirators, save only he,
> Did that they did in envy of great Caesar:
> He only in a general honest thought
> And common good to all, made one of them.

The quarrel between Brutus and Cassius is managed in a masterly way. The dramatic fluctuation of passion, the calmness of Brutus, the heat of Cassius, are admirably described; and the exclamation of Cassius on hearing of the death of Portia, which he does not learn till after the reconciliation, 'How 'scap'd I killing when I crost you so?' gives double force to all that has gone before. The scene between Brutus and Portia, where she endeavours to extort the secret of the conspiracy from him, is conceived in the most heroical spirit, and the burst of tenderness in Brutus :

> You are my true and honourable wife ;
> As dear to me as are the ruddy drops
> That visit my sad heart—

is justified by her whole behaviour. Portia's breathless impatience to learn the event of the conspiracy, in the dialogue with Lucius, is full of passion. The interest which Portia takes in Brutus and that which Calphurnia takes in the fate of Caesar are discriminated with the nicest precision. Mark Antony's speech over the dead body of Caesar has been justly admired for the mixture of pathos and artifice in it : that of Brutus certainly is not so good. The entrance of the conspirators to the house of Brutus at midnight is rendered very impressive. In the midst of this scene we meet with one of those careless and natural digressions which occur so frequently and beautifully in Shakespeare. After Cassius has introduced his friends one by one, Brutus says :

> They are all welcome.
> What watchful cares do interpose themselves
> Betwixt your eyes and night ?
> *Cassius.* Shall I entreat a word ? (*They whisper*).
> *Decius.* Here lies the east : doth not the day break here ?
> *Casca.* No.
> *Cinna.* O pardon, Sir, it doth ; and yon grey lines,
> That fret the clouds, are messengers of day.
> *Casca.* You shall confess, that you are both deceiv'd :
> Here, as I point my sword, the sun arises,
> Which is a great way growing on the south,
> Weighing the youthful season of the year.
> Some two months hence, up higher toward the north
> He first presents his fire, and the high east
> Stands as the Capitol, directly here.

We cannot help thinking this graceful familiarity better than all the formality in the world. The truth of history in *Julius Caesar* is very ably worked up with dramatic effect. The councils of generals, the doubtful turns of battles, are represented to the life. The death of Brutus is worthy of him—it has the dignity of the Roman senator with the firmness of the Stoic philosopher. But what is perhaps better than either, is the little incident of his boy, Lucius, falling asleep over his instrument, as he is playing to his master in his tent, the night before the battle. Nature had played him the same forgetful trick once before on the night of the conspiracy. The humanity of Brutus is the same on both occasions.

——It is no matter :
Enjoy the honey-heavy dew of slumber.
Thou hast no figures nor no fantasies,
Which busy care draws in the brains of men.
Therefore thou sleep'st so sound.

# *Othello*

It has been said that tragedy purifies the affections by terror and pity. That is, it substitutes imaginary sympathy for mere selfishness. It gives us a high and permanent interest, beyond ourselves, in humanity as such. It raises the great, the remote, and the possible to an equality with the real, the little and the near. It makes man a partaker with his kind. It subdues and softens the stubbornness of his will. It teaches him that there are and have been others like himself, by showing him as in a glass what they have felt, thought, and done. It opens the chambers of the human heart. It leaves nothing indifferent to us that can affect our common nature. It excites our sensibility by exhibiting the passions wound up to the utmost pitch by the power of imagination or the temptation of circumstances; and corrects their fatal excesses in ourselves by pointing to the greater extent of sufferings and of crimes to which they have led others. Tragedy creates a balance of the affections. It makes us thoughtful spectators in the lists of life. It is the refiner of the species; a discipline of humanity. The habitual study of poetry and works of imagination is one chief part of a well-grounded education. A taste for liberal art is necessary to complete the character of a gentleman. Science alone is hard and mechanical. It exercises the understanding upon things out of ourselves, while it leaves the affections unemployed, or engrossed with our own immediate, narrow interests.—*Othello* furnishes an illustration of these remarks. It excites our sympathy in an extraordinary degree. The moral it conveys has a closer application to the concerns of human life than that of any other of Shakespeare's plays. 'It comes directly home to the bosoms and business of men'. The pathos in *Lear* is indeed more dreadful and overpowering: but it is less natural, and less of every day's occurrence. We have not the same degree of sympathy with the passions described in *Macbeth*. The interest in *Hamlet* is more remote and reflex. That of *Othello* is at once equally profound and affecting.

The picturesque contrasts of character in this play are almost as remarkable as the depth of the passion. The Moor Othello, the gentle Desdemona, the villain Iago, the good-natured Cassio, the fool Roderigo, present a range and variety of character as striking and palpable as that produced by the opposition of costume in a picture. Their distinguishing qualities stand out to the mind's eye, so that even when we are not thinking of their actions or sentiments, the idea of their persons is still as present to us as ever. These characters and the images they stamp upon the mind are the farthest asunder possible, the distance between them is immense: yet the compass of knowledge and invention which the poet has shown in embodying these extreme creations of his genius is only greater than the truth and felicity with which he has identified each character with itself, or blended their different qualities together in the same story. What a contrast the character of Othello forms to that of Iago: at the same time, the force of conception with which these two figures are opposed to each other is rendered still more intense by the complete consistency with which the traits of each character are brought out in a state of the highest finishing. The making one black and the other white, the one unprincipled, the other unfortunate in the extreme, would have answered the common purposes of effect, and satisfied the ambition of an ordinary painter of character.

Shakespeare has laboured the finer shades of difference in both with as much care and skill as if he had had to depend on the execution alone for the success of his design. On the other hand, Desdemona and Aemilia are not meant to be opposed with anything like strong contrast to each other. Both are, to outward appearance, characters of common life, not more distinguished than women usually are, by difference of rank and situation. The difference of their thoughts and sentiments is, however, laid as open, their minds are separated from each other by signs as plain and as little to be mistaken as the complexions of their husbands.

The movement of the passion in Othello is exceedingly different from that of Macbeth. In Macbeth there is a violent struggle between opposite feelings, between ambition and the stings of conscience, almost from first to last: in Othello, the doubtful conflict between contrary passions, though dreadful, continues only for a short time, and the chief interest is excited by the alternate ascendancy of different passions, the entire and unforeseen change from the fondest love and most unbounded confidence to the tortures of jealousy and the madness of hatred. The revenge of Othello, after it has once taken thorough possession of his mind, never quits it, but grows stronger and stronger at every moment of its delay. The nature of the Moor is noble, confiding, tender, and generous; but his blood is of the most inflammable kind; and being once roused by a sense of his wrongs, he is stopped by no considerations of remorse or pity till he has given a loose to all the dictates of his rage and his despair. It is in working his noble nature up to this extremity through rapid but gradual transitions, in raising passion to its height from the smallest beginnings and in spite of all obstacles, in painting the expiring conflict between love and hatred, tenderness and resentment, jealousy and remorse, in unfolding the strength and the weaknesses of our nature, in uniting sublimity of thought with the anguish of the keenest woe, in putting in motion the various impulses that agitate this our mortal being, and at last blending them in that noble tide of deep and sustained passion, impetuous but majestic, that ' flows on to the Propontic, and knows no ebb ', that Shakespeare has shown the mastery of his genius and of his power over the human heart. The third act of *Othello* is his master-piece, not of knowledge or passion separately, but of the two combined, of the knowledge of character with the expression of passion, of consummate art in the keeping up of appearances with the profound workings of nature, and the convulsive movements of uncontrollable agony, of the power of inflicting torture and of suffering it. Not only is the tumult of passion heaved up from the very bottom of the soul, but every the slightest undulation of feeling is seen on the surface, as it arises from the impulses of imagination or the different probabilities maliciously suggested by Iago. The progressive preparation for the catastrophe is wonderfully managed from the Moor's first gallant recital of the story of his love, of ' the spells and witchcraft he had used ', from his unlooked-for and romantic success, the fond satisfaction with which he dotes on his own happiness, the unreserved tenderness of Desdemona and her innocent importunities in favour of Cassio, irritating the suspicions instilled into her husband's mind by the perfidy of Iago, and rankling there to poison, till he loses all command of himself, and his rage can only be appeased by blood. She is introduced, just before Iago begins to put his scheme in practice, pleading for Cassio with all the thoughtless gaiety of friendship and winning confidence in the love of Othello.

> What ! Michael Cassio ?
> That came a wooing with you, and so many a time,

When I have spoke of you dispraisingly,
Hath ta'en your part, to have so much to do
To bring him in?—Why this is not a boon:
'Tis as I should entreat you wear your gloves,
Or feed on nourishing meats, or keep you warm;
Or sue to you to do a peculiar profit
To your person. Nay, when I have a suit,
Wherein I mean to touch your love indeed,
It shall be full of poise, and fearful to be granted.

Othello's confidence, at first only staggered by broken hints and insinuations, recovers itself at sight of Desdemona; and he exclaims

If she be false, O then Heav'n mocks itself:
I'll not believe it.

But presently after, on brooding over his suspicions by himself, and yielding to his apprehensions of the worst, his smothered jealousy breaks out into open fury, and he returns to demand satisfaction of Iago like a wild beast stung with the envenomed shaft of the hunters. 'Look where he comes', &c. In this state of exasperation and violence, after the first paroxysms of his grief and tenderness have had their vent in that passionate apostrophe, 'I felt not Cassio's kisses on her lips', Iago by false aspersions, and by presenting the most revolting images to his mind,[1] easily turns the storm of passion from himself against Desdemona, and works him up into a trembling agony of doubt and fear, in which he abandons all his love and hopes in a breath.

Now do I see 'tis true. Look here, Iago,
All my fond love thus do I blow to Heav'n. 'Tis gone.
Arise, black vengeance, from the hollow hell;
Yield up, O love, thy crown and hearted throne
To tyrannous hate! Swell, bosom, with thy fraught;
For 'tis of aspicks' tongues.

[1] See the passage beginning, 'It is impossible you should see this, were they as prime as goats', &c.

From this time, his raging thoughts 'never look back, ne'er ebb to humble love' till his revenge is sure of its object, the painful regrets and involuntary recollections of past circumstances which cross his mind amidst the dim trances of passion, aggravating the sense of his wrongs, but not shaking his purpose. Once indeed, where Iago shows him Cassio with the handkerchief in his hand, and making sport (as he thinks) of his misfortunes, the intolerable bitterness of his feelings, the extreme sense of shame, makes him fall to praising her accomplishments and relapse into a momentary fit of weakness, 'Yet, oh, the pity of it, Iago, the pity of it!' This returning fondness, however, only serves, as it is managed by Iago, to whet his revenge, and set his heart more against her. In his conversations with Desdemona, the persuasion of her guilt and the immediate proofs of her duplicity seem to irritate his resentment and aversion to her; but in the scene immediately preceding her death, the recollection of his love returns upon him in all its tenderness and force; and after her death, he all at once forgets his wrongs in the sudden and irreparable sense of his loss:

> My wife! My wife! What wife? I have no wife.
> Oh insupportable! Oh heavy hour!

This happens before he is assured of her innocence; but afterwards his remorse is as dreadful as his revenge has been, and yields only to fixed and death-like despair. His farewell speech, before he kills himself, in which he conveys his reasons to the senate for the murder of his wife, is equal to the first speech in which he gave them an account of his courtship of her, and 'his whole course of love'. Such an ending was alone worthy of such a commencement.

If anything could add to the force of our sympathy with Othello, or compassion for his fate, it would be the frankness and generosity of his nature, which so little deserve it. When Iago first begins to practise upon his unsuspecting friendship, he answers:

> ——'Tis not to make me jealous,
> To say my wife is fair, feeds well, loves company
> Is free of speech, sings, plays, and dances well;
> Where virtue is, these are most virtuous.
> Nor from my own weak merits will I draw
> The smallest fear or doubt of her revolt,
> For she had eyes and chose me.

This character is beautifully (and with affecting simplicity) confirmed by what Desdemona herself says of him to Aemilia after she has lost the handkerchief, the first pledge of his love to her:

> Believe me, I had rather have lost my purse
> Full of cruzadoes. And but my noble Moor
> Is true of mind, and made of no such baseness,
> As jealous creatures are, it were enough
> To put him to ill thinking.
> *Aemilia.* Is he not jealous?
> *Desdemona.* Who he? I think the sun where he was born
> Drew all such humours from him.

In a short speech of Aemilia's there occurs one of those side-intimations of the fluctuations of passion which we seldom meet with but in Shakespeare. After Othello has resolved upon the death of his wife, and bids her dismiss her attendant for the night, she answers:

> I will, my Lord.
> *Aemilia.* How goes it now? *He looks gentler than he did.*

Shakespeare has here put into half a line what some authors would have spun out into ten set speeches.

The character of Desdemona herself is inimitable both in itself, and as it contrasts with Othello's groundless jealousy, and with the foul conspiracy of which she is the innocent victim. Her beauty and external graces are only indirectly glanced at;

we see 'her visage in her mind'; her character everywhere predominates over her person:

> A maiden never bold:
> Of spirit so still and quiet, that her motion
> Blushed at itself.

There is one fine compliment paid to her by Cassio, who exclaims triumphantly when she comes ashore at Cyprus after the storm:

> Tempests themselves, high seas, and howling winds,
> As having sense of beauty, do omit
> Their mortal natures, letting safe go by
> The divine Desdemona.

In general, as is the case with most of Shakespeare's females, we lose sight of her personal charms in her attachment and devotedness to her husband. 'She is subdued even to the very quality of her lord'; and to Othello's 'honours and his valiant parts her soul and fortunes consecrates'. The lady protests so much herself, and she is as good as her word. The truth of conception, with which timidity and boldness are united in the same character, is marvellous. The extravagance of her resolutions, the pertinacity of her affections, may be said to arise out of the gentleness of her nature. They imply an unreserved reliance on the purity of her own intentions, an entire surrender of her fears to her love, a knitting of herself (heart and soul) to the fate of another. Bating the commencement of her passion, which is a little fantastical and headstrong (though even that may perhaps be consistently accounted for from her inability to resist a rising inclination[1]) her whole character consists in having no will of her own, no prompter but her obedience. Her romantic turn is only a consequence of the domestic and

[1] *Iago*. Ay, too gentle.
*Othello*. Nay, that's certain.

practical part of her disposition; and instead of following Othello to the wars, she would gladly have 'remained at home a moth of peace', if her husband could have stayed with her. Her resignation and angelic sweetness of temper do not desert her at the last. The scenes in which she laments and tries to account for Othello's estrangement from her are exquisitely beautiful. After he has struck her, and called her names, she says:

——Alas, Iago,
What shall I do to win my lord again?
Good friend, go to him; for by this light of heaven,
I know not how I lost him. Here I kneel;
If e'er my will did trespass 'gainst his love,
Either in discourse, or thought, or actual deed,
Or that mine eyes, mine ears, or any sense
Delighted them on any other form;
Or that I do not, and ever did,
And ever will, though he do shake me off
To beggarly divorcement, love him dearly,
Comfort forswear me. Unkindness may do much,
And his unkindness may defeat my life,
But never taint my love.
*Iago.* I pray you be content: 'tis but his humour.
The business of the state does him offence.
*Desdemona.* If 'twere no other!—

The scene which follows with Aemilia and the song of the Willow are equally beautiful, and show the author's extreme power of varying the expression of passion, in all its moods and in all circumstances:

*Aemilia.* Would you had never seen him.
*Desdemona.* So would not I: my love doth so approve him,
That even his stubbornness, his checks, his frowns,
Have grace and favour in them, &c.

Not the unjust suspicions of Othello, not Iago's treachery, place Desdemona in a more amiable or interesting light than the casual conversation (half earnest, half jest) between her and Aemilia on the common behaviour of women to their husbands.

This dialogue takes place just before the last fatal scene. If Othello had overheard it, it would have prevented the whole catastrophe ; but then it would have spoiled the play.

The character of Iago is one of the supererogations of Shakespeare's genius. Some persons, more nice than wise, have thought this whole character unnatural, because his villany is *without a sufficient motive.* Shakespeare, who was as good a philosopher as he was a poet, thought otherwise. He knew that the love of power, which is another name for the love of mischief, is natural to man. He would know this as well or better than if it had been demonstrated to him by a logical diagram, merely from seeing children paddle in the dirt or kill flies for sport. Iago in fact belongs to a class of characters common to Shakespeare and at the same time peculiar to him ; whose heads are as acute and active as their hearts are hard and callous. Iago is, to be sure, an extreme instance of the kind ; that is to say, of diseased intellectual activity, with an almost perfect indifference to moral good or evil, or rather with a decided preference of the latter, because it falls more readily in with his favourite propensity, gives greater zest to his thoughts and scope to his actions. He is quite or nearly as indifferent to his own fate as to that of others ; he runs all risks for a trifling and doubtful advantage ; and is himself the dupe and victim of his ruling passion—an insatiable craving after action of the most difficult and dangerous kind. 'Our ancient' is a philosopher, who fancies that a lie that kills has more point in it than an alliteration or an antithesis ; who thinks a fatal experiment on the peace of a family a better thing than watching the palpitations in the heart of a flea in a microscope ; who plots the ruin of his friends as an exercise for his ingenuity, and stabs men in the dark to prevent *ennui.* His gaiety, such as it is, arises from the success of his treachery ;

his ease from the torture he has inflicted on others. He is an amateur of tragedy in real life; and instead of employing his invention on imaginary characters, or long-forgotten incidents, he takes the bolder and more desperate course of getting up his plot at home, casts the principal parts among his nearest friends and connexions, and rehearses it in downright earnest, with steady nerves and unabated resolution. We will just give an illustration or two.

One of his most characteristic speeches is that immediately after the marriage of Othello.

> *Roderigo.* What a full fortune does the thick lips owe,
> If he can carry her thus!
> *Iago.* Call up her father:
> Rouse him (*Othello*), make after him, poison his delight,
> Proclaim him in the streets, incense her kinsmen,
> And tho' he in a fertile climate dwell,
> Plague him with flies: Tho' that his joy be joy,
> Yet throw such changes of vexation on it,
> As it may lose some colour.

In the next passage, his imagination runs riot in the mischief he is plotting, and breaks out into the wildness and impetuosity of real enthusiasm.

> *Roderigo.* Here is her father's house: I'll call aloud.
> *Iago.* Do, with like timorous accent and dire yell,
> As when, by night and negligence, the fire
> Is spied in populous cities.

One of his most favourite topics, on which he is rich indeed, and in descanting on which his spleen serves him for a Muse, is the disproportionate match between Desdemona and the Moor. This is a clue to the character of the lady which he is by no means ready to part with. It is brought forward in the first scene, and he recurs to it, when in answer to his insinuations against Desdemona, Roderigo says:

> I cannot believe that in her—she's full of most blest conditions.
> *Iago.* Bless'd fig's end. The wine she drinks is made of grapes.
> If she had been blest, she would never have married the Moor.

And again with still more spirit and fatal effect afterwards, when he turns this very suggestion arising in Othello's own breast to her prejudice.

> *Othello.* And yet how nature erring from itself—
> *Iago.* Aye, there's the point ;—as to be bold with you,
> Not to affect many proposed matches
> Of her own clime, complexion, and degree, &c.

This is probing to the quick. Iago here turns the character of poor Desdemona, as it were, inside out. It is certain that nothing but the genius of Shakespeare could have preserved the entire interest and delicacy of the part, and have even drawn an additional elegance and dignity from the peculiar circumstances in which she is placed. The habitual licentiousness of Iago's conversation is not to be traced to the pleasure he takes in gross or lascivious images, but to his desire of finding out the worst side of everything, and of proving himself an over-match for appearances. He has none of 'the milk of human kindness' in his composition. His imagination rejects everything that has not a strong infusion of the most unpalatable ingredients; his mind digests only poisons. Virtue or goodness or whatever has the least 'relish of salvation in it' is, to his depraved appetite, sickly and insipid : and he even resents the good opinion entertained of his own integrity, as if it were an affront cast on the masculine sense and spirit of his character. Thus at the meeting between Othello and Desdemona, he exclaims, 'Oh, you are well tuned now : but I'll set down the pegs that make this music, *as honest as I am*'—his character of *bonhommie* not sitting at all easily upon him. In the scenes where he tries to work Othello to his purpose, he is proportionably guarded, insidious, dark, and deliberate. We believe nothing ever came up to the profound dissimulation and dexterous artifice of the well-known dialogue in the third act, where he first enters upon the execution of his design.

*Iago.* My noble lord.
*Othello.* What dost thou say, Iago ?
*Iago.* Did Michael Cassio,
When you woo'd my lady, know of your love ?
*Othello.* He did from first to last.
Why dost thou ask ?
*Iago.* But for a satisfaction of my thought,
No further harm.
*Othello.* Why of thy thought, Iago ?
*Iago.* I did not think he had been acquainted with it.
*Othello.* O yes, and went between us very oft—
*Iago.* Indeed !
*Othello.* Indeed ? Ay, indeed. Discern'st thou aught of that ?
Is he not honest ?
*Iago.* Honest, my lord ?
*Othello.* Honest ? Ay, honest.
*Iago.* My lord, for aught I know.
*Othello.* What do'st thou think ?
*Iago.* Think, my lord !
*Othello.* Think, my lord ! Alas, thou echo'st me,
As if there was some monster in thy thought
Too hideous to be shown.

The stops and breaks, the deep workings of treachery under the mask of love and honesty, the anxious watchfulness, the cool earnestness, and if we may so say, the *passion* of hypocrisy marked in every line, receive their last finishing in that inconceivable burst of pretended indignation at Othello's doubts of his sincerity.

O grace ! O Heaven forgive me !
Are you a man ? Have you a soul or sense ?
God be wi' you ; take mine office. O wretched fool,
That lov'st to make thine honesty a vice !
Oh monstrous world ! take note, take note, O world !
To be direct and honest, is not safe.
I thank you for this profit, and from hence
I'll love no friend, since love breeds such offence.

If Iago is detestable enough when he has business on his hands and all his engines at work, he is still worse when he has nothing to do, and we only see into the hollowness of his heart. His indifference when Othello falls into a swoon, is perfectly diabolical.

> *Iago*. How is it, General? Have you not hurt your head?
> *Othello*. Dost thou mock me?
> *Iago*, I mock you not, by Heaven, &c.

The part indeed would hardly be tolerated, even as a foil to the virtue and generosity of the other characters in the play, but for its indefatigable industry and inexhaustible resources, which divert the attention of the spectator (as well as his own) from the end he has in view to the means by which it must be accomplished.—Edmund the Bastard in *Lear* is something of the same character, placed in less prominent circumstances. Zanga is a vulgar caricature of it.

# *Timon of Athens*

Timon of Athens always appeared to us to be written with as intense a feeling of his subject as any one play of Shakespeare. It is one of the few in which he seems to be in earnest throughout, never to trifle nor go out of his way. He does not relax in his efforts, nor lose sight of the unity of his design. It is the only play of our author in which spleen is the predominant feeling of the mind. It is as much a satire as a play: and contains some of the finest pieces of invective possible to be conceived, both in the snarling, captious answers of the cynic Apemantus, and in the impassioned and more terrible imprecations of Timon. The latter remind the classical reader of the force and swelling impetuosity of the moral declamations in *Juvenal*, while the former have all the keenness and caustic severity of the old Stoic philosophers. The soul of Diogenes appears to have been seated on the lips of Apemantus. The churlish profession of misanthropy in the cynic is contrasted with the profound feeling of it in Timon, and also with the soldierlike and determined resentment of Alcibiades against his countrymen, who have banished him, though this forms only an incidental episode in the tragedy.

The fable consists of a single event—of the transition from the highest pomp and profusion of artificial refinement to the most abject state of savage life, and privation of all social intercourse. The change is as rapid as it is complete; nor is the description of the rich and generous Timon, banqueting in gilded palaces, pampered by every luxury, prodigal of his hospitality, courted by crowds of flatterers, poets, painters, lords, ladies, who :

Follow his strides, his lobbies fill with tendance,
Rain sacrificial whisperings in his ear ;
And through him drink the free air—

more striking than that of the sudden falling off of his friends and fortune, and his naked exposure in a wild forest digging roots from the earth for his sustenance, with a lofty spirit of self-denial, and bitter scorn of the world, which raise him higher in our esteem than the dazzling gloss of prosperity could do. He grudges himself the means of life, and is only busy in preparing his grave. How forcibly is the difference between what he was and what he is described in Apemantus's taunting questions, when he comes to reproach him with the change in his way of life !

——What, think'st thou,
That the bleak air, thy boisterous chamberlain,
Will put thy shirt on warm ? will these moist trees
That have out-liv'd the eagle, page thy heels,
And skip when thou point'st out ? will the cold brook,
Candied with ice, caudle thy morning taste
To cure thy o'er-night's surfeit ? Call the creatures,
Whose naked natures live in all the spight
Of wreakful heav'n, whose bare unhoused trunks,
To the conflicting elements expos'd,
Answer mere nature, bid them flatter thee.

The manners are everywhere preserved with distinct truth. The poet and painter are very skilfully played off against one another, both affecting great attention to the other, and each taken up with his own vanity, and the superiority of his own art. Shakespeare has put into the mouth of the former a very lively description of the genius of poetry and of his own in particular.

——A thing slipt idly from me.
Our poesy is as a gum, which issues

From whence 'tis nourish'd. The fire i' th' flint
Shows not till it be struck : our gentle flame
Provokes itself—and like the current flies
Each bound it chafes.

The hollow friendship and shuffling evasions of the Athenian lords, their smooth professions and pitiful ingratitude, are very satisfactorily exposed, as well as the different disguises to which the meanness of self-love resorts in such cases to hide a want of generosity and good faith. The lurking selfishness of Apemantus does not pass undetected amidst the grossness of his sarcasms and his contempt for the pretentions of others. Even the two courtezans who accompany Alcibiades to the cave of Timon are very characteristically sketched ; and the thieves who come to visit him are also 'true men' in their way.—An exception to this general picture of selfish depravity is found in the old and honest steward, Flavius, to whom Timon pays a full tribute of tenderness. Shakespeare was unwilling to draw a picture '*all over ugly with hypocrisy*'. He owed this character to the good-natured solicitations of his Muse. His mind was well said by Ben Jonson to be the 'sphere of humanity'.

The moral sententiousness of this play equals that of Lord Bacon's *Treatise on the Wisdom of the Ancients*, and is indeed seasoned with greater variety. Every topic of contempt or indignation is here exhausted ; but while the sordid licentiousness of Apemantus, which turns everything to gall and bitterness, shows only the natural virulence of his temper and antipathy to good or evil alike, Timon does not utter an imprecation without betraying the extravagant workings of disappointed passion, of love altered to hate. Apemantus sees nothing good in any object, and exaggerates whatever is disgusting : Timon is tormented with the perpetual contrast between things and appearances, between the fresh, tempting outside and the rottenness within, and invokes mischiefs on the heads of mankind proportioned to the sense of his wrongs and of their treacheries. He impatiently cries out, when he finds the gold,

> This yellow slave
> Will knit and break religions ; bless the accurs'd ;
> Make the hoar leprosy ador'd ; place thieves,
> And give them title, knee, and approbation,
> With senators on the bench ; this is it,
> That makes the wappen'd widow wed again ;
> She, whom the spital-house
> Would cast the gorge at, *this embalms and spices*
> *To th' April day again.*

One of his most dreadful imprecations is that which occurs immediately on his leaving Athens.

> Let me look back upon thee, O thou wall,
> That girdlest in those wolves ! Dive in the earth,
> And fence not Athens ! Matrons, turn incontinent ;
> Obedience fail in children ; slaves and fools
> Pluck the grave wrinkled senate from the bench,
> And minister in their steads. To general filths
> Convert o' th' instant green virginity !
> Do't in your parents' eyes. Bankrupts, hold fast ;
> Rather than render back, out with your knives,
> And cut your trusters' throats ! Bound servants, steal :
> Large-handed robbers your grave masters are,
> And pill by law. Maid, to thy master's bed :
> Thy mistress is o' th' brothel. Son of sixteen,
> Pluck the lin'd crutch from thy old limping sire,
> And with it beat his brains out ! Fear and piety,
> Religion to the Gods, peace, justice, truth,
> Domestic awe, night-rest, and neighbourhood,
> Instructions, manners, mysteries and trades,
> Degrees, observances, customs and laws,
> Decline to your confounding contraries ;
> And let confusion live !—Plagues, incident to men,
> Your potent and infectious fevers heap
> On Athens, ripe for stroke ! Thou cold sciatica,
> Cripple our senators, that their limbs may halt
> As lamely as their manners ! Lust and liberty
> Creep in the minds and manners of our youth,
> That 'gainst the stream of virtue they may strive,

And drown themselves in riot ! Itches, blains,
Sow all th' Athenian bosoms ; and their crop
Be general leprosy : breath infect breath,
That their society (as their friendship) may
Be merely poison !

Timon is here just as ideal in his passion for ill as he had before been in his belief of good. Apemantus was satisfied with the mischief existing in the world, and with his own ill-nature. One of the most decisive intimations of Timon's morbid jealousy of appearances is in his answer to Apemantus, who asks him :

What things in the world can'st thou nearest compare with thy flatterers ?

*Timon.* Women nearest : but men, men are the things themselves.

Apemantus, it is said, 'loved few things better than to abhor himself'. This is not the case with Timon, who neither loves to abhor himself nor others. All his vehement misanthropy is forced, up-hill work. From the slippery turns of fortune, from the turmoils of passion and adversity, he wishes to sink into the quiet of the grave. On that subject his thoughts are intent, on that he finds time and place to grow romantic. He digs his own grave by the sea-shore ; contrives his funeral ceremonies amidst the pomp of desolation, and builds his mausoleum of the elements.

Come not to me again ; but say to Athens,
Timon hath made his everlasting mansion
Upon the beached verge of the salt flood ;
Which once a-day with his embossed froth
The turbulent surge shall cover.—Thither come,
And let my grave stone be your oracle.

And again, Alcibiades, after reading his epitaph, says of him :

These well express in thee thy latter spirits :
Though thou abhorred'st in us our human griefs,

Scorn'd'st our brain's flow, and those our droplets, which
From niggard nature fall ; yet rich conceit
Taught thee to make vast Neptune weep for aye
On thy low grave——

thus making the winds his funeral dirge, his mourner the murmuring ocean ; and seeking in the everlasting solemnities of nature oblivion of the transitory splendour of his lifetime.

## *Coriolanus*

Shakespeare has in this play shown himself well versed in history and state affairs. *Coriolanus* is a store-house of political commonplaces. Any one who studies it may save himself the trouble of reading Burke's *Reflections*, or Paine's *Rights of Man*, or the Debates in both Houses of Parliament since the French Revolution or our own. The arguments for and against aristocracy or democracy, on the privileges of the few and the claims of the many, on liberty and slavery, power and the abuse of it, peace and war, are here very ably handled, with the spirit of a poet and the acuteness of a philosopher. Shakespeare himself seems to have had a leaning to the arbitrary side of the question, perhaps from some feeling of contempt for his own origin; and to have spared no occasion of baiting the rabble. What he says of them is very true: what he says of their betters is also very true, though he dwells less upon it.—The cause of the people is indeed but little calculated as a subject for poetry: it admits of rhetoric, which goes into argument and explanation, but it presents no immediate or distinct images to the mind, 'no jutting frieze, buttress, or coigne of vantage' for poetry 'to make its pendant bed and procreant cradle in'. The language of poetry naturally falls in with the language of power. The imagination is an exaggerating and exclusive faculty: it takes from one thing to add to another: it accumulates circumstances together to give the greatest possible effect to a favourite object. The understanding is a dividing and measuring faculty: it judges of things, not according to their immediate impression on the mind, but according to their relations to one another. The one is a monopolizing faculty, which seeks the greatest quantity of present excitement by inequality and disproportion; the other is a distributive faculty, which seeks the greatest quantity of ultimate good, by justice and proportion. The one is an aristocratical, the other a republican faculty. The principle of poetry is a very anti-levelling principle. It aims at effect, it exists by contrast. It admits of no medium. It is everything by excess. It rises above the ordinary standard of sufferings and crimes. It presents a dazzling appearance. It shows its head turretted, crowned, and crested. Its front is gilt and blood-stained. Before it 'it carries noise, and behind it tears'. It has its altars and its victims, sacrifices, human sacrifices. Kings, priests, nobles, are its train-bearers, tyrants and slaves its executioners.—'Carnage is its daughter'. Poetry is right-royal. It puts the individual for the species, the one above the infinite many, might before right. A lion hunting a flock of sheep or a herd of wild asses is a more poetical object than they; and we even take part with the lordly beast, because our vanity or some other feeling makes us disposed to place ourselves in the situation of the strongest party. So we feel some concern for the poor citizens of Rome when they meet together to compare their wants and grievances, till Coriolanus comes in and with blows and big words drives this set of 'poor rats', this rascal scum, to their homes and beggary before him. There is nothing heroical in a multitude of miserable rogues not wishing to be starved, or complaining that they are like to be so; but when a single man comes forward to brave their cries and to make them submit to the last indignities, from mere pride and self-will, our admiration of his prowess is immediately converted into contempt for their pusillanimity. The insolence of power is stronger than the plea of necessity. The tame submission to usurped authority or even the natural resistance to it has nothing to excite or flatter the imagination: it is the assumption of a right to insult or oppress others that carries an imposing air of superiority with it. We had rather be the oppressor than the oppressed. The love of power in ourselves and the admiration of it in others are both natural to man: the one makes him a tyrant, the other a slave. Wrong dressed out in pride, pomp, and circumstance has more attraction than abstract right.—Coriolanus complains of the fickleness of the people: yet the instant he cannot gratify his pride and obstinacy at their expense, he turns his arms against his country. If his country was not worth defending, why did he build his pride on its defence? He is a conqueror and a hero; he conquers other countries, and makes this a plea for enslaving his own; and when he is prevented from doing so, he leagues with its enemies to destroy his country. He rates the people 'as if he were a God to punish, and not a man of their infirmity'. He scoffs at one of their tribunes for maintaining their rights and franchises: 'Mark you his absolute *shall*?' not marking his own absolute *will* to take everything from them, his impatience of the slightest opposition to his own pretensions being in proportion to their arrogance and absurdity. If the great and powerful had the beneficence and wisdom of Gods, then all this would have been well: if with a greater knowledge of what is good for the people, they had as great a care for their interest as they have themselves, if they were seated above the world, sympathizing with the welfare, but not feeling the passions of men, receiving neither good nor hurt from them, but bestowing their benefits as free gifts on them, they might then rule over them like another Providence. But this is not the case. Coriolanus is unwilling that the senate should show their ' cares ' for the people, lest their ' cares ' should be construed into ' fears ', to the subversion of all due authority ; and he is no sooner disappointed in his schemes to deprive the people not only of the cares of the state, but of all power to redress themselves, than Volumnia is made madly to exclaim :

> Now the red pestilence strike all trades in Rome,
> And occupations perish.

This is but natural : it is but natural for a mother to have more regard for her son than for a whole city ; but then the city should be left to take some care of itself. The care of the state cannot, we here see, be safely entrusted to maternal affection, or to the domestic charities of high life. The great have private feelings of their own, to which the interests of humanity and justice must curtsy. Their interests are so far from being the same as those of the community, that they are in direct and necessary opposition to them ; their power is at the expense of *our* weakness ; their riches of *our* poverty ; their pride of *our* degradation ; their splendour of *our* wretchedness ; their tyranny of *our* servitude. If they had the superior knowledge ascribed to them (which they have not) it would only render them so much more formidable ; and from Gods would convert them into Devils. The whole dramatic moral of *Coriolanus* is that those who have little shall have less, and that those who have much shall take all that others have left. The people are poor ; therefore they ought to be starved. They are slaves ; therefore they ought to be beaten. They work hard ; therefore they ought to be treated like beasts of burden. They are ignorant ; therefore they ought not to be allowed to feel that they want food, or clothing, or rest, that they are enslaved, oppressed, and miserable.

This is the logic of the imagination and the passions; which seek to aggrandize what excites admiration and to heap contempt on misery, to raise power into tyranny, and to make tyranny absolute; to thrust down that which is low still lower, and to make wretches desperate: to exalt magistrates into kings, kings into gods; to degrade subjects to the rank of slaves, and slaves to the condition of brutes. The history of mankind is a romance, a mask, a tragedy, constructed upon the principles of *poetical justice*; it is a noble or royal hunt, in which what is sport to the few is death to the many, and in which the spectators halloo and encourage the strong to set upon the weak, and cry havoc in the chase, though they do not share in the spoil. We may depend upon it that what men delight to read in books, they will put in practice in reality.

One of the most natural traits in this play is the difference of the interest taken in the success of Coriolanus by his wife and mother. The one is only anxious for his honour; the other is fearful for his life.

> *Volumnia.* Methinks I hither hear your husband's drum:
> I see him pluck Aufidius down by th' hair:
> Methinks I see him stamp thus—and call thus—
> Come on, ye cowards; ye were got in fear
> Though you were born in Rome; his bloody brow
> With his mail'd hand then wiping, forth he goes
> Like to a harvest man, that's task'd to mow
> Or all, or lose his hire.
> *Virgilia.* His bloody brow! Oh, Jupiter, no blood.
> *Volumnia.* Away, you fool; it more becomes a man
> Than gilt his trophy. The breast of Hecuba,
> When she did suckle Hector, look'd not lovelier
> Than Hector's forehead, when it spit forth blood
> At Grecian swords contending.

When she hears the trumpets that proclaim her son's return, she says in the true spirit of a Roman matron:

These are the ushers of Martius: before him
He carries noise, and behind him he leaves tears.
Death, that dark spirit, in's nervy arm doth lie,
Which being advanc'd, declines, and then men die.

Coriolanus himself is a complete character: his love of reputation, his contempt of popular opinion, his pride and modesty, are consequences of each other. His pride consists in the inflexible sternness of his will: his love of glory is a determined desire to bear down all opposition, and to extort the admiration both of friends and foes. His contempt for popular favour, his unwillingness to hear his own praises, spring from the same source. He cannot contradict the praises that are bestowed upon him; therefore he is impatient at hearing them. He would enforce the good opinion of others by his actions, but does not want their acknowledgements in words.

Pray now, no more: my mother,
Who has a charter to extol her blood,
When she does praise me, grieves me.

His magnanimity is of the same kind. He admires in an enemy that courage which he honours in himself: he places himself on the hearth of Aufidius with the same confidence that he would have met him in the field, and feels that by putting himself in his power, he takes from him all temptation for using it against him.

In the title-page of *Coriolanus* it is said at the bottom of the Dramatis Personae, 'The whole history exactly followed, and many of the principal speeches copied from the life of Coriolanus in Plutarch'. It will be interesting to our readers to see how far this is the case. Two of the principal scenes, those between Coriolanus and Aufidius and between Coriolanus and his mother, are thus given in Sir Thomas North's translation of Plutarch, dedicated to Queen Elizabeth, 1579. The first is as follows:

It was even twilight when he entered the city of Antium, and many people met him in the streets, but no man knew him. So he went directly to Tullus Aufidius' house, and when he came thither, he got him up straight to the chimney-hearth, and sat him down, and spake not a word to any man, his face all muffled over. They of the house spying him, wondered what he should be, and yet they durst not bid him rise. For ill-favouredly muffled and disguised as he was, yet there appeared a certain majesty in his countenance and in his silence: whereupon they went to Tullus, who was at supper, to tell him of the strange disguising of this man. Tullus rose presently from the board, and coming towards him, asked him what he was, and wherefore he came. Then Martius unmuffled himself, and after he had paused awhile, making no answer, he said unto himself, If thou knowest me not yet, Tullus, and seeing me, dost not perhaps believe me to be the man I am indeed, I must of necessity discover myself to be that I am. 'I am Caius Martius, who hath 'done to thyself particularly, and to all the Volsces generally, 'great hurt and mischief, which I cannot deny for my surname of 'Coriolanus that I bear. For I never had other benefit nor 'recompence of the true and painful service I have done, and the 'extreme dangers I have been in, but this only surname: a good 'memory and witness of the malice and displeasure thou 'shouldest bear me. Indeed the name only remaineth with me; 'for the rest, the envy and cruelty of the people of Rome have 'taken from me, by the sufferance of the dastardly nobility and 'magistrates, who have forsaken me, and let me be banished by 'the people. This extremity hath now driven me to come as a 'poor suitor, to take thy chimney-hearth, not of any hope I have 'to save my life thereby. For if I had feared death, I would 'not have come hither to put myself in hazard: but pricked 'forward with desire to be revenged of them that thus have 'banished me, which now I do begin, in putting my person into 'the hands of their enemies. Wherefore if thou hast any heart 'to be wrecked of the injuries thy enemies have done thee, speed 'thee now, and let my misery serve thy turn, and so use it as my 'service may be a benefit to the Volsces: promising thee, that 'I will fight with better good will for all you, than I did when 'I was against you, knowing that they fight more valiantly 'who know the force of the enemy, than such as have never 'proved it. And if it be so that thou dare not, and that thou 'art weary to prove fortune any more, then am I also weary 'to live any longer. And it were no wisdom in thee to save the 'life of him who hath been heretofore thy mortal enemy, and 'whose service now can nothing help, nor pleasure thee.'
Tullus hearing what he said, was a marvellous glad man, and taking him by the hand, he said unto him: 'Stand up, O Martius,

'and be of good cheer, for in proffering thyself unto us, thou 'doest us great honour: and by this means thou mayest hope 'also of greater things at all the Volsces' hands.' So he feasted him for that time, and entertained him in the honourablest manner he could, talking with him of no other matter at that present: but within few days after, they fell to consultation together in what sort they should begin their wars.

## The meeting between Coriolanus and his mother is also nearly the same as in the play.

Now was Martius set then in the chair of state, with all the honours of a general, and when he had spied the women coming afar off, he marvelled what the matter meant: but afterwards knowing his wife which came foremost, he determined at the first to persist in his obstinate and inflexible rancour. But overcome in the end with natural affection, and being altogether altered to see them, his heart would not serve him to tarry their coming to his chair, but coming down in haste, he went to meet them, and first he kissed his mother, and embraced her a pretty while, then his wife and little children. And nature so wrought with him, that the tears fell from his eyes, and he could not keep himself from making much of them, but yielded to the affection of his blood, as if he had been violently carried with the fury of a most swift-running stream. After he had thus lovingly received them, and perceiving that his mother Volumnia would begin to speak to him, he called the chiefest of the council of the Volsces to hear what she would say. Then she spake in this sort: 'If we held our peace, my son, and determined not to speak, the 'state of our poor bodies, and present sight of our raiment, would 'easily betray to thee what life we have led at home, since thy 'exile and abode abroad; but think now with thyself, how much 'more unfortunate than all the women living, we are come hither, 'considering that the sight which should be most pleasant to all 'others to behold, spiteful fortune had made most fearful to us: 'making myself to see my son, and my daughter here her husband, 'besieging the walls of his native country: so as that which is 'the only comfort to all others in their adversity and misery, to 'pray unto the Gods, and to call to them for aid, is the only 'thing which plungeth us into most deep perplexity. For we 'cannot, alas, together pray, both for victory to our country, and 'for safety of thy life also: but a world of grievous curses, yea 'more than any mortal enemy can heap upon us, are forcibly 'wrapped up in our prayers. For the bitter sop of most hard 'choice is offered thy wife and children, to forgo one of the two: 'either to lose the person of thyself, or the nurse of their native 'country. For myself, my son, I am determined not to tarry 'till fortune in my lifetime do make an end of this war. For if 'I cannot persuade thee rather to do good unto both parties, than 'to overthrow and destroy the one, preferring love and nature 'before the malice and calamity of wars, thou shalt see, my son, 'and trust unto it, thou shalt no sooner march forward to assault 'thy country, but thy foot shall tread upon thy mother's womb, 'that brought thee first into this world. And I may not defer 'to see the day, either that my son be led prisoner in triumph 'by his natural countrymen, or that he himself do triumph of 'them, and of his natural country. For if it were so, that my 'request tended to save thy country, in destroying the Volsces, 'I must confess, thou wouldest hardly and doubtfully resolve 'on that. For as to destroy thy natural country, it is altogether 'unmeet and unlawful, so were it not just and less honourable 'to betray those that put their trust in thee. But my only 'demand consisteth, to make a gaol delivery of all evils, which 'delivereth equal benefit and safety, both to the one and the 'other, but most honourable for the Volsces. For it shall appear, 'that having victory in their hands, they have of special favour 'granted us singular graces, peace and amity, albeit themselves 'have no less part of both than we. Of which good, if so it came 'to pass, thyself is the only author, and so hast thou the only 'honour. But if it fail, and fall out contrary, thyself alone 'deservedly shalt carry the shameful reproach and burthen of 'either party. So, though the end of war be uncertain, yet this 'notwithstanding is most certain, that if it be thy chance to 'conquer, this benefit shalt thou reap of thy goodly conquest, 'to be chronicled the plague and destroyer of thy country. And 'if fortune overthrow thee, then the world will say, that through 'desire to revenge thy private injuries, thou hast for ever undone 'thy good friends, who did most lovingly and courteously receive 'thee'. Martius gave good ear unto his mother's words, without interrupting her speech at all, and after she had said what she would, he held his peace a pretty while, and answered not a word. Hereupon she began again to speak unto him, and said: 'My son, 'why dost thou not answer me? Dost thou think it good alto'gether to give place unto thy choler and desire of revenge, and 'thinkest thou it not honesty for thee to grant thy mother's 'request in so weighty a cause? Dost thou take it honourable 'for a nobleman, to remember the wrongs and injuries done him, 'and dost not in like case think it an honest nobleman's part to 'be thankful for the goodness that parents do show to their 'children, acknowledging the duty and reverence they ought 'to bear unto them? No man living is more bound to show 'himself thankful in all parts and respects than thyself; who so 'universally showest all ingratitude. Moreover, my son, thou 'has sorely taken of thy country, exacting grievous payments 'upon them, in revenge of the injuries offered thee; besides, 'thou hast not hitherto showed thy poor mother any courtesy. 'And therefore it is not only honest, but due unto me, that 'without compulsion I should obtain my so just and reasonable 'request of thee. But since by reason I cannot persuade thee 'to it, to what purpose do I defer my last hope?' And with these words herself, his wife and children, fell down upon their knees before him: Martius seeing that, could refrain no longer, but went straight and lifted her up, crying out, 'Oh mother, 'what have you done to me?' And holding her hard by the right hand, 'Oh mother,' said he, 'you have won a happy victory 'for your country, but mortal and unhappy for your son: for 'I see myself vanquished by you alone'. These words being spoken openly, he spake a little apart with his mother and wife, and then let them return again to Rome, for so they did request him; and so remaining in the camp that night, the next morning he dislodged, and marched homeward unto the Volsces' country again.

Shakespeare has, in giving a dramatic form to this passage, adhered very closely and properly to the text. He did not think it necessary to improve upon the truth of nature. Several of the scenes in *Julius Caesar*, particularly Portia's appeal to the confidence of her husband by showing him the wound she had given herself, and the appearance of the ghost of Caesar to Brutus, are, in like manner, taken from the history.

## *Troilus and Cressida*

This is one of the most loose and desultory of our author's plays: it rambles on just as it happens, but it overtakes, together with some indifferent matter, a prodigious number of fine things in its way. Troilus himself is no character: he is merely a common lover: but Cressida and her uncle Pandarus are hit off with proverbial truth. By the speeches given to the leaders of the Grecian host, Nestor, Ulysses, Agamemnon, Achilles, Shakespeare seems to have known them as well as if he had been a spy sent by the Trojans into the enemy's camp—to say nothing of their being very lofty examples of didactic eloquence. The following is a very stately and spirited declamation:

*Ulysses.* Troy, yet upon her basis, had been down,
And the great Hector's sword had lack'd a master,
But for these instances.
The speciality of rule hath been neglected.

* * *

The heavens themselves, the planets, and this centre,
Observe degree, priority, and place,
Insisture, course, proportion, season, form,
Office, and custom, in all line of order:
And therefore is the glorious planet, Sol,
In noble eminence, enthron'd and spher'd
Amidst the other, whose med'cinable eye
Corrects the ill aspects of planets evil,
And posts, like the commandment of a king,
Sans check, to good and bad. But, when the planets,
In evil mixture to disorder wander.
What plagues and what portents? what mutinies?
What raging of the sea? shaking of earth?
Commotion in the winds? frights, changes, horrors,
Divert and crack, rend and deracinate
The unity and married calm of states

Quite from their fixture ! O, when degree is shaken,
(Which is the ladder to all high designs)
The enterprise is sick ! How could communities,
Degrees in schools, and brotherhoods in cities,
Peaceful commerce from dividable shores,
The primogenitive and due of birth,
Prerogative of age, crowns, sceptres, laurels,
(But by degree) stand in authentic place ?
Take but degree away, untune that string,
And hark what discord follows ! each thing meets
In mere oppugnancy. The bounded waters
Would lift their bosoms higher than the shores,
And make a sop of all this solid globe :
Strength would be lord of imbecility,
And the rude son would strike his father dead :
Force would be right ; or rather, right and wrong
(Between whose endless jar Justice resides)
Would lose their names, and so would Justice too.
Then everything includes itself in power,
Power into will, will into appetite ;
And appetite (an universal wolf,
So doubly seconded with will and power)
Must make perforce an universal prey,
And last, eat up himself. Great Agamemnon,
This chaos, when degree is suffocate,
Follows the choking :
And this neglection of degree it is,
That by a pace goes backward, in a purpose
It hath to climb. The general's disdained
By him one step below ; he, by the next ;
That next, by him beneath : so every step,
Exampled by the first pace that is sick
Of his superior, grows to an envious fever
Of pale and bloodless emulation ;
And 'tis this fever that keeps Troy on foot,
Not her own sinews. To end a tale of length,
Troy in our weakness lives, not in her strength.

It cannot be said of Shakespeare, as was said of some one, that he was ' without o'erflowing full '. He was full, even to o'erflowing. He gave heaped measure, running over. This was his greatest fault. He was only in danger ' of losing distinction in his thoughts ' (to borrow his own expression)

As doth a battle when they charge on heaps
The enemy flying.

There is another passage, the speech of Ulysses to Achilles, showing him the thankless nature of popularity, which has a still greater depth of moral observation and richness of illustration than the former. It is long, but worth the quoting. The sometimes giving an entire extract from the unacted plays of our author may with one class of readers have almost the use of restoring a lost passage; and may serve to convince another class of critics, that the poet's genius was not confined to the production of stage effect by preternatural means.—

*Ulysses.* Time hath, my lord, a wallet at his back,
Wherein he puts alms for Oblivion;
A great-siz'd monster of ingratitudes:
Those scraps are good deeds past,
Which are devour'd as fast as they are made,
Forgot as soon as done: Persev'rance, dear my lord,
Keeps Honour bright: to have done, is to hang
Quite out of fashion, like a rusty mail
In monumental mockery. Take the instant way;
For Honour travels in a strait so narrow,
Where one but goes abreast; keep then the path,
For Emulation hath a thousand sons,
That one by one pursue; if you give way,
Or hedge aside from the direct forth-right,
Like to an entered tide, they all rush by,
And leave you hindmost;—
Or, like a gallant horse fall'n in first rank,
O'er-run and trampled on: then what they do in present,
Tho' less than yours in past, must o'ertop yours:
For Time is like a fashionable host,
That slightly shakes his parting guest by th' hand,
And with his arms out-stretch'd, as he would fly,
Grasps in the comer: the Welcome ever smiles,
And Farewell goes out sighing. O, let not virtue seek
Remuneration for the thing it was; for beauty, wit,
High birth, vigour of bone, desert in service,
Love, friendship, charity, are subjects all
To envious and calumniating time:
One touch of nature makes the whole world kin,
That all, with one consent, praise new-born gauds,
Tho' they are made and moulded of things past.

The present eye praises the present object.
Then marvel not, thou great and complete man,
That all the Greeks begin to worship Ajax;
Since things in motion sooner catch the eye,
Than what not stirs. The cry went out on thee,
And still it might, and yet it may again,
If thou would'st not entomb thy self alive,
And case thy reputation in thy tent.—

The throng of images in the above lines is prodigious; and though they sometimes jostle against one another, they everywhere raise and carry on the feeling, which is metaphysically true and profound. The debates between the Trojan chiefs on the restoring of Helen are full of knowledge of human motives and character. Troilus enters well into the philosophy of war, when he says in answer to something that falls from Hector:

Why there you touch'd the life of our design:
Were it not glory that we more affected,
Than the performance of our heaving spleens,
I would not wish a drop of Trojan blood
Spent more in her defence. But, worthy Hector,
She is a theme of honour and renown,
A spur to valiant and magnanimous deeds.

The character of Hector, in the few slight indications which appear of it, is made very amiable. His death is sublime, and shows in a striking light the mixture of barbarity and heroism of the age. The threats of Achilles are fatal; they carry their own means of execution with them.

Come here about me, you my Myrmidons,
Mark what I say.—Attend me where I wheel:
Strike not a stroke, but keep yourselves in breath;
And when I have the bloody Hector found,
Empale him with your weapons round about:
In fellest manner execute your arms.
Follow me, sirs, and my proceeding eye.

He then finds Hector and slays him, as if he had been hunting down a wild beast. There is something revolting as well as terrific in the ferocious coolness with which he singles out his prey: nor does the splendour of the achievement reconcile us to the cruelty of the means.

The characters of Cressida and Pandarus are very amusing and instructive. The disinterested willingness of Pandarus to serve his friend in an affair which lies next his heart is immediately brought forward. 'Go thy way, Troilus, go thy way; had I a sister were a grace, or a daughter were a goddess, he should take his choice. O admirable man! Paris, Paris is dirt to him, and I warrant Helen, to change, wou'd give money to boot'. This is the language he addresses to his niece: nor is she much behindhand in coming into the plot. Her head is as light and fluttering as her heart. 'It is the prettiest villain, she fetches her breath so short as a new ta'en sparrow'. Both characters are originals, and quite different from what they are in Chaucer. In Chaucer, Cressida is represented as a grave, sober, considerate personage (a widow—he cannot tell her age, nor whether she has children or no) who has an alternate eye to her character, her interest, and her pleasure: Shakespeare's Cressida is a giddy girl, an unpractised jilt, who falls in love with Troilus, as she afterwards deserts him, from mere levity and thoughtlessness of temper. She may be wooed and won to anything and from anything, at a moment's warning: the other knows very well what she would be at, and sticks to it, and is more governed by substantial reasons than by caprice or vanity. Pandarus again, in Chaucer's story, is a friendly sort of go-between, tolerably busy, officious, and forward in bringing matters to bear: but in Shakespeare he has 'a stamp exclusive and professional'; he wears the badge of his trade; he is a regular knight of the game. The difference of the manner in which the subject is treated arises perhaps less from intention, than from the different genius of the two poets. There is no *double entendre* in the characters of Chaucer: they are either quite serious or quite comic. In Shakespeare the ludicrous and ironical are constantly blended with the stately and the impassioned. We see Chaucer's characters as they saw themselves, not as they appeared to others or might have appeared to the poet. He is as deeply implicated in the affairs of his personages as they could be themselves. He had to go a long journey with each of them, and became a kind of necessary confidant. There is little relief, or light and shade in his pictures. The conscious smile is not seen lurking under the brow of grief or impatience. Everything with him is intense and continuous—a working out of what went before.—Shakespeare never committed himself to his characters. He trifled, laughed, or wept with them as he chose. He has no prejudices for or against them; and it seems a matter of perfect indifference whether he shall be in jest or earnest. According to him, 'the web of our lives is of a mingled yarn, good and ill together'. His genius was dramatic, as Chaucer's was historical. He saw both sides of a question, the different views taken of it according to the different interests of the parties concerned, and he was at once an actor and spectator in the scene. If anything, he is too various and flexible; too full of transitions, of glancing lights, of salient points. If Chaucer followed up his subject too doggedly, perhaps Shakespeare was too volatile and heedless. The Muse's wing too often lifted him off his feet. He made infinite excursions to the right and the left.

——He hath done
Mad and fantastic execution,
Engaging and redeeming of himself
With such a careless force and forceless care,
As if that luck in very spite of cunning
Bade him win all.

Chaucer attended chiefly to the real and natural, that is, to the involuntary and inevitable impressions on the mind in given circumstances: Shakespeare exhibited also the possible and the fantastical,—not only what things are in themselves, but whatever they might seem to be, their different reflections, their endless combinations. He lent his fancy, wit, invention, to others, and borrowed their feelings in return. Chaucer excelled in the force of habitual sentiment; Shakespeare added to it every variety of passion, every suggestion of thought or accident. Chaucer described external objects with the eye of a painter, or he might be said to have embodied them with the hand of a sculptor, every part is so thoroughly made out, and tangible: Shakespeare's imagination threw over them a lustre

—Prouder than when blue Iris bends.

Everything in Chaucer has a downright reality. A simile or a sentiment is as if it were given in upon evidence. In Shakespeare the commonest matter-of-fact has a romantic grace about it; or seems to float with the breath of imagination in a freer element. No one could have more depth of feeling or observation than Chaucer, but he wanted resources of invention to lay open the stores of nature or the human heart with the same radiant light that Shakespeare has done. However fine or profound the thought, we know what was coming, whereas the effect of reading Shakespeare is 'like the eye of vassalage encountering majesty'. Chaucer's mind was consecutive, rather than discursive. He arrived at truth through a certain process; Shakespeare saw everything by intuition, Chaucer had great variety of power, but he could do only one thing at once. He set himself to work on a particular subject. His ideas were kept separate, labelled, ticketed and parcelled out in a set form, in pews and compartments by themselves. They did not play into one another's hands. They did not re-act upon one another, as the blower's breath moulds the yielding glass. There is something hard and dry in them. What is the most wonderful thing in Shakespeare's faculties is their excessive sociability, and how they gossiped and compared notes together.

We must conclude this criticism; and we will do it with a quotation or two. One of the most beautiful passages in Chaucer's tale is the description of Cresseide's first avowal of her love:

And as the new abashed nightingale,
That stinteth first when she beginneth sing,
When that she heareth any herde's tale,
Or in the hedges any wight stirring,
And, after, sicker doth her voice outring;
Right so Cresseide, when that her dread stent,
Opened her heart, and told him her intent.

See also the two next stanzas, and particularly that divine one beginning.

Her armes small, her back both straight and soft, &c.

Compare this with the following speech of Troilus to Cressida in the play.

O, that I thought it could be in a woman;
And if it can, I will presume in you,
To feed for aye her lamp and flame of love,
To keep her constancy in plight and youth,
Out-living beauties outward, with a mind
That doth renew swifter than blood decays.
Or, that persuasion could but thus convince me,
That my integrity and truth to you
Might be affronted with the match and weight
Of such a winnow'd purity in love;
How were I then uplifted! But alas,
I am as true as Truth's simplicity,
And simpler than the infancy of Truth.

These passages may not seem very characteristic at first sight, though we think they are so. We will give two, that cannot be mistaken. Patroclus says to Achilles :

> ——Rouse yourself ; and the weak wanton Cupid
> Shall from your neck unloose his amorous fold,
> And like a dew-drop from the lion's mane,
> Be shook to air.

Troilus, addressing the God of Day on the approach of the morning that parts him from Cressida, says with much scorn :

> What ! proffer'st thou thy light here for to sell ?
> Go, sell it them that smallé selés grave.

If nobody but Shakespeare could have written the former, nobody but Chaucer would have thought of the latter.—Chaucer was the most literal of poets, as Richardson was of prose-writers.

## *Anthony and Cleopatra*

This is a very noble play. Though not in the first class of Shakespeare's productions, it stands next to them, and is, we think, the finest of his historical plays, that is, of those in which he made poetry the organ of history, and assumed a certain tone of character and sentiment, in conformity to known facts, instead of trusting to his observations of general nature or to the unlimited indulgence of his own fancy. What he has added to the history, is upon a par with it. His genius was, as it were, a match for history as well as nature, and could grapple at will with either. This play is full of that pervading comprehensive power by which the poet could always make himself master of time and circumstances. It presents a fine picture of Roman pride and Eastern magnificence: and in the struggle between the two, the empire of the world seems suspended, 'like the swan's down feather:

> That stands upon the swell at full of tide,
> And neither way inclines'.

The characters breathe, move, and live. Shakespeare does not stand reasoning on what his characters would do or say, but at once *becomes* them, and speaks and acts for them. He does not present us with groups of stage-puppets or poetical machines making set speeches on human life, and acting from a calculation of ostensible motives, but he brings living men and women on the scene, who speak and act from real feelings, according to the ebbs and flows of passion, without the least tincture of the pedantry of logic or rhetoric.



Q

Nothing is made out by inference and analogy, by climax and antithesis, but everything takes place just as it would have done in reality, according to the occasion.—The character of Cleopatra is a master-piece. What an extreme contrast it affords to Imogen! One would think it almost impossible for the same person to have drawn both. She is voluptuous, ostentatious, conscious, boastful of her charms, haughty, tyrannical, fickle. The luxurious pomp and gorgeous extravagance of the Egyptian queen are displayed in all their force and lustre, as well as the irregular grandeur of the soul of Mark Antony. Take only the first four lines that they speak as an example of the regal style of love-making.

> *Cleopatra.* If it be love, indeed, tell me how much?
> *Antony.* There's beggary in the love that can be reckon'd.
> *Cleopatra.* I'll set a bourn how far to be belov'd.
> *Antony.* Then must thou needs find out new heav'n, new earth.

The rich and poetical description of her person, beginning:

> The barge she sat in, like a burnish'd throne,
> Burnt on the water; the poop was beaten gold,
> Purple the sails, and so perfumed, that
> The winds were love-sick—

seems to prepare the way for, and almost to justify the subsequent infatuation of Antony when in the sea-fight at Actium, he leaves the battle, and 'like a doting mallard' follows her flying sails.

Few things in Shakespeare (and we know of nothing in any other author like them) have more of that local truth of imagination and character than the passage in which Cleopatra is represented conjecturing what were the employments of Antony in his absence. 'He's speaking now, or murmuring—*Where's my serpent of old Nile*?' Or again, when she says to Antony, after the defeat at Actium, and his summoning up resolution to risk another fight—'It is my birthday; I had thought to have held it poor; but since my lord is Antony again, I will be Cleopatra'. Perhaps the finest burst of all is Antony's rage after his final defeat when he comes in, and surprises the messenger of Caesar kissing her hand:

> To let a fellow that will take rewards,
> And say, God quit you, be familiar with
> My play-fellow, your hand; this kingly seal,
> And plighter of high hearts.

It is no wonder that he orders him to be whipped; but his low condition is not the true reason: there is another feeling which lies deeper, though Antony's pride would not let him show it, except by his rage; he suspects the fellow to be Caesar's proxy.

Cleopatra's whole character is the triumph of the voluptuous, of the love of pleasure, and the power of giving it, over every other consideration. Octavia is a dull foil to her, and Fulvia a shrew and shrill-tongued. What a picture do those lines give of her:

> Age cannot whither her, nor custom stale
> Her infinite variety. Other women cloy
> The appetites they feed, but she makes hungry
> Where most she satisfies.

What a spirit and fire in her conversation with Antony's messenger who brings her the unwelcome news of his marriage with Octavia! How all the pride of beauty and of high rank breaks out in her promised reward to him:

> ——There's gold, and here
> My bluest veins to kiss!

She had great and unpardonable faults, but the beauty of her death almost redeems them. She learns from the depth of despair the strength of her affections. She keeps her queen-like state in the last disgrace, and her sense of the pleasurable in the last moments of her life. She tastes a luxury in death. After applying the asp, she says with fondness :

> Dost thou not see my baby at my breast,
> That sucks the nurse asleep ?
> As sweet as balm, as soft as air, as gentle.
> Oh Antony !

It is worth while to observe that Shakespeare has contrasted the extreme magnificence of the descriptions in this play with pictures of extreme suffering and physical horror, not less striking—partly perhaps to excuse the effeminacy of Mark Antony to whom they are related as having happened, but more to preserve a certain balance of feeling in the mind. Caesar says, hearing of his conduct at the court of Cleopatra :

> ——Antony,
> Leave thy lascivious wassails. When thou once
> Wert beaten from Mutina, where thou slew'st
> Hirtius and Pansa, consuls, at thy heel
> Did famine follow, whom thou fought'st against,
> Though daintily brought up, with patience more
> Than savages could suffer. Thou did'st drink
> The stale of horses, and the gilded puddle
> Which beast would cough at. Thy palate then did deign
> The roughest berry on the rudest hedge,
> Yea, like the stag, when snow the pasture sheets,
> The barks of trees thou browsed'st. On the Alps,
> It is reported, thou did'st eat strange flesh,
> Which some did die to look on : and all this,
> It wounds thine honour, that I speak it now,
> Was borne so like a soldier, that thy cheek
> So much as lank'd not.

The passage after Antony's defeat by Augustus where he is made to say :

> Yes, yes ; he at Philippi kept
> His sword e'en like a dancer ; while I struck
> The lean and wrinkled Cassius, and 'twas I
> That the mad Brutus ended.

is one of those fine retrospections which show us the winding and eventful march of human life. The jealous attention which has been paid to the unities both of time and place has taken away the principle of perspective in the drama, and all the interest which objects derive from distance, from contrast, from privation, from change of fortune, from long-cherished passion; and contracts our view of life from a strange and romantic dream, long, obscure, and infinite, into a smartly contested, three hours' inaugural disputation on its merits by the different candidates for theatrical applause.

The latter scenes of *Antony and Cleopatra* are full of the changes of accident and passion. Success and defeat follow one another with startling rapidity. Fortune sits upon her wheel more blind and giddy than usual. This precarious state and the approaching dissolution of his greatness are strikingly displayed in the dialogue between Antony and Eros:

> *Antony*. Eros, thou yet behold'st me?
> *Eros*. Ay, noble lord.
> *Antony*. Sometime we see a cloud that's dragonish,
> A vapour sometime, like a bear or lion,
> A towered citadel, a pendant rock,
> A forked mountain, or blue promontory
> With trees upon't, that nod unto the world
> And mock our eyes with air. Thou hast seen these signs,
> They are black vesper's pageants.
> *Eros*. Ay, my lord.
> *Antony*. That which is now a horse, even with a thought
> The rack dislimns, and makes it indistinct
> As water is in water.
> *Eros*. It does, my lord.
> *Antony*. My good knave, Eros, now thy captain is
> Even such a body, &c.

This is, without doubt, one of the finest pieces of poetry in Shakespeare. The splendour of the imagery, the semblance of reality, the lofty range of picturesque objects hanging over the world their evanescent nature, the total uncertainty o what is left behind, are just like the mouldering schemes of human greatness. It is finer than Cleopatra's passionate lamentation over his fallen grandeur, because it is more dim, unstable, unsubstantial. Antony's headstrong presumption and infatuated determination to yield to Cleopatra's wishes to fight by sea instead of land, meet a merited punishment; and the extravagance of his resolutions, increasing with the desperateness of his circumstances, is well commented upon by Enobarbus:

——I see men's judgements are
A parcel of their fortunes, and things outward
Do draw the inward quality after them
To suffer all alike.

The repentance of Enobarbus after his treachery to his master is the most affecting part of the play. He cannot recover from the blow which Antony's generosity gives him, and he dies broken-hearted 'a master-leaver and a fugitive'.

Shakespeare's genius has spread over the whole play a richness like the overflowing of the Nile.

# *Hamlet*

This is that Hamlet the Dane, whom we read of in our youth, and whom we seem almost to remember in our after-years; he who made that famous soliloquy on life, who gave the advice to the players, who thought 'this goodly frame, the earth, a sterile promontory, and this brave o'er-hanging firmament, the air, this majestical roof fretted with golden fire, a foul and pestilent congregation of vapours'; whom 'man delighted not, nor woman neither'; he who talked with the grave-diggers, and moralized on Yorick's skull; the school-fellow of Rosencrans and Guildenstern at Wittenberg; the friend of Horatio; the lover of Ophelia; he that was mad and sent to England; the slow avenger of his father's death; who lived at the court of Horwendillus five hundred years before we were born, but all whose thoughts we seem to know as well as we do our own, because we have read them in Shakespeare.

Hamlet is a name: his speeches and sayings but the idle coinage of the poet's brain. What then, are they not real? They are as real as our own thoughts. Their reality is in the reader's mind. It is *we* who are Hamlet. This play has a prophetic truth, which is above that of history. Whoever has become thoughtful and melancholy through his own mishaps or those of others; whoever has borne about with him the clouded brow of reflection, and thought himself 'too much i' th' sun'; whoever has seen the golden lamp of day dimmed by envious mists rising in his own breast, and could find in the world before him only a dull blank with nothing left remarkable in it; whoever has known 'the pangs of despised love, the insolence of office, or the spurns which patient merit of the unworthy takes'; he who has felt his mind sink within him, and sadness cling to his heart like a malady, who has had his hopes blighted and his youth staggered by the apparitions of strange things; who cannot be well at ease, while he sees evil hovering near him like a spectre; whose powers of action have been eaten up by thought, he to whom the universe seems infinite, and himself nothing; whose bitterness of soul makes him careless of consequences, and who goes to a play as his best resource to shove off, to a second remove, the evils of life by a mock-presentation of them—this is the true Hamlet.

We have been so used to this tragedy that we hardly know how to criticize it any more than we should know how to describe our own faces. But we must make such observations as we can. It is the one of Shakespeare's plays that we think of oftenest, because it abounds most in striking reflections on human life, and because the distresses of Hamlet are transferred, by the turn of his mind, to the general account of humanity. Whatever happens to him, we apply to ourselves, because he applies it so himself as a means of general reasoning. He is a great moralizer; and what makes him worth attending to is, that he moralizes on his own feelings and experience. He is not a commonplace pedant. If *Lear* shows the greatest depth of passion, *Hamlet* is the most remarkable for the ingenuity, originality, and unstudied development of character. Shakespeare had more magnanimity than any other poet, and he has shown more of it in this play than in any other. There is no attempt to force an interest: everything is left for time and circumstances to unfold. The attention is excited without effort, the incidents succeed each other as matters of course, the characters think and speak and act just as they might do, if left entirely to themselves. There is no set purpose, no straining at a point. The observations are suggested by the passing scene—the gusts of passion come and go like sounds of music borne on the wind. The whole play is an exact transcript of what might be supposed to have taken place at the court of Denmark, at the remote period of time fixed upon, before the modern refinements in morals and manners were heard of. It would have been interesting enough to have been admitted as a bystander in such a scene, at such a time, to have heard and seen something of what was going on. But here we are more than spectators. We have not only 'the outward pageants and the signs of grief;' but 'we have that within which passes show.' We read the thoughts of the heart, we catch the passions living as they rise. Other dramatic writers give us very fine versions and paraphrases of nature: but Shakespeare, together with his own comments, gives us the original text, that we may judge for ourselves. This is a very great advantage.

The character of Hamlet is itself a pure effusion of genius. It is not a character marked by strength of will or even of passion, but by refinement of thought and sentiment. Hamlet is as little of the hero as a man can well be: but he is a young and princely novice, full of high enthusiasm and quick sensibility—the sport of circumstances, questioning with fortune and refining on his own feelings, and forced from the natural bias of his disposition by the strangeness of his situation. He seems incapable of deliberate action, and is only hurried into extremities on the spur of the occasion, when he has no time to reflect, as in the scene where he kills Polonius, and again, where he alters the letters which Rosencraus and Guildenstern are taking with them to England, purporting his death. At other times, when he is most bound to act, he remains puzzled, undecided, and sceptical, dallies with his purposes, till the occasion is lost, and always finds some pretence to relapse into indolence and thoughtfulness again. For this reason he refuses to kill the King when he is at his prayers, and by a refinement in malice, which is in truth only an excuse for his own want of resolution, defers his revenge to some more fatal opportunity, when he shall be engaged in some act 'that has no relish of salvation in it':

He kneels and prays,
And now I'll do 't, and so he goes to heaven,
And so am I reveng'd: *that would be scann'd.*
He kill'd my father, and for that,
I, his sole son, send him to heaven.
Why this is reward, not revenge.
Up sword and know thou a more horrid time,
When he is drunk, asleep, or in a rage.

He is the prince of philosophical speculators, and because he cannot have his revenge perfect, according to the most refined idea his wish can form, he misses it altogether. So he scruples to trust the suggestions of the Ghost, contrives the scene of the play to have surer proof of his uncle's guilt, and then rests satisfied with this confirmation of his suspicions, and the success of his experiment, instead of acting upon it. Yet he is sensible of his own weakness, taxes himself with it, and tries to reason himself out of it:

How all occasions do inform against me,
And spur my dull revenge! What is a man,
If his chief good and market of his time
Be but to sleep and feed? A beast; no more.
Sure he that made us with such large discourse,
Looking before and after, gave us not
That capability and god-like reason
To rust in us unus'd: now whether it be
Bestial oblivion, or some craven scruple
Of thinking too precisely on th' event,—
A thought which quarter'd, hath but one part wisdom,

And ever three parts coward ;—I do not know
Why yet I live to say, this thing's to do ;
Sith I have cause, and will, and strength, and means
To do it. Examples gross as earth excite me :
Witness this army of such mass and charge,
Led by a delicate and tender prince,
Whose spirit with divine ambition puff'd,
Makes mouths at the invisible event,
Exposing what is mortal and unsure
To all that fortune, death, and danger dare,
Even for an egg-shell. 'Tis not to be great,
Never to stir without great argument ;
But greatly to find quarrel in a straw,
When honour's at the stake. How stand I then,
That have a father kill'd, a mother stain'd,
Excitements of my reason and my blood,
And let all sleep, while to my shame I see
The imminent death of twenty thousand men,
That for a fantasy and trick of fame,
Go to their graves like beds, fight for a plot
Whereon the numbers cannot try the cause,
Which is not tomb enough and continent
To hide the slain ?—O, from this time forth,
My thoughts be bloody or be nothing worth.

Still he does nothing ; and this very speculation on his own infirmity only affords him another occasion for indulging it. It is not for any want of attachment to his father or abhorrence of his murder that Hamlet is thus dilatory, but it is more to his taste to indulge his imagination in reflecting upon the enormity of the crime and refining on his schemes of vengeance, than to put them into immediate practice. His ruling passion is to think, not to act : and any vague pretence that flatters this propensity instantly diverts him from his previous purposes.

The moral perfection of this character has been called in question, we think, by those who did not understand it. It is more interesting than according to rules ; amiable, though not faultless. The ethical delineations of 'that noble and liberal casuist' (as Shakespeare has been well called) do not exhibit the drab-coloured quakerism of morality. His plays are not copied either from *The Whole Duty of Man*, or from *The Academy of Compliments*! We confess, we are a little shocked at the want of refinement in those who are shocked at the want of refinement in Hamlet. The want of punctilious exactness in his behaviour either partakes of the 'license of the time,' or else belongs to the very excess of intellectual refinement in the character, which makes the common rules of life, as well as his own purposes, sit loose upon him. He may be said to be amenable only to the tribunal of his own thoughts, and is too much taken up with the airy world of contemplation to lay as much stress as he ought on the practical consequences of things. His habitual principles of action are unhinged and out of joint with the time. (His conduct to Ophelia is quite natural in his circumstances. It is that of assumed severity only. It is the effect of disappointed hope, of bitter regrets, of affection suspended, not obliterated, by the distractions of the scene around him! Amidst the natural and preternatural horrors of his situation, he might be excused in delicacy from carrying on a regular courtship. When 'his father's spirit was in arms', it was not a time for the son to make love in. He could neither marry Ophelia, nor wound her mind by explaining the cause of his alienation, which he durst hardly trust himself to think of. It would have taken him years to have come to a direct explanation on the point. In the harassed state of his mind, he could not have done otherwise than he did. His conduct does not contradict what he says when he sees her funeral:

I loved Ophelia: forty thousand brothers
Could not with all their quantity of love
Make up my sum

Nothing can be more affecting or beautiful than the Queen's apostrophe to Ophelia on throwing flowers into the grave :

> ——Sweets to the sweet, farewell.
> I hop'd thou should'st have been my Hamlet's wife :
> I thought thy bride-bed to have deck'd, sweet maid,
> And not have strew'd thy grave.

Shakespeare was thoroughly a master of the mixed motives of human character, and he here shows us the Queen, who was so criminal in some respects, not without sensibility and affection in other relations of life.—Ophelia is a character almost too exquisitely touching to be dwelt upon. Oh rose of May, oh flower too soon faded! Her love, her madness, her death, are described with the truest touches of tenderness and pathos. It is a character which nobody but Shakespeare could have drawn in the way that he has done, and to the conception of which there is not even the smallest approach, except in some of the old romantic ballads. Her brother, Laertes, is a character we do not like so well: he is too hot and choleric, and somewhat rodomontade. Polonius is a perfect character in its kind; nor is there any foundation for the objections which have been made to the consistency of this part. It is said that he acts very foolishly and talks very sensibly. There is no inconsistency in that. Again, that he talks wisely at one time and foolishly at another; that his advice to Laertes is very sensible, and his advice to the King and Queen on the subject of Hamlet's madness very ridiculous. But he gives the one as a father, and is sincere in it; he gives the other as a mere courtier, a busy-body, and is accordingly officious, garrulous, and impertinent. In short, Shakespeare has been accused of inconsistency in this and other characters, only because he has kept up the distinction which there is in nature, between the understandings and the moral habits of men, between the absurdity of their ideas and the absurdity of their motives. Polonius is not a fool, but he makes himself so. His folly, whether in his actions or speeches, comes under the head of impropriety of intention.

We do not like to see our author's plays acted, and least of all, *Hamlet*. There is no play that suffers so much in being transferred to the stage. Hamlet himself seems hardly capable of being acted. Mr. Kemble unavoidably fails in this character from a want of ease and vanity. The character of Hamlet is made up of undulating lines; it has the yielding flexibility of 'a wave o' th' sea'. Mr. Kemble plays it like a man in armour, with a determined inveteracy of purpose, in one undeviating straight line, which is as remote from the natural grace and refined susceptibility of the character as the sharp angles and abrupt starts which Mr. Kean introduces into the part. Mr. Kean's Hamlet is as much too splenetic and rash as Mr. Kemble's is too deliberate and formal. His manner is too strong and pointed. He throws a severity, approaching to virulence, into the common observations and answers. There is nothing of this in Hamlet. He is, as it were, wrapped up in his reflections, and only *thinks aloud*. There should therefore be no attempt to impress what he says upon others by a studied exaggeration of emphasis or manner; no *talking at* his hearers. There should be as much of the gentleman and scholar as possible infused into the part, and as little of the actor. A pensive air of sadness should sit reluctantly upon his brow, but no appearance of fixed and sullen gloom. He is full of weakness and melancholy, but there is no harshness in his nature. He is the most amiable of misanthropes.

# *The Tempest*

There can be little doubt that Shakespeare was the most universal genius that ever lived. 'Either for tragedy, comedy, history, pastoral, pastoral-comical, historical-pastoral, scene individable or poem unlimited, he is the only man. Seneca cannot be too heavy, nor Plautus too light for him.' He has not only the same absolute command over our laughter and our tears, all the resources of passion, of wit, of thought, of observation, but he has the most unbounded range of fanciful invention, whether terrible or playful, the same insight into the world of imagination that he has into the world of reality; and over all there presides the same truth of character and nature, and the same spirit of humanity. His ideal beings are as true and natural as his real characters; that is, as consistent with themselves, or if we suppose such beings to exist at all, they could not act, speak, or feel otherwise than as he makes them. He has invented for them a language, manners, and sentiments of their own, from the tremendous imprecations of the Witches in *Macbeth*, when they do 'a deed without a name', to the sylph-like expressions of Ariel, who 'does his spiriting gently'; the mischievous tricks and gossiping of Robin Goodfellow, or the uncouth gabbling and emphatic gesticulations of Caliban in this play.

*The Tempest* is one of the most original and perfect of Shakespeare's productions, and he has shown in it all the variety of his powers. It is full of grace and grandeur. The human and imaginary characters, the dramatic and the grotesque, are blended together with the greatest art, and without any appearance of it. Though he has here given 'to airy nothing a local habitation and a name', yet that part which is only the fantastic creation of his mind, has the same palpable texture, and coheres 'semblably' with the rest. As the preternatural part has the air of reality, and almost haunts the imagination with a sense of truth, the real characters and events partake of the wildness of a dream. The stately magician, Prospero, driven from his dukedom, but around whom (so potent is his art) airy spirits throng numberless to do his bidding; his daughter Miranda ('worthy of that name') to whom all the power of his art points, and who seems the goddess of the isle; the princely Ferdinand, cast by fate upon the haven of his happiness in this idol of his love; the delicate Ariel; the savage Caliban, half brute, half demon; the drunken ship's crew—are all connected parts of the story, and can hardly be spared from the place they fill. Even the local scenery is of a piece and character with the subject. Prospero's enchanted island seems to have risen up out of the sea; the airy music, the tempest-tossed vessel, the turbulent waves, all have the effect of the landscape background of some fine picture. Shakespeare's pencil is (to use an illusion of his own) 'like the dyer's hand, subdued to what it works in'. Everything in him, though it partakes of 'liberty of wit', is also subjected to 'the law' of the understanding. For instance, even the drunken sailors, who are made reeling-ripe, share, in the disorder of their minds and bodies, in the tumult of the elements, and seem on shore to be as much at the mercy of chance as they were before at the mercy of the winds and waves. These fellows with their sea-wit are the least to our taste of any part of the play: but they are as like drunken sailors as they can be, and are an indirect foil to Caliban, whose figure acquires a classical dignity in the comparison.

The character of Caliban is generally thought (and justly so) to be one of the author's masterpieces. It is not indeed pleasant to see this character on the stage any more than it is to see the God Pan personated there. But in itself it is one of the wildest and most abstracted of all Shakespeare's characters, whose deformity whether of body or mind is redeemed by the power and truth of the imagination displayed in it. It is the essence of grossness, but there is not a particle of vulgarity in it. Shakespeare has described the brutal mind of Caliban in contact with the pure and original forms of nature; the character grows out of the soil where it is rooted uncontrolled, uncouth and wild, uncramped by any of the meannesses of custom. It is 'of the earth, earthy'. It seems almost to have been dug out of the ground, with a soul instinctively superadded to it answering to its wants and origin. Vulgarity is not natural coarseness, but conventional coarseness, learnt from others, contrary to, or without an entire conformity of natural power and disposition; as fashion is the commonplace affectation of what is elegant and refined without any feeling of the essence of it. Schlegel, the admirable German critic on Shakespeare observes that Caliban is a poetical character, and 'always speaks in blank verse'. He first comes in thus:

> *Caliban.* As wicked dew as e'er my mother brush'd
> With raven's feather from unwholesome fen,
> Drop on you both: a south-west blow on ye,
> And blister you all o'er!
> *Prospero.* For this, be sure, to-night thou shalt have cramps,
> Side-stitches that shall pen thy breath up; urchins
> Shall for that vast of night that they may work,
> All exercise on thee: thou shalt be pinch'd
> As thick as honey-combs, each pinch more stinging
> Than bees that made 'em.

*Caliban.* I must eat my dinner.
This island's mine by Sycorax my mother,
Which thou tak'st from me. When thou camest first,
Thou strok'dst me, and mad'st much of me; would'st give me
Water with berries in't; and teach me how
To name the bigger light and how the less
That burn by day and night; and then I lov'd thee,
And show'd thee all the qualities o' th' isle,
The fresh springs, brine-pits, barren place and fertile:
Curs'd be I that I did so! All the charms
Of Sycorax, toads, beetles, bats, light on you!
For I am all the subjects that you have,
Who first was mine own king; and here you sty me
In this hard rock, whiles you do keep from me
The rest o' th' island.

And again, he promises Trinculo his services thus, if he will free him from his drudgery.

I'll show thee the best springs; I'll pluck thee berries,
I'll fish for thee, and get thee wood enough.
I pr'ythee let me bring thee where crabs grow,
And I with my long nails will dig thee pig-nuts:
Show thee a jay's nest, and instruct thee how
To snare the nimble marmozet: I'll bring thee
To clust'ring filberds; and sometimes I'll get thee
Young scamels from the rock.

In conducting Stephano and Trinculo to Prospero's cell, Caliban shows the superiority of natural capacity over greater knowledge and greater folly; and in a former scene, when Ariel frightens them with his music, Caliban to encourage them accounts for it in the eloquent poetry of the senses:

Be not afraid, the isle is full of noises,
Sounds, and sweet airs, that give delight and hurt not.
Sometimes a thousand twanging instruments
Will hum about mine ears, and sometimes voices,
That if I then had waked after long sleep,
Would make me sleep again; and then in dreaming,
The clouds methought would open, and show riches
Ready to drop upon me: when I wak'd
I cried to dream again.

This is not more beautiful than it is true. The poet here shows us the savage with the simplicity of a child, and makes the strange monster amiable. Shakespeare had to paint the human animal rude and without choice in its pleasures, but not without the sense of pleasure or some germ of the affections. Master Barnardine in *Measure for Measure*, the savage of civilized life, is an admirable philosophical counterpart to Caliban.

Shakespeare has, as it were by design, drawn off from Caliban the elements of whatever is ethereal and refined, to compound them in the unearthly mould of Ariel. Nothing was ever more finely conceived than this contrast between the material and the spiritual, the gross and delicate. Ariel is imaginary power, the swiftness of thought personified. When told to make good speed by Prospero, he says, 'I drink the air before me'. This is something like Puck's boast on a similar occasion, 'I'll put a girdle round about the earth in forty minutes'. But Ariel differs from Puck in having a fellow-feeling in the interests of those he is employed about. How exquisite is the following dialogue between him and Prospero!

> *Ariel*. Your charm so strongly works 'em,
> That if you now beheld them, your affections
> Would become tender.
> *Prospero*. Dost thou think so, spirit?
> *Ariel*. Mine would, sir, were I human.
> *Prospero*. And mine shall.
> Hast thou, which art but air, a touch, a feeling
> Of their afflictions, and shall not myself,
> One of their kind, that relish all as sharply,
> Passion'd as they, be kindlier moved than thou art?

It has been observed that there is a peculiar charm in the songs introduced in Shakespeare, which, without conveying any distinct images, seem to recall all the feelings connected with them, like snatches of half-forgotten music heard indistinctly and at intervals. There is this effect produced by Ariel's songs, which (as we are told) seem to sound in the air, and as if the person playing them were invisible. We shall give one instance out of many of this general power.

*Enter* FERDINAND ; *and* ARIEL *invisible, playing and singing.*

ARIEL'S SONG

Come unto these yellow sands,
And then take hands ;
Curt'sied when you have, and kiss'd,
(The wild waves whist ;)
Foot it featly here and there ;
And sweet sprites the burden bear.
[*Burden dispersedly.*

Hark, hark ! bowgh-wowgh : the watch dogs bark,
Bowgh-wowgh.
*Ariel.* Hark, hark ! I hear
The strain of strutting chanticleer
Cry cock-a-doodle-doo.

*Ferdinand.* Where should this music be ? in air or earth ?
It sounds no more : and sure it waits upon
Some god o' th' island. Sitting on a bank
Weeping against the king my father's wreck,
This music crept by me upon the waters,
Allaying both their fury and my passion
With its sweet air ; thence I have follow'd it,
Or it hath drawn me rather :—but 'tis gone.—
No, it begins again.

ARIEL'S SONG

Full fathom five thy father lies,
Of his bones are coral made :
Those are pearls that were his eyes,
Nothing of him that doth fade,
But doth suffer a sea change,
Into something rich and strange.
Sea-nymphs hourly ring his knell—
Hark ! now I hear them, ding-dong bell.
[*Burden ding-dong.*

*Ferdinand.* The ditty does remember my drown'd father.
This is no mortal business, nor no sound
That the earth owns : I hear it now above me.

The courtship between Ferdinand and Miranda is one of the chief beauties of this play. It is the very purity of love. The pretended interference of Prospero with it heightens its interest, and is in character with the magician, whose sense of preternatural power makes him arbitrary, tetchy, and impatient of opposition.

*The Tempest* is a finer play than the *Midsummer Night's Dream*, which has sometimes been compared with it; but it is not so fine a poem. There are a greater number of beautiful passages in the latter. Two of the most striking in *The Tempest* are spoken by Prospero. The one is that admirable one when the vision which he has conjured up disappears, beginning, 'The cloud-capp'd towers, the gorgeous palaces', &c., which has so often been quoted that every schoolboy knows it by heart; the other is that which Prospero makes in adjuring his art:

> Ye elves of hills, brooks, standing lakes, and groves,
> And ye that on the sands with printless foot
> Do chase the ebbing Neptune, and do fly him
> When he comes back; you demi-puppets, that
> By moonshine do the green sour ringlets make,
> Whereof the ewe not bites; and you whose pastime
> Is to make midnight mushrooms, that rejoice
> To hear the solemn curfew, by whose aid
> (Weak masters tho' ye be) I have be-dimm'd
> The noon-tide sun, call'd forth the mutinous winds,
> And 'twixt the green sea and the azur'd vault
> Set roaring war; to the dread rattling thunder
> Have I giv'n fire, and rifted Jove's stout oak
> With his own bolt; the strong-bas'd promontory
> Have I made shake, and by the spurs pluck'd up
> The pine and cedar: graves at my command
> Have wak'd their sleepers; op'd, and let 'em forth
> By my so potent art. But this rough magic
> I here abjure; and when I have requir'd
> Some heav'nly music, which ev'n now I do,
> (To work mine end upon their senses that
> This airy charm is for) I'll break my staff,
> Bury it certain fadoms in the earth,

And deeper than did ever plummet sound,
I'll drown my book.

We must not forget to mention among other things in this play, that Shakespeare has anticipated nearly all the arguments on the Utopian schemes of modern philosophy :

*Gonzalo.* Had I the plantation of this isle, my lord—
*Antonio.* He'd sow't with nettle-seed.
*Sebastian.* Or docks or mallows.
*Gonzalo.* And were the king on't, what would I do ?
*Sebastian.* 'Scape being drunk, for want of wine.
*Gonzalo.* I' th' commonwealth I would by contraries
Execute all things : for no kind of traffic
Would I admit ; no name of magistrate ;
Letters should not be known ; wealth, poverty,
And use of service, none ; contract, succession,
Bourn, bound of land, tilth, vineyard, none ;
No use of metal, corn, or wine, or oil ;
No occupation, all men idle, all,
And women too ; but innocent and pure :
No sov'reignty.
*Sebastian.* And yet he would be king on't.
*Antonio.* The latter end of his commonwealth forgets the beginning.
*Gonzalo.* All things in common nature should produce
Without sweat or endeavour. Treason, felony,
Sword, pike, knife, gun, or need of any engine
Would I not have ; but nature should bring forth,
Of its own kind, all foison, all abundance
To feed my innocent people !
*Sebastian.* No marrying 'mong his subjects ?
*Antonio.* None, man ; all idle ; whores and knaves.
*Gonzalo.* I would with such perfection govern, sir,
T' excel the golden age.
*Sebastian.* Save his majesty !

## *The Midsummer Night's Dream*

Bottom the Weaver is a character that has not had justice done him. He is the most romantic of mechanics. And what a list of companions he has—Quince the Carpenter, Snug the Joiner, Flute the Bellows-mender, Snout the Tinker, Starveling the Tailor; and then again, what a group of fairy attendants, Puck, Peaseblossom, Cobweb, Moth, and Mustard-seed! It has been observed that Shakespeare's characters are constructed upon deep physiological principles; and there is something in this play which looks very like it. Bottom the Weaver, who takes the lead of

> This crew of patches, rude mechanicals,
> That work for bread upon Athenian stalls,

follows a sedentary trade, and he is accordingly represented as conceited, serious, and fantastical. He is ready to undertake anything and everything, as if it was as much a matter of course as the motion of his loom and shuttle. He is for playing the tyrant, the lover, the lady, the lion. 'He will roar that it shall do any man's heart good to hear him'; and this being objected to as improper, he still has a resource in his good opinion of himself, and 'will roar you an 'twere any nightingale'. Snug the Joiner is the moral man of the piece, who proceeds by measurement and discretion in all things. You see him with his rule and compasses in his hand. 'Have you the lion's part written? Pray you, if it be, give it me, for I am slow of study'.—'You may do it extempore', says Quince, 'for it is nothing but roaring'. Starveling the Tailor keeps the peace, and objects to the lion and the drawn sword. 'I believe we must leave the killing out when all's done'. Starveling, however, does not start the objections himself, but seconds them when made by others, as if he had not spirit to express his fears without encouragement. It is too much to suppose all this intentional: but it very luckily falls out so. Nature includes all that is implied in the most subtle analytical distinctions; and the same distinctions will be found in Shakespeare. Bottom, who is not only chief actor, but stage-manager for the occasion, has a device to obviate the danger of frightening the ladies: 'Write me a prologue, and let the prologue seem to say, we will do no harm with our swords, and that Pyramus is not killed indeed; and for better assurance, tell them that I, Pyramus, am not Pyramus, but Bottom the Weaver; this will put them out of fear'. Bottom seems to have understood the subject of dramatic illusion at least as well as any modern essayist. If our holiday mechanic rules the roast among his fellows, he is no less at home in his new character of an ass, 'with amiable cheeks, and fair large ears'. He instinctively acquires a most learned taste, and grows fastidious in the choice of dried peas and bottled hay. He is quite familiar with his new attendants, and assigns them their parts with all due gravity. 'Monsieur Cobweb, good Monsieur, get your weapon in your hand, and kill me a red-hipt humble-bee on the top of a thistle, and, good Monsieur, bring me the honey-bag'. What an exact knowledge is here shown of natural history!

Puck, or Robin Goodfellow, is the leader of the fairy band. He is the Ariel of the *Midsummer Night's Dream*; and yet as unlike as can be to the Ariel in *The Tempest*. No other poet could have made two such different characters out of the same fanciful materials and situations. Ariel is a minister of retribution, who is touched with a sense of pity at the woes he inflicts. Puck is a mad-cap sprite, full of wantonness and mischief, who laughs at those whom he misleads—'Lord, what fools these mortals be!' Ariel cleaves the air, and executes his mission with the zeal of a winged messenger; Puck is borne along on his fairy errand like the light and glittering gossamer before the breeze. He is, indeed, a most Epicurean little gentleman, dealing in quaint devices and faring in dainty delights. Prospero and his world of spirits are a set of moralists: but with Oberon and his fairies we are launched at once into the empire of the butterflies. How beautifully is this race of beings contrasted with the men and women actors in the scene, by a single epithet which Titania gives to the latter, 'the human mortals'! It is astonishing that Shakespeare should be considered, not only by foreigners, but by many of our own critics, as a gloomy and heavy writer, who painted nothing but 'gorgons and hydras, and chimeras dire'. His subtlety exceeds that of all other dramatic writers, insomuch that a celebrated person of the present day said that he regarded him rather as a metaphysician than a poet. His delicacy and sportive gaiety are infinite. In the *Midsummer Night's Dream* alone, we should imagine, there is more sweetness and beauty of description than in the whole range of French poetry put together. What we mean is this, that we will produce out of that single play ten passages, to which we do not think any ten passages in the works of the French poets can be opposed, displaying equal fancy and imagery. Shall we mention the remonstrance of Helena to Hermia, or Titania's description of her fairy train, or her disputes with Oberon about the Indian boy, or Puck's account of himself and his employments, or the Fairy Queen's exhortation to the elves to pay due attendance upon her favourite, Bottom; or Hippolita's description of a chace, or Theseus's answer? The two last are as heroical and spirited as the others are full of luscious tenderness. The reading of this play is like wandering in a grove by moonlight: the descriptions breathe a sweetness like odours thrown from beds of flowers.

Titania's exhortation to the fairies to wait upon Bottom, which is remarkable for a certain cloying sweetness in the repetition of the rhymes, is as follows:

> Be kind and courteous to this gentleman.
> Hop in his walks, and gambol in his eyes,
> Feed him with apricocks and dewberries,
> With purple grapes, green figs and mulberries;
> The honey-bags steal from the humble bees,
> And for night tapers crop their waxen thighs,
> And light them at the fiery glow-worm's eyes,
> To have my love to bed, and to arise:
> And pluck the wings from painted butterflies,
> To fan the moon-beams from his sleeping eyes;
> Nod to him, elves, and do him courtesies.

The sounds of the lute and of the trumpet are not more distinct than the poetry of the foregoing passage, and of the conversation between Theseus and Hippolital:

> *Theseus.* Go, one of you, find out the forester,
> For now our observation is perform'd;
> And since we have the vaward of the day,
> My love shall hear the music of my hounds.
> Uncouple in the western valley, go,
> Dispatch, I say, and find the forester.
> We will, fair Queen, up to the mountain's top,
> And mark the musical confusion
> Of hounds and echo in conjunction.
> *Hippolita.* I was with Hercules and Cadmus once,
> When in a wood of Crete they bay'd the bear
> With hounds of Sparta; never did I hear
> Such gallant chiding. For besides the groves,
> The skies, the fountains, every region near
> Seem'd all one mutual cry. I never heard
> So musical a discord, such sweet thunder.
> *Theseus.* My hounds are bred out of the Spartan kind,

So flew'd, so sanded, and their heads are hung
With ears that sweep away the morning dew ;
Crook-knee'd and dew-lap'd, like Thessalian bulls,
Slow in pursuit, but matched in mouth like bells,
Each under each. A cry more tuneable
Was never halloo'd to, nor cheer'd with horn,
In Crete, in Sparta, nor in Thessaly :
Judge when you hear.

Even Titian never made a hunting-piece of a *gusto* so fresh and lusty, and so near the first ages of the world as this.—

It had been suggested to us, that the *Midsummer Night's Dream* would do admirably to get up as a Christmas after-piece ; and our prompter proposed that Mr. Kean should play the part of Bottom, as worthy of his great talents. He might, in the discharge of his duty, offer to play the lady like any of our actresses that he pleased, the lover or the tyrant like any of our actors that he pleased, and the lion like ' the most fearful wild-fowl living '. The carpenter, the tailor, and joiner, it was thought, would hit the galleries. The young ladies in love would interest the side-boxes ; and Robin Goodfellow and his companions excite a lively fellow-feeling in the children from school. There would be two courts, an empire within an empire, the Athenian and the Fairy King and Queen, with their attendants, and with all their finery. What an opportunity for processions, for the sound of trumpets and glittering of spears ! What a fluttering of urchins' painted wings ; what a delightful profusion of gauze clouds and airy spirits floating on them !

Alas, the experiment has been tried, and has failed ; not through the fault of Mr. Kean, who did not play the part of Bottom, nor of Mr. Liston, who did, and who played it well, but from the nature of things. The *Midsummer Night's Dream*, when acted, is converted from a delightful fiction into a dull pantomime. All that is finest in the play is lost in the representation. The spectacle was grand; but the spirit was evaporated, the genius was fled.—Poetry and the stage do not agree well together. The attempt to reconcile them in this instance fails not only of effect, but of decorum. The *ideal* can have no place upon the stage, which is a picture without perspective: everything there is in the foreground. That which was merely an airy shape, a dream, a passing thought, immediately becomes an unmanageable reality. Where all is left to the imagination (as is the case in reading) every circumstance, near or remote, has an equal chance of being kept in mind, and tells according to the mixed impression of all that has been suggested. But the imagination cannot sufficiently qualify the actual impressions of the senses. Any offence given to the eye is not to be got rid of by explanation. Thus Bottom's head in the play is a fantastic illusion, produced by magic spells: on the stage, it is an ass's head, and nothing more; certainly a very strange costume for a gentleman to appear in. Fancy cannot be embodied any more than a simile can be painted; and it is as idle to attempt it as to personate *Wall* or *Moonshine*. Fairies are not incredible, but fairies six feet high are so. Monsters are not shocking, if they are seen at a proper distance. When ghosts appear at midday, when apparitions stalk along Cheapside, then may the *Midsummer Night's Dream* be represented without injury at Covent Garden or at Drury Lane. The boards of a theatre and the regions of fancy are not the same thing.

## *Romeo and Juliet*

Romeo and Juliet is the only tragedy which Shakespeare has written entirely on a love-story. It is supposed to have been his first play, and it deserves to stand in that proud rank. There is the buoyant spirit of youth in every line, in the rapturous intoxication of hope, and in the bitterness of despair. It has been said of *Romeo and Juliet* by a great critic, that 'whatever is most intoxicating in the odour of a southern spring, languishing in the song of the nightingale, or voluptuous in the first opening of the rose, is to be found in this poem'. The description is true; and yet it does not answer to our idea of the play. For if it has the sweetness of the rose, it has its freshness too; if it has the languor of the nightingale's song, it has also its giddy transport; if it has the softness of a southern spring, it is as glowing and as bright. There is nothing of a sickly and sentimental cast. Romeo and Juliet are in love, but they are not love-sick. Everything speaks the very soul of pleasure, the high and healthy pulse of the passions: the heart beats, the blood circulates and mantles throughout. Their courtship is not an insipid interchange of sentiments lip-deep, learnt at second-hand from poems and plays,—made up of beauties of the most shadowy kind, of 'fancies wan that hang the pensive head', of evanescent smiles and sighs that breathe not, of delicacy that shrinks from the touch and feebleness that scarce supports itself, an elaborate vacuity of thought, and an artificial dearth of sense, spirit, truth, and nature! It is the reverse of all this.

It is Shakespeare all over, and Shakespeare when he was young.

We have heard it objected to *Romeo and Juliet* that it is founded on an idle passion between a boy and a girl, who have scarcely seen and can have but little sympathy or rational esteem for one another, who have had no experience of the good or ills of life, and whose raptures or despair must be therefore equally groundless and fantastical. Whoever objects to the youth of the parties in this play as 'too unripe and crude' to pluck the sweets of love, and wishes to see a first-love carried on into a good old age, and the passions taken at the rebound, when their force is spent, may find all this done in the *Stranger* and in other German plays, where they do things by contraries, and transpose nature to inspire sentiment and create philosophy. Shakespeare proceeded in a more straightforward and, we think, effectual way. He did not endeavour to extract beauty from wrinkles, or the wild throb of passion from the last expiring sigh of indifference. He did not 'gather grapes of thorns nor figs of thistles'. It was not his way. But he has given a picture of human life, such as it is in the order of nature. He has founded the passion of the two lovers not on the pleasures they had experienced, but on all the pleasures they had *not* experienced. All that was to come of life was theirs. At that untried source of promised happiness they slaked their thirst, and the first eager draught made them drunk with love and joy. They were in full possession of their senses and their affections. Their hopes were of air, their desires of fire. Youth is the season of love, because the heart is then first melted in tenderness from the touch of novelty, and kindled to rapture, for it knows no end of its enjoyments or its wishes. Desire has no limit but itself. Passion, the love and expectation of pleasure, is infinite, extravagant, inexhaustible, till experience comes to check and kill it. Juliet exclaims on her first interview with Romeo:

> My bounty is as boundless as the sea,
> My love as deep.

And why should it not? What was to hinder the thrilling tide of pleasure, which had just gushed from her heart, from flowing on without stint or measure, but experience which she was yet without? What was to abate the transport of the first sweet sense of pleasure, which her heart and her senses had just tasted, but indifference which she was yet a stranger to? What was there to check the ardour of hope, of faith, of constancy, just rising in her breast, but disappointment which she had not yet felt? As are the desires and the hopes of youthful passion, such is the keenness of its disappointments, and their baleful effect. Such is the transition in this play from the highest bliss to the lowest despair, from the nuptial couch to an untimely grave. The only evil that even in apprehension befalls the two lovers is the loss of the greatest possible felicity; yet this loss is fatal to both, for they had rather part with life than bear the thought of surviving all that had made life dear to them. In all this, Shakespeare has but followed nature, which existed in his time, as well as now. The modern philosophy, which reduces the whole theory of the mind to habitual impressions, and leaves the natural impulses of passion and imagination out of the account, had not then been discovered; or if it had, would have been little calculated for the uses of poetry.

It is the inadequacy of the same false system of philosophy to account for the strength of our earliest attachments, which has led Mr. Wordsworth to indulge in the mystical visions of Platonism in his Ode on the Progress of Life. He has very admirably described the vividness of our impressions in youth and childhood, and how 'they fade by degrees into the light of common day', and he ascribes the change to the supposition of a pre-existent state, as if our early thoughts were nearer heaven, reflections of former trails of glory, shadows of our past being. This is idle. It is not from the knowledge of the past that the first impressions of things derive their gloss and splendour, but from our ignorance of the future, which fills the void to come with the warmth of our desires, with our gayest hopes, and brightest fancies. It is the obscurity spread before it that colours the prospect of life with hope, as it is the cloud which reflects the rainbow. There is no occasion to resort to any mystical union and transmission of feeling through different states of being to account for the romantic enthusiasm of youth; nor to plant the root of hope in the grave, nor to derive it from the skies. Its root is in the heart of man: it lifts its head above the stars. Desire and imagination are inmates of the human breast. The heaven 'that lies about us in our infancy' is only a new world, of which we know nothing but what we wish it to be, and believe all that we wish. In youth and boyhood, the world we live in is the world of desire, and of fancy: it is experience that brings us down to the world of reality. What is it that in youth sheds a dewy light round the evening star? That makes the daisy look so bright? That perfumes the hyacinth? That embalms the first kiss of love? It is the delight of novelty, and the seeing no end to the pleasure that we fondly believe is still in store for us. The heart revels in the luxury of its own thoughts, and is unable to sustain the weight of hope and love that presses upon it.—The effects of the passion of love alone might have dissipated Mr. Wordsworth's theory, if he means anything more by it than an ingenious and poetical allegory. *That* at least is not a link in the chain let down from other worlds ; 'the purple light of love ' is not a dim reflection of the smiles of celestial bliss. It does not appear till the middle of life, and then seems like ' another morn risen on mid-day '. In this respect the soul comes into the world ' in utter nakedness '. Love waits for the ripening of the youthful blood. The sense of pleasure precedes the love of pleasure, but with the sense of pleasure, as soon as it is felt, come thronging infinite desires and hopes of pleasure, and love is mature as soon as born. It withers and it dies almost as soon !

This play presents a beautiful *coup d'oeil* of the progress of human life. In thought it occupies years, and embraces the circle of the affections from childhood to old age. Juliet has become a great girl, a young woman since we first remember her a little thing in the idle prattle of the nurse, Lady Capulet was about her age when she became a mother, and old Capulet somewhat impatiently tells his younger visitors :

——I've seen the day,
That I have worn a visor, and could tell
A whispering tale in a fair lady's ear,
Such as would please : 'tis gone, 'tis gone, 'tis gone.

Thus one period of life makes way for the following, and one generation pushes another off the stage. One of the most striking passages to show the intense feeling of youth in this play is Capulet's invitation to Paris to visit his entertainment.

At my poor house, look to behold this night
Earth-treading stars that make dark heav'n light ;
Such comfort as do lusty young men feel
When well-apparel'd April on the heel
Of limping winter treads, even such delight
Among fresh female-buds shall you this night
Inherit at my house.

The feelings of youth and of the spring are here blended together like the breath of opening flowers. Images of vernal beauty appear to have floated before the author's mind, in writing this poem, in profusion. Here is another of exquisite beauty, brought in more by accident than by necessity. Montague declares of his son smit with a hopeless passion, which he will not reveal :

> But he, his own affection's counsellor,
> Is to himself so secret and so close,
> So far from sounding and discovery,
> As is the bud bit with an envious worm,
> Ere he can spread his sweet leaves to the air,
> Or dedicate his beauty to the sun.

This casual description is as full of passionate beauty as when Romeo dwells in frantic fondness on 'the white wonder of his Juliet's hand'. The reader may, if he pleases, contrast the exquisite pastoral simplicity of the above lines with the gorgeous description of Juliet when Romeo first sees her at her father's house, surrounded by company and artificial splendour.

> What lady's that which doth enrich the hand
> Of yonder knight ?
> O she doth teach the torches to burn bright ;
> Her beauty hangs upon the cheek of night,
> Like a rich jewel in an Aethiop's ear.

It would be hard to say which of the two garden scenes is the finest, that where he first converses with his love, or takes leave of her the morning after their marriage. Both are like a heaven upon earth : the blissful bowers of Paradise let down upon this lower world. We will give only one passage of these well-known scenes to show the perfect refinement and delicacy of Shakespeare's conception of the female character. It is wonderful how Collins, who was a critic and a poet of great sensibility, should have encouraged the common error on this subject by saying—' But stronger Shakespeare felt for man alone '.

The passage we mean is Juliet's apology for her maiden boldness.

Thou know'st the mask of night is on my face ;
Else would a maiden blush bepaint my cheek
For that which thou hast heard me speak to-night.
Fain would I dwell on form, fain, fain deny
What I have spoke—but farewell compliment :
Dost thou love me ? I know thou wilt say, aye,
And I will take thee at thy word—Yet if thou swear'st,
Thou may'st prove false ; at lovers' perjuries
They say Jove laughs. Oh gentle Romeo,
If thou dost love, pronounce it faithfully ;
Or if thou think I am too quickly won,
I'll frown and be perverse, and say thee nay,
So thou wilt woo : but else not for the world.
In truth, fair Montague, I am too fond ;
And therefore thou may'st think my 'haviour light ;
But trust me, gentleman, I'll prove more true
Than those that have more cunning to be strange.
I should have been more strange, I must confess,
But that thou over-heard'st, ere I was ware,
My true love's passion ; therefore pardon me,
And not impute this yielding to light love,
Which the dark night hath so discovered.

In this and all the rest her heart, fluttering between pleasure, hope, and fear, seems to have dictated to her tongue, and ' calls true love spoken simple modesty '. Of the same sort, but bolder in virgin innocence, is her soliloquy after her marriage with Romeo.

Gallop apace, you fiery-footed steeds,
Towards Phoebus' mansion ; such a wagoner
As Phaëton would whip you to the west,
And bring in cloudy night immediately.
Spread thy close curtain, love-performing night ;
That run-aways' eyes may wink ; and Romeo
Leap to these arms, untalked of, and unseen !—
Lovers can see to do their amorous rites
By their own beautie : or if love be blind,
It best agrees with night.—Come, civil night,

Thou sober-suited matron, all in black,
And learn me how to lose a winning match,
Play'd for a pair of stainless maidenhoods:
Hood my unmann'd blood bating in my cheeks,
With thy black mantle; till strange love, grown bold,
Thinks true love acted, simple modesty.
Come night!—Come, Romeo! come, thou day in night;
For thou wilt lie upon the wings of night
Whiter than new snow on a raven's back.—
Come, gentle night; come, loving, black-brow'd night,
Give me my Romeo: and when he shall die,
Take him and cut him out in little stars,
And he will make the face of heaven so fine,
That all the world shall be in love with night,
And pay no worship to the garish sun.—
O, I have bought the mansion of a love,
But not possess'd it; and though I am sold,
Not yet enjoy'd: so tedious is this day,
As is the night before some festival
To an impatient child, that hath new robes,
And may not wear them.

We the rather insert this passage here, inasmuch as we have no doubt it has been expunged from the Family Shakespeare. Such critics do not perceive that the feelings of the heart sanctify, without disguising, the impulses of nature. Without refinement themselves, they confound modesty with hypocrisy. Not so the German critic, Schlegel. Speaking of *Romeo and Juliet*, he says, 'It was reserved for Shakespeare to unite purity of heart and the glow of imagination, sweetness and dignity of manners and passionate violence, in one ideal picture'. The character is indeed one of perfect truth and sweetness. It has nothing forward, nothing coy, nothing affected or coquettish about it;—it is a pure effusion of nature. It is as frank as it is modest, for it has no thought that it wishes to conceal. It reposes in conscious innocence on the strength of its affections. Its delicacy does not consist in coldness and reserve, but in combining warmth of imagination and tenderness of heart with the most voluptuous sensibility. Love is a gentle flame that rarefies and expands her whole being. What an idea of trembling haste and airy grace, borne upon the thoughts of love, does the Friar's exclamation give of her, as she approaches his cell to be married :

> Here comes the lady. Oh, so light of foot
> Will ne'er wear out the everlasting flint :
> A lover may bestride the gossamer,
> That idles in the wanton summer air,
> And yet not fall, so light is vanity.

The tragic part of this character is of a piece with the rest. It is the heroic founded on tenderness and delicacy. Of this kind are her resolution to follow the Friar's advice, and the conflict in her bosom between apprehension and love when she comes to take the sleeping poison. Shakespeare is blamed for the mixture of low characters. If this is a deformity, it is the source of a thousand beauties. One instance is the contrast between the guileless simplicity of Juliet's attachment to her first love, and the convenient policy of the nurse in advising her to marry Paris, which excites such indignation in her mistress. 'Ancient damnation ! oh most wicked fiend ', &c.

Romeo is Hamlet in love. There is the same rich exuberance of passion and sentiment in the one, that there is of thought and sentiment in the other. Both are absent and self-involved, both live out of themselves in a world of imagination. Hamlet is abstracted from everything ; Romeo is abstracted from everything but his love, and lost in it. His 'frail thoughts dally with faint surmise ', and are fashioned out of the suggestions of hope, 'the flatteries of sleep '. He is himself only in his Juliet ; she is his only reality, his heart's true home and idol. The rest of the world is to him a passing dream. How finely is this character portrayed where he recollects himself on seeing Paris slain at the tomb of Juliet !

What said my man when my betossed soul
Did not attend him as we rode ? I think
He told me Paris should have married Juliet.

And again, just before he hears the sudden tidings of her death :

If I may trust the flattery of sleep,
My dreams presage some joyful news at hand ;
My bosom's lord sits lightly on his throne,
And all this day an unaccustom'd spirit
Lifts me above the ground with cheerful thoughts.
I dreamt my lady came and found me dead,
(Strange dream ! that gives a dead man leave to think)
And breath'd such life with kisses on my lips,
That I reviv'd and was an emperor.
Ah me ! how sweet is love itself possess'd,
When but love's shadows are so rich in joy !

Romeo's passion for Juliet is not a first love : it succeeds and drives out his passion for another mistress, Rosaline, as the sun hides the stars. This is perhaps an artifice (not absolutely necessary) to give us a higher opinion of the lady, while the first absolute surrender of her heart to him enhances the richness of the prize. The commencement, progress, and ending of his second passion are however complete in themselves, not injured, if they are not bettered by the first. The outline of the play is taken from an Italian novel ; but the dramatic arrangement of the different scenes between the lovers, the more than dramatic interest in the progress of the story, the development of the characters with time and circumstances, just according to the degree and kind of interest excited, are not inferior to the expression of passion and nature. It has been ingeniously remarked among other proofs of skill in the contrivance of the fable, that the improbability of the main incident in the piece, the administering of the sleeping-potion, is softened and obviated from the beginning by the introduction of the Friar on his first appearance culling simples and descanting on their virtues.

Of the passionate scenes in this tragedy, that between the Friar and Romeo when he is told of his sentence of banishment, that between Juliet and the Nurse when she hears of it, and of the death of her cousin Tybalt (which bear no proportion in her mind, when passion after the first shock of surprise throws its weight into the scale of her affections), and the last scene at the tomb, are among the most natural and overpowering. In all of these it is not merely the force of any one passion that is given, but the slightest and most unlooked-for transitions from one to another, the mingling currents of every different feeling rising up and prevailing in turn, swayed by the master-mind of the poet, as the waves undulate beneath the gliding storm. Thus when Juliet has by her complaints encouraged the Nurse to say, 'Shame come to Romeo', she instantly repels the wish, which she had herself occasioned, by answering:

Blister'd be thy tongue
For such a wish, he was not born to shame.
Upon his brow shame is ashamed to sit,
For 'tis a throne where honour may be crown'd
Sole monarch of the universal earth!
O, what a beast was I to chide him so!
*Nurse.* Will you speak well of him that kill'd you cousin?
*Juliet.* Shall I speak ill of him that is my husband?
Ah my poor lord, what tongue shall smooth thy name,
When I, thy three-hours' wife, have mangled it?

And then follows on the neck of her remorse and returning fondness, that wish treading almost on the brink of impiety, but still held back by the strength of her devotion to her lord, that 'father, mother, nay, or both were dead', rather than Romeo banished. If she requires any other excuse, it is in the manner in which Romeo echoes her frantic grief and disappointment in the next scene at being banished from her.—Perhaps one of the finest pieces of acting that ever was witnessed on the stage, is Mr. Kean's manner of doing this scene and his repetition of the word, *Banished.* He treads close indeed upon the genius of his author.

A passage which this celebrated actor and able commentator on Shakespeare (actors are the best commentators on the poets) did not give with equal truth or force of feeling was the one which Romeo makes at the tomb of Juliet, before he drinks the poison.

——Let me peruse this face—
Mercutio's kinsman ! noble county Paris !
What said my man, when my betossed soul
Did not attend him as we rode ! I think,
He told me, Paris should have married Juliet !
Said he not so ? or did I dream it so ?
Or am I mad, hearing him talk of Juliet,
To think it was so ?—O, give me thy hand,
One writ with me in sour misfortune's book !
I'll bury thee in a triumphant grave——
For here lies Juliet.

* * *

——O, my love ! my wife !
Death that hath suck'd the honey of thy breath,
Hath had no power yet upon thy beauty :
Thou art not conquer'd ; beauty's ensign yet
Is crimson in thy lips, and in thy cheeks,
And Death's pale flag is not advanced there.——
Tybalt, ly'st thou there in thy bloody sheet ?
O, what more favour can I do to thee,
Than with that hand that cut thy youth in twain,
To sunder his that was thine enemy ?
Forgive me, cousin ! Ah, dear Juliet,
Why art thou yet so fair ! I will believe
That unsubstantial death is amorous ;
And that the lean abhorred monster keeps
Thee here in dark to be his paramour.
For fear of that, I will stay still with thee ;
And never from this palace of dim night
Depart again : here, here will I remain
With worms that are thy chamber-maids ; O, here
Will I set up my everlasting rest ;
And shake the yoke of inauspicious stars
From this world-wearied flesh.—Eyes, look your last !
Arms, take your last embrace ! and lips, O you

The doors of breath, seal with a righteous kiss
A dateless bargain to engrossing death !——
Come, bitter conduct, come unsavoury guide !
Thou desperate pilot, now at once run on
The dashing rocks my sea-sick weary bark !
Here's to my love !—[*Drinks.*] O, true apothecary !
Thy drugs are quick.—Thus with a kiss I die.

The lines in this speech describing the loveliness of Juliet, who is supposed to be dead, have been compared to those in which it is said of Cleopatra after her death, that she looked 'as she would take another Antony in her strong toil of grace ;' and a question has been started which is the finest, that we do not pretend to decide. We can more easily decide between Shakespeare and any other author, than between him and himself.—Shall we quote any more passages to show his genius or the beauty of *Romeo and Juliet* ? At that rate, we might quote the whole. The late Mr. Sheridan, on being shown a volume of the Beauties of Shakespeare, very properly asked—' But where are the other eleven ? ' The character of Mercutio in this play is one of the most mercurial and spirited of the productions of Shakespeare's comic muse.

## *Lear*

We wish that we could pass this play over, and say nothing about it. All that we can say must fall far short of the subject; or even of what we ourselves conceive of it. To attempt to give a description of the play itself or of its effect upon the mind, is mere impertinence: yet we must say something.—It is then the best of all Shakespeare's plays, for it is the one in which he was the most in earnest. He was here fairly caught in the web of his own imagination. The passion which he has taken as his subject is that which strikes its root deepest into the human heart; of which the bond is the hardest to be unloosed; and the cancelling and tearing to pieces of which gives the greatest revulsion to the frame. This depth of nature, this force of passion, this tug of war of the elements of our being, this firm faith in filial piety, and the giddy anarchy and whirling tumult of the thoughts at finding this prop failing it, the contrast between the fixed, immoveable basis of natural affection, and the rapid, irregular starts of imagination, suddenly wrenched from all its accustomed holds and resting-places in the soul, this is what Shakespeare has given, and what nobody else but he could give. So we believe.—The mind of Lear staggering between the weight of attachment and the hurried movements of passion is like a tall ship driven about by the winds, buffeted by the furious waves, but that still rides above the storm, having its anchor fixed in the bottom of the sea; or it is like the sharp rock circled by the eddying whirlpool that foams and beats against it, or like the solid promontory pushed from its basis by the force of an earthquake.

The character of Lear itself is very finely conceived for the purpose. It is the only ground on which such a story could be built with the greatest truth and effect. It is his rash haste, his violent impetuosity, his blindness to everything but the dictates of his passions or affections, that produces all his misfortunes, that aggravates his impatience of them, that enforces our pity for him. The part which Cordelia bears in the scene is extremely beautiful: the story is almost told in the first words she utters. We see at once the precipice on which the poor old king stands from his own extravagant and credulous importunity, the indiscreet simplicity of her love (which, to be sure, has a little of her father's obstinacy in it) and the hollowness of her sisters' pretensions. Almost the first burst of that noble tide of passion, which runs through the play, is in the remonstrance of Kent to his royal master on the injustice of his sentence against his youngest daughter—'Be Kent unmannerly, when Lear is mad!' This manly plainness which draws down on him the displeasure of the unadvised king is worthy of the fidelity with which he adheres to his fallen fortunes. The true character of the two eldest daughters, Regan and Gonerill (they are so thoroughly hateful that we do not even like to repeat their names) breaks out in their answer to Cordelia who desires them to treat their father well—'Prescribe not us our duties'—their hatred of advice being in proportion to their determination to do wrong, and to their hypocritical pretensions to do right. Their deliberate hypocrisy adds the last finishing to the odiousness of their characters. It is the absence of this detestable quality that is the only relief in the character of Edmund the Bastard, and that at times reconciles us to him. We are not tempted to exaggerate the guilt of his conduct, when he himself gives it up as a bad business, and writes himself down 'plain villain'. Nothing more can be said about it. His religious honesty in this respect is admirable. One speech of his is worth a million. His father, Gloster, whom he has just deluded with a forged story of his brother Edgar's designs against his life, accounts for his unnatural behaviour and the strange depravity of the times from the late eclipses in the sun and moon. Edmund, who is in the secret, says when he is gone: 'This is the excellent foppery of the world, that when we are sick in fortune (often the surfeits of our own behaviour) we make guilty of our disasters the sun, the moon, and stars: as if we were villains on necessity; fools by heavenly compulsion; knaves, thieves, and treacherous by spherical predominance; drunkards, liars, and adulterers by an enforced obedience of planetary influence; and all that we are evil in, by a divine thrusting on. An admirable evasion of whore-master man, to lay his goatish disposition on the charge of a star! My father compounded with my mother under the Dragon's tail, and my nativity was under Ursa Major: so that it follows, I am rough and lecherous. I should have been what I am, had the maidenliest star in the firmament twinkled on my bastardizing.'—The whole character, its careless, light-hearted villany, contrasted with the sullen, rancorous malignity of Regan and Gonerill, its connexion with the conduct of the under-plot, in which Gloster's persecution of one of his sons and the ingratitude of another, form a counterpart to the mistakes and misfortunes of Lear—his double amour with the two sisters, and the share which he has in bringing about the fatal catastrophe, are all managed with an uncommon degree of skill and power.

It has been said, and we think justly, that the

third act of *Othello*, and the three first acts of *Lear*, are Shakespeare's great masterpieces in the logic of passion: that they contain the highest examples not only of the force of individual passion, but of its dramatic vicissitudes and striking effects arising from the different circumstances and characters of the persons speaking. We see the ebb and flow of the feeling, its pauses and feverish starts, its impatience of opposition, its accumulating force when it has time to recollect itself, the manner in which it avails itself of every passing word or gesture, its haste to repel insinuation, the alternate contraction and dilation of the soul, and all 'the dazzling fence of controversy' in this mortal combat with poisoned weapons, aimed at the heart, where each wound is fatal. We have seen in *Othello*, how the unsuspecting frankness and impetuous passions of the Moor are played upon and exasperated by the artful dexterity of Iago. In the present play, that which aggravates the sense of sympathy in the reader, and of uncontrollable anguish in the swollen heart of Lear, is the petrifying indifference, the cold, calculating, obdurate selfishness of his daughters. His keen passions seem whetted on their stony hearts. The contrast would be too painful, the shock too great, but for the intervention of the Fool, whose well-timed levity comes in to break the continuity of feeling when it can no longer be borne, and to bring into play again the fibres of the heart just as they are growing rigid from over-strained excitement. The imagination is glad to take refuge in the half-comic, half-serious comments of the Fool, just as the mind under the extreme anguish of a surgical operation vents itself in sallies of wit. The character was also a grotesque ornament of the barbarous times, in which alone the tragic ground-work of the story could be laid. In another point of view it is indispensable, inasmuch as while it is a diversion to the too great intensity of our disgust, it carries the pathos to the highest pitch of which it is capable, by showing the pitiable weakness of the old king's conduct and its irretrievable consequences in the most familiar point of view. Lear may well 'beat at the gate which let his folly in', after, as the Fool says, 'he has made his daughters his mothers.' The character is dropped in the third act to make room for the entrance of Edgar as Mad Tom, which well accords with the increasing bustle and wildness of the incidents; and nothing can be more complete than the distinction between Lear's real and Edgar's assumed madness, while the resemblance in the cause of their distresses, from the severing of the nearest ties of natural affection, keeps up a unity of interest. Shakespeare's mastery over his subject, if it was not art, was owing to a knowledge of the connecting links of the passions, and their effect upon the mind, still more wonderful than any systematic adherence to rules, and that anticipated and outdid all the efforts of the most refined art, not inspired and rendered instinctive by genius.

One of the most perfect displays of dramatic power is the first interview between Lear and his daughter, after the designed affronts upon him, which till one of his knights reminds him of them, his sanguine temperament had led him to overlook. He returns with his train from hunting, and his usual impatience breaks out in his first words, 'Let me not stay a jot for dinner; go, get it ready'. He then encounters the faithful Kent in disguise, and retains him in his service; and the first trial of his honest duty is to trip up the heels of the officious Steward who makes so prominent and despicable a figure through the piece. On the entrance of Gonerill the following dialogue takes place:

*Lear.* How now, daughter? what makes that frontlet on? Methinks, you are too much of late i' the frown.

*Fool.* Thou wast a pretty fellow, when thou had'st no need to care for her frowning; now thou art an O without a figure: I am better than thou art now; I am a fool, thou art nothing.—— Yes, forsooth, I will hold my tongue; [*To Gonerill.*] so your face bids me, though you say nothing. Mum, mum.

He that keeps nor crust nor crum,
Weary of all, shall want some——

That's a sheal'd peascod! [*Pointing to Lear.*

*Gonerill.* Not only, sir, this your all-licens'd fool,
But other of your insolent retinue
Do hourly carp and quarrel; breaking forth
In rank and not-to-be-endured riots.
I had thought, by making this well known unto you,
To have found a safe redress; but now grow fearful,
By what yourself too late have spoke and done,
That you protect this course, and put it on
By your allowance; which if you should, the fault
Would not 'scape censure, nor the redresses sleep,
Which in the tender of a wholesome weal,
Might in their working do you that offence,
(Which else were shame) that then necessity
Would call discreet proceeding.

*Fool.* For you trow, nuncle,

The hedge sparrow fed the cuckoo so long,
That it had its head bit off by its young.

So out went the candle, and we were left darkling.

*Lear.* Are you our daughter?

*Gonerill.* Come, sir.
I would, you would make use of that good wisdom
Whereof I know you are fraught; and put away
These dispositions, which of late transform you
From what you rightly are.

*Fool.* May not an ass know when the cart draws the horse?
——Whoop, Jug, I love thee.

*Lear.* Does any here know me?——Why, this is not Lear:
Does Lear walk thus? speak thus?—Where are his eyes?
Either his notion weakens, or his discernings
Are lethargy'd——Ha! waking?—'Tis not so.——
Who is it that can tell me who I am?—Lear's shadow?
I would learn that: for by the marks
Of sov'reignty, of knowledge, and of reason,
I should be false persuaded I had daughters.——
Your name, fair gentlewoman?

*Gonerill.* Come, sir :
This admiration is much o' the favour
Of other your new pranks. I do beseech you
To understand my purposes aright :
As you are old and reverend, you should be wise :
Here do you keep a hundred knights and squires ;
Men so disorder'd, so debauch'd, and bold,
That this our court, infected with their manners,
Shows like a riotous inn : epicurism and lust
Make it more like a tavern, or a brothel,
Than a grac'd palace. The shame itself doth speak
For instant remedy : be then desir'd
By her, that else will take the thing she begs,
A little to disquantity your train ;
And the remainder, that shall still depend,
To be such men as may besort your age,
And know themselves and you.
*Lear.* Darkness and devils !——
Saddle my horses ; call my train together.——
Degenerate bastard ! I'll not trouble thee ;
Yet have I left a daughter.
*Gonerill.* You strike my people ; and your disorder'd rabble
Make servants of their betters.

*Enter* ALBANY.

*Lear.* Woe, that too late repents—O, sir, are you come ?
Is it your will ? speak, sir.—Prepare my horses.——
[*To Albany.*
Ingratitude ! thou marble-hearted fiend,
More hideous, when thou show'st thee in a child,
Than the sea-monster !
*Albany.* Pray, sir, be patient.
*Lear.* Detested kite ! thou liest. [*To Gonerill.*
My train are men of choice and rarest parts,
That all particulars of duty know ;
And in the most exact regard support
The worships of their name.——O most small fault,
How ugly didst thou in Cordelia show !
Which, like an engine, wrench'd my frame of nature
From the fixt place ; drew from my heart all love,
And added to the gall. O Lear, Lear, Lear !
Beat at the gate, that let thy folly in.
[*Striking his head.*
And thy dear judgement out !—Go, go, my people !
*Albany.* My lord, I am guiltless, as I am ignorant
Of what hath mov'd you.
*Lear.* It may be so, my lord——

Hear, nature, hear: dear goddess, hear!
Supend thy purpose, if thou didst intend
To make this creature fruitful!
Into her womb convey sterility;
Dry up in her the organs of increase;
And from her derogate body never spring
A babe to honour her! If she must teem,
Create her child of spleen: that it may live,
To be a thwart disnatur'd torment to her!
Let it stamp wrinkles in her brow of youth;
With cadent tears fret channels in her cheeks;
Turn all her mother's pains, and benefits,
To laughter and contempt; that she may feel
How sharper than a serpent's tooth it is
To have a thankless child!——Away, away! [*Exit.*
*Albany*. Now, gods, that we adore, whereof comes this?
*Gonerill*. Never afflict yourself to know the cause;
But let his disposition have that scope
That dotage gives it.

*Re-enter* LEAR.

*Lear*. What, fifty of my followers at a clap!
Within a fortnight!
*Albany*. What's the matter, sir?
*Lear*. I'll tell thee; life and death! I am asham'd
That thou hast power to shake my manhood thus:
[*To Gonerill.*
That these hot tears, which break from me perforce,
Should make thee worth them.——Blasts and fogs upon thee!
The untented woundings of a father's curse
Pierce every sense about thee!——Old fond eyes,
Beweep this cause again, I'll pluck you out;
And cast you, with the waters that you lose,
To temper clay.——Ha! is it come to this?
Let it be so:——Yet have I left a daughter,
Who, I am sure, is kind and comfortable;
When she shall hear this of thee, with her nails
She'll flay thy wolfish visage. Thou shalt find
That I'll resume the shape, which thou dost think
I have cast off forever.
[*Exeunt, Lear, Kent, and Attendants.*

This is certainly fine: no wonder that Lear says after it, 'O let me not be mad, not mad, sweet heavens,' feeling its effects by anticipation: but fine as is this burst of rage and indignation at the first blow aimed at his hopes and expectations, it is nothing near so fine as what follows from his double disappointment, and his lingering efforts to see which of them he shall lean upon for support and find comfort in, when both his daughters turn against his age and weakness. It is with some difficulty that Lear gets to speak with his daughter Regan, and her husband, at Gloster's castle. In concert with Gonerill they have left their own home on purpose to avoid him. His apprehensions are first alarmed by this circumstance, and when Gloster, whose guests they are, urges the fiery temper of the Duke of Cornwall as an excuse for not importtuning him a second time, Lear breaks out :

> Vengeance ! Plague ! Death ! Confusion !
> Fiery ? What fiery quality ? Why, Gloster,
> I'd speak with the Duke of Cornwall and his wife.

Afterwards, feeling perhaps not well himself, he is inclined to admit their excuse from illness, but then recollecting that they have set his messenger (Kent) in the stocks, all his suspicions are roused again, and he insists on seeing them.

> *Enter* CORNWALL, REGAN, GLOSTER, *and Servants.*
> *Lear.* Good-morrow to you both.
> *Cornwall.* Hail to your grace !
> [*Kent is set at liberty.*
> *Regan.* I am glad to see your highness.
> *Lear.* Regan, I think you are ; I know what reason
> I have to think so : if thou should'st not be glad,
> I would divorce me from thy mother's tomb,
> Sepulch'ring an adultress.——O, are you free ?
> [*To Kent.*
> Some other time for that.——Beloved Regan,
> Thy sister's naught : O Regan, she hath tied
> Sharp-tooth'd unkindness, like a vulture, here——
> [*Points to his heart.*
> I can scarce speak to thee ; thou'lt not believe,
> Of how deprav'd a quality——O Regan !
> *Regan.* I pray you, sir, take patience ; I have hope
> You less know how to value her desert,
> Than she to scant her duty.

*Lear.* Say, how is that ?

*Regan.* I cannot think my sister in the least
Would fail her obligation ; if, sir, perchance,
She have restrain'd the riots of your followers,
'Tis on such ground, and to such wholesome end,
As clears her from all blame.

*Lear.* My curses on her !

*Regan.* O, sir, you are old ;
Nature in you stands on the very verge
Of her confine : you should be rul'd, and led
By some discretion, that discerns your state
Better than you yourself : therefore, I pray you,
That to our sister you do make return ;
Say, you have wrong'd her, sir.

*Lear.* Ask her forgiveness ?
Do you but mark how this becomes the use ?
*Dear daughter, I confess that I am old ;*
*Age is unnecessary ; on my knees I beg,*
*That you'll vouchsafe me raiment, bed, and food.*

*Regan.* Good sir, no more ; these are unsightly tricks :
Return you to my sister.

*Lear.* Never, Regan :
She hath abated me of half my train ;
Look'd blank upon me ; struck me with her tongue,
Most serpent-like, upon the very heart :——
All the stor'd vengeances of heaven fall
On her ungrateful top ! Strike her young bones,
You taking airs, with lameness !

*Cornwall.* Fie, sir, fie !

*Lear.* You nimble lightnings, dart your blinding flames
Into her scornful eyes ! Infect her beauty,
You fen-suck'd fogs, drawn by the powerful sun,
To fall, and blast her pride !

*Regan.* O the blest gods !
So will you wish on me, when the rash mood is on.

*Lear.* No, Regan, thou shalt never have my curse ;
Thy tender-hefted nature shall not give
Thee o'er to harshness ; her eyes are fierce, but thine
Do comfort, and not burn : 'Tis not in thee
To grudge my pleasures, to cut off my train,
To bandy hasty words, to scant my sizes,
And, in conclusion, to oppose the bolt
Against my coming in : thou better know'st
The offices of nature, bond of childhood,
Effects of courtesy, dues of gratitude ;
Thy half o' the kingdom thou hast not forgot,

Wherein I thee endow'd.
*Regan.* Good sir, to the purpose. [*Trumpets within.*
*Lear.* Who put my man i' the stocks?
*Cornwall.* What trumpet's that?

*Enter Steward.*

*Regan.* I know't, my sister's; this approves her letter.
That she would soon be here.—Is your lady come?
*Lear.* This is a slave, whose easy-borrow'd pride
Dwells in the fickle grace of her he follows:——
Out, varlet, from my sight!
*Cornwall.* What means your grace?
*Lear.* Who stock'd my servant? Regan, I have good hope
Thou did'st not know on't.—Who comes here? O heavens,

*Enter* GONERILL.

If you do love old men, if your sweet sway
Allow obedience, if yourselves are old,
Make it your cause; send down, and take my part!—
Art not asham'd to look upon this beard?— [*To Gonerill.*
O, Regan, wilt thou take her by the hand?
*Gonerill.* Why not by the hand, sir? How have I offended?
All's not offence, that indiscretion finds,
And dotage terms so.
*Lear.* O, sides, you are too tough!
Will you yet hold?—How came my man i' the stocks?
*Cornwall.* I set him there, sir: but his own disorders
Deserv'd much less advancement.
*Lear.* You! did you?
*Regan.* I pray you, father, being weak, seem so.
If, till the expiration of your month,
You will return and sojourn with my sister,
Dismissing half your train, come then to me;
I am now from home, and out of that provision
Which shall be needful for your entertainment.
*Lear.* Return to her, and fifty men dismiss'd?
No, rather I adjure all roofs, and choose
To be a comrade with the wolf and owl——
To wage against the enmity o' the air,
Necessity's sharp pinch!——Return with her!
Why, the hot-blooded France, that dowerless took
Our youngest born, I could as well be brought
To knee his throne, and squire-like pension beg
To keep base life afoot.——Return with her!
Persuade me rather to be slave and sumpter
To this detested groom. [*Looking on the Steward.*

*Gonerill.* At your choice, sir.

*Lear.* Now, I pr'ythee, daughter, do not make me mad;
I will not trouble thee, my child; farewell:
We'll no more meet, no more see one another:——
But yet thou art my flesh, my blood, my daughter;
Or, rather, a disease that's in my flesh,
Which I must needs call mine: thou art a bile,
A plague-sore, an embossed carbuncle,
In my corrupted blood. But I'll not chide thee:
Let shame come when it will, I do not call it:
I did not bid the thunder-bearer shoot,
Nor tell tales of thee to high-judging Jove:
Mend when thou canst; be better, at thy leisure:
I can be patient; I can stay with Regan,
I, and my hundred knights.

*Regan.* Not altogether so, sir;
I look'd not for you yet, nor am provided
For your fit welcome: Give ear, sir, to my sister;
For those that mingle reason with your passion
Must be content to think you old, and so——
But she knows what she does.

*Lear.* Is this well spoken now?

*Regan.* I dare avouch it, sir: What, fifty followers?
Is it not well? What should you need of more?
Yea, or so many? Sith that both charge and danger
Speak 'gainst so great a number? How, in one house,
Should many people, under two commands,
Hold amity? 'Tis hard; almost impossible.

*Gonerill.* Why might you not, my lord, receive attendance
From those that she calls servants, or from mine?

*Regan.* Why not, my lord? If then they chanc'd to slack you,
We would control them: if you will come to me
(For now I spy a danger) I entreat you
To bring but five-and-twenty; to no more
Will I give place, or notice.

*Lear.* I gave you all——

*Regan.* And in good time you gave it.

*Lear.* Made you my guardians, my depositaries;
But kept a reservation to be follow'd
With such a number: what, must I come to you
With five-and-twenty, Regan! said you so?

*Regan.* And speak it again, my lord; no more with me.

*Lear.* Those wicked creatures yet do look well-favour'd,
When others are more wicked; not being the worst,
Stands in some rank of praise:——I'll go with thee;
[*To Gonerill.*

Thy fifty yet doth double five-and-twenty,
And thou art twice her love.
*Gonerill.* Hear me, my lord ;
What need you five-and-twenty, ten, or five,
To follow in a house, where twice so many
Have a command to tend you ?
*Regan.* What need one ?
*Lear.* O, reason not the need : our basest beggars
Are in the poorest thing superfluous :
Allow not nature more than nature needs,
Man's life is cheap as beast's : thou art a lady ;
If only to go warm were gorgeous,
Why, nature needs not what thou gorgeous wear'st ;
Which scarcely keeps thee warm.——But, for true need——
You heavens, give me that patience which I need !
You see me here, you gods ; a poor old man,
As full of grief as age ; wretched in both !
If it be you that stir these daughters' hearts
Against their father, fool me not so much
To bear it tamely ; touch me with noble anger !
O, let no woman's weapons, water-drops,
Stain my man's cheeks !——No, you unnatural hags,
I will have such revenges on you both,
That all the world shall—I will do such things——
What they are, yet I know not ; but they shall be
The terrors of the earth. You think, I'll weep :
No, I'll not weep :——
I have full cause of weeping ; but this heart
Shall break into a hundred thousands flaws,
Or e'er I'll weep ;——O, fool, I shall go mad !
[*Exeunt Lear, Gloster, Kent and Fool.*

If there is anything in any author like this yearning of the heart, these throes of tenderness, this profound expression of all that can be thought and felt in the most heart-rending situations, we are glad of it ; but it is in some author that we have not read.

The scene in the storm, where he is exposed to all the fury of the elements, though grand and terrible, is not so fine, but the moralizing scenes with Mad Tom, Kent, and Gloster, are upon a par with the former. His exclamation in the supposed trial-scene of his daughters, 'See the little dogs and all Tray, Blanch, and Sweetheart, see they bark at me', his issuing his orders, 'Let them anatomize Regan, see what breeds about her heart', and his reflection when he sees the misery of Edgar, 'Nothing but his unkind daughters could have brought him to this', are in a style of pathos, where the extremest resources of the imagination are called in to lay open the deepest movements of the heart, which was peculiar to Shakespeare. In the same style and spirit is his interrupting the Fool who asks, 'whether a madman be a gentleman or a yeoman', by answering 'A king, a king!'

The indirect part that Gloster takes in these scenes where his generosity leads him to relieve Lear and resent the cruelty of his daughters, at the very time that he is himself instigated to seek the life of his son, and suffering under the sting of his supposed ingratitude, is a striking accompaniment to the situation of Lear. Indeed, the manner in which the threads of the story are woven together is almost as wonderful in the way of art as the carrying on the tide of passion, still varying and unimpaired, is on the score of nature. Among the remarkable instances of this kind are Edgar's meeting with his old blind father; the deception he practises upon him when he pretends to lead him to the top of Dover-cliff—'Come on, sir, here's the place', to prevent his ending his life and miseries together; his encounter with the perfidious Steward whom he kills, and his finding the letter from Gonerill to his brother upon him which leads to the final catastrophe, and brings the wheel of Justice 'full circle home' to the guilty parties. The bustle and rapid succession of events in the last scenes is surprising. But the meeting between Lear and Cordelia is by far the most affecting part of them. It has all the wildness of poetry, and all the heartfelt truth of nature. The previous account of her reception of the news of his unkind treatment, her involuntary reproaches to her sisters, 'Shame, ladies, shame', Lear's backwardness to see his daughter, the picture of the desolate state to which is reduced, 'Alack, 'tis he; why he was met even now, as mad as the vex'd sea, singing aloud', only prepare the way for and heighten our expectation of what follows, and assuredly this expectation is not disappointed when through the tender care of Cordelia he revives and recollects her.

*Cordelia.* How does my royal lord? How fares your majesty!
*Lear.* You do me wrong, to take me out o' the grave:
Thou art a soul in bliss; but I am bound
Upon a wheel of fire, that mine own tears
Do scald like molten lead.
*Cordelia.* Sir, do you know me?
*Lear.* You are a spirit I know: when did you die?
*Cordelia.* Still, still, far wide!
*Physician.* He's scarce awake; let him alone awhile.
*Lear.* Where have I been? Where am I?—Fair daylight?——
I am mightily abus'd.—I should even die with pity,
To see another thus.—I know not what to say.——
I will not swear these are my hands:—let's see;
I feel this pin prick. 'Would I were assur'd
Of my condition.
*Cordelia.* O, look upon me, sir,
And hold your hands in benediction o'er me:——
No, sir, you must not kneel.
*Lear.* Pray, do not mock me:
I am a very foolish fond old man,
Fourscore and upward;
Not an hour more, nor less: and, to deal plainly,
I fear, I am not in my perfect mind.
Methinks, I shou'd know you, and know this man;
Yet I am doubtful: for I am mainly ignorant
What place this is; and all the skill I have
Remembers not these garments; nor I know not
Where I did lodge last night: do not laugh at me;
For, as I am a man, I think this lady
To be my child Cordelia.
*Cordelia.* And so I am, I am!

Almost equal to this in awful beauty is their consolation of each other when, after the triumph of their enemies, they are led to prison.

*Cordelia.* We are not the first.
Who, with best meaning, have incurr'd the worst.
For thee, oppressed king, am I cast down;
Myself could else out-frown false fortune's frown.—
Shall we not see these daughters, and these sisters?
*Lear.* No, no, no, no! Come, let's away to prison:
We two alone will sing like birds i' the cage:
When thou dost ask me blessing, I'll kneel down,
And ask of thee forgiveness: so we'll live,
And pray, and sing, and tell old tales, and laugh
At gilded butterflies, and hear poor rogues
Talk of court news; and we'll talk with them too—
Who loses, and who wins; who's in, who's out;—
And take upon us the mystery of things,
As if we were God's spies: and we'll wear out,
In a wall'd prison, packs and sects of great ones,
That ebb and flow by the moon.
*Edmund.* Take them away.
*Lear.* Upon such sacrifices, my Cordelia,
The gods themselves throw incense.

The concluding events are sad, painfully sad; but their pathos is extreme. The oppression of the feelings is relieved by the very interest we take in the misfortunes of others, and by the reflections to which they give birth. Cordelia is hanged in prison by the orders of the bastard Edmund, which are known too late to be countermanded, and Lear dies broken-hearted, lamenting over her.

*Lear.* And my poor fool is hang'd! No, no, no life:
Why should a dog, a horse, a rat, have life,
And thou no breath at all? O, thou wilt come no more,
Never, never, never, never, never!——
Pray you, undo this button: thank you, sir.——

He dies, and indeed we feel the truth of what Kent says on the occasion—

Vex not his ghost: O, let him pass! he hates him,
That would upon the rack of the rough world
Stretch him out longer.

Yet a happy ending has been contrived for this play, which is approved of by Dr. Johnson and condemned by Schlegel. A better authority than either, on any subject in which poetry and feeling are concerned, has given it in favour of Shakespeare, in some remarks on the acting of Lear, with which we shall conclude this account.

'The *Lear* of Shakespeare cannot be acted. The contemptible machinery with which they mimic the storm which he goes out in, is not more inadequate to represent the horrors of the real elements than any actor can be to represent Lear. The greatness of Lear is not in corporal dimension, but in intellectual; the explosions of his passions are terrible as a volcano: they are storms turning up and disclosing to the bottom that rich sea, his mind, with all its vast riches. It is his mind which is laid bare. This case of flesh and blood seems too insignificant to be thought on; even as he himself neglects it. On the stage we see nothing but corporal infirmities and weakness, the impotence of rage; while we read it, we see not Lear, but we are Lear;—we are in his mind, we are sustained by a grandeur, which baffles the malice of daughters and storms; in the aberrations of his reason, we discover a mighty irregular power of reasoning, immethodized from the ordinary purposes of life, but exerting its powers, as the wind blows where it listeth, at will on the corruptions and abuses of mankind. What have looks or tones to do with that sublime identification of his age with that of *the heavens themselves,* when in his reproaches to them for conniving at the injustice of his children, he reminds them that 'they themselves are old!' What gesture shall we appropriate to this? What has the voice or the eye to do with such things? But the play is beyond all art, as the tamperings with it show: it is too hard and stony: it must have love-scenes, and a happy ending. It is not enough that Cordelia is a daughter, she must shine as a lover too. Tate has put his hook in the nostrils of this Leviathan, for Garrick and his followers, the showmen of the scene, to draw it about more easily. A happy ending !—as if the living martyrdom that Lear had gone through,—the flaying of his feelings alive, did not make a fair dismissal from the stage of life the only decorous thing for him. If he is to live and be happy after, if he could sustain this world's burden after, why all this pudder and preparation—why torment us with all this unnecessary sympathy ? As if the childish pleasure of getting his gilt robes and sceptre again could tempt him to act over again his misused station—as if at his years and with his experience anything was left but to die '.[1]

Four things have struck us in reading *Lear* :

1. That poetry is an interesting study, for this reason, that it relates to whatever is most interesting in human life. Whoever therefore has a contempt for poetry, has a contempt for himself and humanity.

2. That the language of poetry is superior to the language of painting ; because the strongest of our recollections relate to feelings, not to faces.

3. That the greatest strength of genius is shown in describing the strongest passions : for the power of the imagination, in works of invention, must be in proportion to the force of the natural impressions, which are the subject of them.

4. That the circumstance which balances the pleasure against the pain in tragedy is, that in proportion to the greatness of the evil, is our sense and desire of the opposite good excited ; and that our sympathy with actual suffering is lost in the strong impulse given to our natural affections, and carried away with the swelling tide of passion, that gushes from and relieves the heart.

[1] See an article, called ' Theatralia ', in the second volume of the *Reflector*, by Charles Lamb.

# *Richard II*

Richard II is a play little known compared with *Richard III*, which last is a play that every unfledged candidate for theatrical fame chooses to strut and fret his hour upon the stage in ; yet we confess that we prefer the nature and feeling of the one to the noise and bustle of the other ; at least, as we are so often forced to see it acted. In *Richard II* the weakness of the king leaves us leisure to take a greater interest in the misfortunes of the man. After the first act, in which the arbitrariness of his behaviour only proves his want of resolution, we see him staggering under the unlooked-for blows of fortune, bewailing his loss of kingly power, not preventing it, sinking under the aspiring genius of Bolingbroke, his authority trampled on, his hopes failing him, and his pride crushed and broken down under insults and injuries, which his own misconduct had provoked, but which he has not courage or manliness to resent. The change of tone and behaviour in the two competitors for the throne according to their change of fortune, from the capricious sentence of banishment passed by Richard upon Bolingbroke, the suppliant offers and modest pretensions of the latter on his return, to the high and haughty tone with which he accepts Richard's resignation of the crown after the loss of all his power, the use which he makes of the deposed king to grace his triumphal progress through the streets of London, and the final intimation of his wish for his death, which immediately finds a servile executioner, is marked throughout with complete effect and without the slightest appearance of effort. The steps by which Bolingbroke mounts the throne are those by which Richard sinks into the grave. We feel neither respect nor love for the deposed monarch; or he is as wanting in energy as in principle: but we pity him, for he pities himself. His heart is by no means hardened against himself, but bleeds afresh at every new stroke of mischance, and his sensibility, absorbed in his own person, and unused to misfortune, is not only tenderly alive to its own sufferings, but without the fortitude to bear them. He is, however, human in his distresses; for to feel pain, and sorrow, weakness, disappointment, remorse and anguish, is the lot of humanity, and we sympathize with him accordingly. The sufferings of the man make us forget that he ever was a king.

The right assumed by sovereign power to trifle at its will with the happiness of others as a matter of course, or to remit its exercise as a matter of favour, is strikingly shown in the sentence of banishment so unjustly pronounced on Bolingbroke and Mowbray, and in what Bolingbroke says when four years of his banishment are taken off, with as little reason:

> How long a time lies in one little word!
> Four lagging winters and four wanton springs
> End in a word: such is the breath of kings.

A more affecting image of the loneliness of a state of exile can hardly be given than by what Bolingbroke afterwards observes of his having 'sighed his English breath in foreign clouds'; or than that conveyed in Mowbray's complaint at being banished for life.

> The language I have learned these forty years,
> My native English, now I must forego;
> And now my tongue's use is to me no more
> Than an unstringed viol or a harp,
> Or like a cunning instrument cas'd up,
> Or being open, put into his hands

That knows no touch to tune the harmony.
I am too old to fawn upon a nurse,
Too far in years to be a pupil now.—

How very beautiful is all this, and at the same time how very *English* too!

*Richard II* may be considered as the first of that series of English historical plays, in which 'is hung armour of the invincible knights of old', in which their hearts seem to strike against their coats of mail, where their blood tingles for the fight, and words are but the harbingers of blows. Of this state of accomplished barbarism the appeal of Bolingbroke and Mowbray is an admirable specimen. Another of these 'keen encounters of their wits', which serve to whet the talkers' swords, is where Aumerle answers in the presence of Bolingbroke to the charge which Bagot brings against him of being an accessory in Gloster's death.

*Fitzwater.* If that thy valour stand on sympathies,
There is my gage, Aumerle, in gage to thine;
By that fair sun that shows me where thou stand'st
I heard thee say, and vauntingly thou spak'st it,
That thou were cause of noble Gloster's death.
If thou deny'st it twenty times thou liest,
And I will turn thy falsehood to thy heart
Where it was forged, with my rapier's point.
*Aumerle.* Thou dar'st not, coward, live to see the day.
*Fitzwater.* Now, by my soul, I would it were this hour.
*Aumerle.* Fitzwater, thou art damn'd to hell for this.
*Percy.* Aumerle, thou liest; his honour is as true,
In this appeal, as thou art all unjust;
And that thou art so, there I throw my gage
To prove it on thee, to th' extremest point
Of mortal breathing. Seize it, if thou dar'st.
*Aumerle.* And if I do not, may my hands rot off,
And never brandish more revengeful steel
Over the glittering helmet of my foe.
Who sets me else? By heav'n, I'll throw at all.
I have a thousand spirits in my breast,
To answer twenty thousand such as you.
*Surrey.* My lord Fitzwater, I remember well
The very time Aumerle and you did talk.

*Fitzwater*. My lord, 'tis true : you were in presence then :
And you can witness with me, this is true.
*Surrey*. As false, by heav'n, as heav'n itself is true.
*Fitzwater*. Surrey, thou liest.
*Surrey*. Dishonourable boy,
That lie shall lie so heavy on my sword,
That it shall render vengeance and revenge,
Till thou the lie-giver and that lie rest
In earth as quiet as thy father's skull.
In proof whereof, there is mine honour's pawn :
Engage it to the trial, if thou dar'st.
*Fitzwater*. How fondly dost thou spur a forward horse :
If I dare eat or drink or breath or live,
I dare meet Surrey in a wilderness,
And spit upon him, whilst I say he lies,
And lies, and lies : there is my bond of faith,
To tie thee to thy strong correction.
As I do hope to thrive in this new world,
Aumerle is guilty of my true appeal.

The truth is, that there is neither truth nor honour in all these noble persons : they answer words with words, as they do blows with blows, in mere self-defence : nor have they any principle whatever but that of courage in maintaining any wrong they dare commit, or any falsehood which they find it useful to assert. How different were these noble knights and 'barons bold' from their more refined descendants in the present day, who instead of deciding questions of right by brute force, refer everything to convenience, fashion and good breeding! In point of any abstract love of truth or justice, they are just the same now that they were then.

The characters of old John of Gaunt and of his brother York, uncles to the King, the one stern and foreboding, the other honest, good-natured, doing all for the best, and therefore doing nothing, are well kept up. The speech of the former, in praise of England, is one of the most eloquent that ever was penned. We should perhaps hardly be disposed to feed the pampered egotism of our countrymen by quoting this description, were it not that the conclusion of it (which looks prophetic) may qualify any improper degree of exultation.

This royal throne of kings, this sceptered isle,
This earth of Majesty, this seat of Mars,
This other Eden, demi-Paradise,
This fortress built by nature for herself
Against infection and the hand of war;
This happy breed of men, this little world,
This precious stone set in the silver sea,
Which serves it in the office of a wall
(Or as a moat defensive to a house)
Against the envy of less happy lands:
This nurse, this teeming womb of royal kings,
Fear'd for their breed and famous for their birth,
Renown'd for their deeds, as far from home,
For Christian service and true chivalry,
As is the sepulchre in stubborn Jewry
Of the world's ransom, blessed Mary's son;
This land of such dear souls, this dear dear land,
Dear for her reputation through the world,
Is now leas'd out (I die pronouncing it)
Like to a tenement or pelting farm.
England bound in with the triumphant sea,
Whose rocky shore beats back the envious surge
Of wat'ry Neptune, is bound in with shame,
With inky-blots and rotten parchment bonds.
That England, that was wont to conquer others,
Hath made a shameful conquest of itself.

The character of Bolingbroke, afterwards Henry IV, is drawn with a masterly hand:—patient for occasion, and steadily availing himself of it, seeing his advantage afar off, but only seizing on it when he has it within his reach, humble, crafty, bold, and aspiring, encroaching by regular but slow degrees, building power on opinion, and cementing opinion by power. His disposition is first unfolded by Richard himself, who however is too self-willed and secure to make a proper use of his knowledge.

Ourself and Bushy, Bagot here and Green,
Observed his courtship of the common people:

How he did seem to dive into their hearts,
With humble and familiar courtesy,
What reverence he did throw away on slaves ;
Wooing poor craftsmen with the craft of smiles,
And patient under-bearing of his fortune,
As 'twere to banish their affections with him.
Off goes his bonnet to an oyster-wench ;
A brace of draymen bid God speed him well,
And had the tribute of his supple knee,
With thanks my countrymen, my loving friends ;
As were our England in reversion his,
And he our subjects' next degree in hope.

Afterwards, he gives his own character to Percy, in these words :

I thank thee, gentle Percy, and be sure
I count myself in nothing else so happy,
As in a soul rememb'ring my good friends ;
And as my fortune ripens with thy love,
It shall be still thy true love's recompense.

We know how he afterwards kept his promise. His bold assertion of his own rights, his pretended submission to the king, and the ascendancy which he tacitly assumes over him without openly claiming it, as soon as he has him in his power, are characteristic traits of this ambitious and politic usurper. But the part of Richard himself gives the chief interest to the play. His folly, his vices, his misfortunes, his reluctance to part with the crown, his fear to keep it, his weak and womanish regrets, his starting tears, his fits of hectic passion, his smothered majesty, pass in succession before us, and make a picture as natural as it is affecting. Among the most striking touches of pathos are his wish, ' O that I were a mockery king of snow to melt away before the sun of Bolingbroke ', and the incident of the poor groom who comes to visit him in prison, and tells him how ' it yearned his heart that Bolingbroke upon his coronation day rode on Roan Barbary '. We shall have occasion to return hereafter to the character of Richard II in speaking of Henry VI. There is only one passage more, the description of his entrance into London with Bolingbroke, which we should like to quote here, if it had not been so used and worn out, so thumbed and got by rote, so praised and painted; but its beauty surmounts all these considerations.

*Duchess.* My lord, you told me you would tell the rest,
When weeping made you break the story off
Of our two cousins coming into London.
*York.* Where did I leave?
*Duchess.* At that sad stop, my lord,
Where rude misgovern'd hands, from window tops,
Threw dust and rubbish on king Richard's head.
*York.* Then, as I said, the duke, great Bolingbroke,
Mounted upon a hot and fiery steed,
Which his aspiring rider seem'd to know,
With slow, but stately pace, kept on his course,
While all tongues cried—God save thee, Bolingbroke!
You would have thought the very windows spake,
So many greedy looks of young and old
Through casements darted their desiring eyes
Upon his visage; and that all the walls,
With painted imag'ry, had said at once—
Jesu preserve thee! welcome, Bolingbroke!
Whilst he, from one side to the other turning,
Bare-headed, lower than his proud steed's neck,
Bespake them thus—I thank you, countrymen:
And thus still doing thus he pass'd along.
*Duchess.* Alas, poor Richard! where rides he the while?
*York.* As in a theatre, the eyes of men,
After a well-grac'd actor leaves the stage,
Are idly bent on him that enters next,
Thinking his prattle to be tedious:
Even so, or with much more contempt, men's eyes
Did scowl on Richard; no man cried God save him!
No joyful tongue gave him his welcome home:
But dust was thrown upon his sacred head!
Which with such gentle sorrow he shook off—
His face still combating with tears and smiles,
The badges of his grief and patience—
That had not God, for some strong purpose, steel'd
The hearts of men, they must perforce have melted.
And barbarism itself have pitied him.

# *Henry IV*

IN TWO PARTS

If Shakespeare's fondness for the ludricrous sometimes led to faults in his tragedies (which was not often the case), he has made us amends by the character of Falstaff. This is perhaps the most substantial comic character that ever was invented. Sir John carries a most portly presence in the mind's eye; and in him, not to speak it profanely, 'we behold the fullness of the spirit of wit and humour bodily'. We are as well acquainted with his person as his mind, and his jokes come upon us with double force and relish from the quantity of flesh through which they make their way, as he shakes his fat sides with laughter, or 'lards the lean earth as he walks along'. Other comic characters seem, if we approach and handle them, to resolve themselves into air, 'into thin air'; but this is embodied and palpable to the grossest apprehension: it lies 'three fingers deep upon the ribs', it plays about the lungs and the diaphragm with all the force of animal enjoyment. His body is like a good estate to his mind, from which he receives rents and revenues of profit and pleasure in kind, according to its extent, and the richness of the soil. Wit is often a meagre substitute for pleasurable sensation; an effusion of spleen and petty spite at the comforts of others, from feeling none in itself. Falstaff's wit is an emanation of a fine constitution; an exuberance of good-humour and good-nature; an overflowing of his love of laughter, and good-fellowship; a giving vent to his heart's ease and over-contentment with himself and others. He would not be in character, if he were not so fat as he is; for there is the greatest keeping in the boundless luxury of his imagination and the pampered self-indulgence of his physical appetites. He manures and nourishes his mind with jests, as he does his body with sack and sugar. He carves out his jokes, as he would a capon, or a haunch of venison, where there is *cut and come again*; and pours out upon them the oil of gladness. His tongue drops fatness, and in the chambers of his brain 'it snows of meat and drink'. He keeps up perpetual holiday and open house, and we live with him in a round of invitations to a rump and dozen.—Yet we are not to suppose that he was a mere sensualist. All this is as much in imagination as in reality. His sensuality does not engross and stupify his other faculties, but 'ascends me into the brain, clears away all the dull, crude vapours that environ it, and makes it full of nimble, fiery, and delectable shapes'. His imagination keeps up the ball after his senses have done with it. He seems to have even a greater enjoyment of the freedom from restraint, of good cheer, of his ease, of his vanity, in the ideal exaggerated descriptions which he gives of them, than in fact. He never fails to enrich his discourse with allusions to eating and drinking, but we never see him at table. He carries his own larder about with him, and he is himself a 'tun of man'. His pulling out the bottle in the field of battle is a joke to show his contempt for glory accompanied with danger, his systematic adherence to his Epicurean philosophy in the most trying circumstances. Again, such is his deliberate exaggeration of his own vices, that it does not seem quite certain whether the account of his hostess's bill, found in his pocket, with such an out-of-the-way charge for capons and sack with only one halfpenny-worth of bread, was not put there by himself as a trick to humour the jest upon his favourite propensities, and as a conscious caricature of himself. He is represented as a liar, a braggart, a coward, a glutton, &c., and yet we are not offended but delighted with him ; for he is all these as much to amuse others as to gratify himself. He openly assumes all these characters to show the humorous part of them. The unrestrained indulgence of his own ease, appetites, and convenience, has neither malice nor hypocrisy in it. In a word, he is an actor in himself almost as much as upon the stage, and we no more object to the character of Falstaff in a moral point of view than we should think of bringing an excellent comedian, who should represent him to the life, before one of the police offices. We only consider the number of pleasant lights in which he puts certain foibles (the more pleasant as they are opposed to the received rules and necessary restraints of society) and do not trouble ourselves about the consequences resulting from them, for no mischievous consequences do result. Sir John is old as well as fat, which gives a melancholy retrospective tinge to the character ; and by the disparity between his inclinations and his capacity for enjoyment, makes it still more ludicrous and fantastical.

The secret of Falstaff's wit is for the most part a masterly presence of mind, an absolute self-possession, which nothing can disturb. His repartees are involuntary suggestions of his self-love ; instinctive evasions of everything that threatens to interrupt the career of his triumphant jollity and self-complacency. His very size floats him out of all his difficulties in a sea of rich conceits ; and he turns round on the pivot of his convenience, with every occasion and at a moment's warning. His natural repugnance to every unpleasant thought or circumstance of itself makes light of objections, and provokes the most extravagant and licentious answers in his own justification. His indifference to truth puts no check upon his invention, and the more improbable and unexpected his contrivances are, the more happily does he seem to be delivered of them, the anticipation of their effect acting as a stimulus to the gaiety of his fancy. The success of one adventurous sally gives him spirits to undertake another: he deals always in round numbers, and his exaggerations and excuses are 'open, palpable, monstrous as the father that begets them'. His dissolute carelessness of what he says discovers itself in the first dialogue with the Prince.

*Falstaff.* By the lord, thou say'st true, lad; and is not mine hostess of the tavern a most sweet wench?

*P. Henry.* As the honey of Hibla, my old lad of the castle; and is not a buff-jerkin a most sweet robe of durance?

*Falstaff.* How now, how now, mad wag, what in thy quips and thy quiddities? what a plague have I to do with a buff-jerkin?

*P. Henry.* Why, what a pox have I to do with mine hostess of the tavern?

In the same scene he afterwards affects melancholy, from pure satisfaction of heart, and professes reform, because it is the farthest thing in the world from his thoughts. He has no qualms of conscience, and therefore would as soon talk of them as of anything else when the humour takes him.

*Falstaff.* But Hal, I pr'ythee trouble me no more with vanity. I would to God thou and I knew where a commodity of good names were to be bought: an old lord of council rated me the other day in the street about you, sir; but I mark'd him not, and yet he talked very wisely, and in the street too.

*P. Henry.* Thou didst well, for wisdom cries out in the street, and no man regards it.

*Falstaff.* O, thou hast damnable iteration, and art indeed able to corrupt a saint. Thou hast done much harm unto me, Hal; God forgive thee for it. Before I knew thee, Hal, I knew nothing, and now I am, if a man should speak truly, little better than one of the wicked. I must give over this life, and I will give it over, by the lord ; an I do not, I am a villain. I'll be damn'd for never a king's son in Christendom.

*P. Henry*. Where shall we take a purse to-morrow, Jack ?

*Falstaff*. Where thou wilt, lad, I'll make one ; an I do not, call me villain, and baffle me.

*P. Henry*. I see good amendment of life in thee, from praying to purse-taking.

*Falstaff*. Why, Hal, 'tis my vocation, Hal. 'Tis no sin for a man to labour in his vocation.

Of the other prominent passages, his account of his pretended resistance to the robbers, 'who grew from four men in buckram into eleven' as the imagination of his own valour increased with his relating it, his getting off when the truth is discovered by pretending he knew the Prince, the scene in which in the person of the old king he lectures the prince and gives himself a good character, the soliloquy on honour, and description of his new-raised recruits, his meeting with the chief justice, his abuse of the Prince and Poins, who overhear him, to Doll Tearsheet, his reconciliation with Mrs. Quickly who has arrested him for an old debt, and whom he persuades to pawn her plate to lend him ten pounds more, and the scenes with Shallow and Silence, are all inimitable. Of all of them, the scene in which Falstaff plays the part, first, of the King, and then of Prince Henry, is the one that has been the most often quoted. We must quote it once more in illustration of our remarks.

*Falstaff*. Harry, I do not only marvel where thou spendest thy time, but also how thou art accompanied : for though the camomile, the more it is trodden on, the faster it grows, yet youth, the more it is wasted, the sooner it wears. That thou art my son, I have partly thy mother's word, partly my own opinion ; but chiefly, a villainous trick of thine eye, and a foolish hanging of thy nether lip, that doth warrant me. If then thou be son to me, here lies the point ;—Why, being son to me, art thou so pointed at ? Shall the blessed son of heaven prove a micher, and eat blackberries ? A question not to be ask'd. Shall the son of England prove a thief, and take purses ? a question not to be ask'd. There is a thing, Harry, which thou hast often heard of, and it is known to many in our land by the name of pitch: this pitch, as ancient writers do report, doth defile; so doth the company thou keepest: for, Harry, now I do not speak to thee in drink, but in tears; not in pleasure, but in passion; not in words only, but in woes also:—and yet there is a virtuous man, whom I have often noted in thy company, but I know not his name.

*P. Henry.* What manner of man, an it like your majesty?

*Falstaff.* A goodly portly man, i' faith, and a corpulent; of a cheerful look, a pleasing eye, and a most noble carriage; and, as I think, his age some fifty, or, by'r-lady, inclining to three-score; and now I do remember me, his name is Falstaff: If that man should be lewdly given, he deceiveth me; for, Harry, I see virtue in his looks. If then the fruit may be known by the tree, as the tree by the fruit, then peremptorily I speak it, there is virtue in that Falstaff: him keep with, the rest banish. And tell me now, thou naughty varlet, tell me, where hast thou been this month?

*P. Henry.* Dost thou speak like a king? Do thou stand for me, and I'll play my father.

*Falstaff.* Depose me? if thou dost it half so gravely, so majestically, both in word and matter, hang me up by the heels for a rabbit-sucker, or a poulterer's hare.

*P. Henry.* Well, here I am set.

*Falstaff.* And here I stand:—judge, my masters.

*P. Henry.* Now, Harry, whence come you?

*Falstaff.* My noble lord, from Eastcheap.

*P. Henry.* The complaints I hear of thee are grievous.

*Falstaff.* S'blood, my lord, they are false:—nay, I'll tickle ye for a young prince, i'faith.

*P. Henry.* Swearest thou, ungracious boy? henceforth ne'er look on me. Thou art violently carried away from grace: there is a devil haunts thee, in the likeness of a fat old man; a tun of man is thy companion. Why dost thou converse with that trunk of humours, that bolting-hutch of beastliness, that swoln parcel of dropsies, that huge bombard of sack, that stuft cloak-bag of guts, that roasted Manning-tree ox with the pudding in his belly, that reverend vice, that grey iniquity, that father ruffian, that vanity in years? wherein is he good, but to taste sack and drink it? wherein neat and cleanly, but to carve a capon and eat it? wherein cunning, but in craft? wherein crafty, but in villainy? wherein villainous, but in all things? wherein worthy, but in nothing?

*Falstaff.* I would, your grace would take me with you: whom means your grace?

*P. Henry.* That villainous, abominable mis-leader of youth,

Falstaff, that old white-bearded Satan.

*Falstaff*. My lord, the man I know.

*P. Henry*. I know thou dost.

*Falstaff*. But to say, I know more harm in him than in myself, were to say more than I know. That he is old (the more the pity) his white hairs do witness it: but that he is (saving your reverence) a whore-master, that I utterly deny. If sack and sugar be a fault, God help the wicked! if to be old and merry be a sin, then many an old host that I know is damned: if to be fat be to be hated, then Pharaoh's lean kine are to be loved. No, my good lord; banish Peto, banish Bardolph, banish Poins; but for sweet Jack Falstaff, kind Jack Falstaff, true Jack Falstaff, valiant Jack Falstaff, and therefore more valiant, being as he is, old Jack Falstaff, banish not him thy Harry's company; banish plump Jack, and banish all the world.

*P. Henry*. I do, I will.

[*Knocking; and Hostess and Bardolph go out.*

*Re-enter* BARDOLPH, *running*.

*Bardolph*. O, my lord, my lord; the sheriff, with a most monstrous watch, is at the door.

*Falstaff*. Out, you rogue! play out the play: I have much to say in the behalf of that Falstaff.

One of the most characteristic descriptions of Sir John is that which Mrs. Quickly gives of him when he asks her, 'What is the gross sum that I owe thee?'

*Hostess*. Marry, if thou wert an honest man, thyself, and the money too. Thou didst swear to me upon a parcel-gilt goblet, sitting in my Dolphin-chamber, at the round table, by a sea-coal fire on Wednesday in Whitsunweek, when the prince broke thy head for likening his father to a singing man of Windsor; thou didst swear to me then, as I was washing thy wound, to marry me, and make me my lady thy wife. Canst thou deny it? Did not goodwife Keech, the butcher's wife, come in then, and call me gossip Quickly? coming in to borrow a mess of vinegar; telling us, she had a good dish of prawns; whereby thou didst desire to eat some; whereby I told thee, they were ill for a green wound? And didst thou not, when she was gone down stairs, desire me to be no more so familiarity with such poor people; saying, that ere long they should call me madam? And didst thou not kiss me, and bid me fetch thee thirty shillings? I put thee now to thy book-oath; deny it, if thou canst.

This scene is to us the most convincing proof of Falstaff's power of gaining over the goodwill of those he was familiar with, except indeed Bardolph's somewhat profane exclamation on hearing the account of his death, 'Would I were with him, wheresoe'er he is, whether in heaven or hell'.

One of the topics of exulting superiority over others most common in Sir John's mouth is his corpulence and the exterior marks of good living which he carries about him, thus 'turning his vices into commodity'. He accounts for the friendship between the Prince and Poins, from 'their legs being both of a bigness'; and compares Justice Shallow to 'a man made after supper of a cheese-paring'. There cannot be a more striking gradation of character than that between Falstaff and Shallow, and Shallow and Silence. It seems difficult at first to fall lower than the squire; but this fool, great as he is, finds an admirer and humble foil in his cousin Silence. Vain of his acquaintance with Sir John, who makes a butt of him, he exclaims, 'Would, cousin Silence, that thou had'st seen that which this knight and I have seen!'—'Aye, Master Shallow, we have heard the chimes at midnight,' says Sir John. To Falstaff's observation, 'I did not think Master Silence had been a man of this mettle', Silence answers, 'Who, I? I have been merry twice and once ere now'. What an idea is here conveyed of a prodigality of living? What good husbandry and economical self-denial in his pleasures? What a stock of lively recollections? It is curious that Shakespeare has ridiculed in Justice Shallow, who was 'in some authority under the king', that disposition to unmeaning tautology, which is the regal infirmity of later times, and which, it may be supposed, he acquired from talking to his cousin Silence, and receiving no answers.

*Falstaff*. You have here a goodly dwelling, and a rich.

*Shallow*. Barren, barren, barren; beggars all, beggars all, Sir

John: marry, good air. Spread Davy, spread Davy. Well said, Davy.

*Falstaff.* This Davy serves you for good uses.

*Shallow.* A good varlet, a good varlet, a very good varlet. By the mass, I have drank too much sack at supper. A good varlet. Now sit down, now sit down. Come, cousin.

The true spirit of humanity, the thorough knowledge of the stuff we are made of, the practical wisdom with the seeming fooleries in the whole of the garden-scene at Shallow's country-seat, and just before in the exquisite dialogue between him and Silence on the death of old Double, have no parallel anywhere else. In one point of view, they are laughable in the extreme; in another they are equally affecting, if it is affecting to show *what a little thing is human life,* what a poor forked creature man is!

The heroic and serious part of these two plays founded on the story of Henry IV is not inferior to the comic and farcical. The characters of Hotspur and Prince Henry are two of the most beautiful and dramatic, both in themselves and from contrast, that ever were drawn. They are the essence of chivalry. We like Hotspur the best upon the whole, perhaps because he was unfortunate.—The characters of their fathers, Henry IV and old Northumberland, are kept up equally well. Henry naturally succeeds by his prudence and caution in keeping what he has got; Northumberland fails in his enterprise from an excess of the same quality, and is caught in the web of his own cold, dilatory policy. Owen Glendower is a masterly character. It is as bold and original as it is intelligible and thoroughly natural. The disputes between him and Hotspur are managed with infinite address and insight into nature. We cannot help pointing out here some very beautiful lines, where Hotspur describes the fight between Glendower and Mortimer.

——When on the gentle Severn's sedgy bank,
In single opposition hand to hand,
He did confound the best part of an hour
In changing hardiment with great Glendower:
Three times they breath'd, and three times did they drink,
Upon agreement, of swift Severn's flood;
Who then affrighted with their bloody looks,
Ran fearfully among the trembling reeds,
And hid his crisp head in the hollow bank,
Blood-stained with these valiant combatants.

The peculiarity and the excellence of Shakespeare's poetry is, that it seems as if he made his imagination the hand-maid of nature, and nature the plaything of his imagination. He appears to have been all the characters, and in all the situations he describes. It is as if either he had had all their feelings, or had lent them all his genius to express themselves. There cannot be stronger instances of this than Hotspur's rage when Henry IV forbids him to speak of Mortimer, his insensibility to all that his father and uncle urge to calm him, and his fine abstacted apostrophe to honour, 'By heaven methinks it were an easy leap to pluck bright honour from the moon', &c. After all, notwithstanding the gallantry, generosity, good temper, and idle freaks of the mad-cap Prince of Wales, we should not have been sorry if Northumberland's force had come up in time to decide the fate of the battle at Shrewsbury; at least, we always heartily sympathize with Lady Percy's grief when she exclaims:

Had my sweet Harry had but half their numbers,
To-day might I (hanging on Hotspur's neck)
Have talked of Monmouth's grave.

The truth is, that we never could forgive the Prince's treatment of Falstaff; though perhaps Shakespeare knew what was best, according to the history, the nature of the times, and of the man. We speak only as dramatic critics. Whatever terror the French in those days might have of Henry V, yet to the readers of poetry at present, Falstaff is the better man of the two. We think of him and quote him oftener.

# *Henry V*

Henry V is a very favourite monarch with the English nation, and he appears to have been also a favourite with Shakespeare, who labours hard to apologize for the actions of the king, by showing us the character of the man, as 'the king of good fellows'. He scarcely deserves this honour. He was fond of war and low company:—we know little else of him. He was careless, dissolute, and ambitious—idle, or doing mischief. In private, he seemed to have no idea of the common decencies of life, which he subjected to a kind of regal license; in public affairs, he seemed to have no idea of any rule of right or wrong, but brute force, glossed over with a little religious hypocrisy and archiepiscopal advice. His principles did not change with his situation and professions. His adventure on Gads-hill was a prelude to the affair of Agincourt, only a bloodless one; Falstaff was a puny prompter of violence and outrage, compared with the pious and politic Archbishop of Canterbury, who gave the king *carte blanche*, in a genealogical tree of his family, to rob and murder in circles of latitude and longitude abroad—to save the possessions of the Church at home. This appears in the speeches in Shakespeare, where the hidden motives that actuate princes and their advisers in war and policy are better laid open than in speeches from the throne or woolsack. Henry, because he did not know how to govern his own kingdom, determined to make war upon his neighbours. Because his own title to the crown was doubtful, he laid claim to that of France. Because he did not know how to exercise the enormous power, which had just dropped into his hands, to any one good purpose, he immediately undertook (a cheap and obvious resource of sovereignty) to do all the mischief he could. Even if absolute monarchs had the wit to find out objects of laudable ambition, they could only 'plume up their wills' in adhering to the more sacred formula of the royal prerogative, 'the right divine of kings to govern wrong', because will is only then triumphant when it is opposed to the will of others, because the pride of power is only then shown, not when it consults the rights and interests of others, but when it insults and tramples on all justice and all humanity. Henry, declares his resolution 'when France is his, to bend it to his awe, or break it all to pieces'—a resolution worthy of a conqueror, to destroy all that he cannot enslave; and what adds to the joke, he lays all the blame of the consequences of his ambition on those who will not submit tamely to his tyranny. Such is the history of kingly power, from the beginning to the end of the world—with this difference, that the object of war formerly, when the people adhered to their allegiance, was to depose kings; the object latterly, since the people swerved from their allegiance, has been to restore kings, and to make common cause against mankind. The object of our late invasion and conquest of France was to restore the legitimate monarch, the descendant of Hugh Capet, to the throne: Henry V in his time made war on and deposed the descendant of this very Hugh Capet, on the plea that he was a usurper and illegitimate. What would the great modern catspaw of legitimacy and restorer of divine right have said to the claim of Henry and the title of the descendants of Hugh Capet? Henry V, it is true, was a hero, a king of England, and the conqueror of the king of France. Yet we feel little love or admiration for him. He was a hero, that is, he was ready to sacrifice his own life for the pleasure of destroying thousands of other lives; he was a king of England, but not a constitutional one, and we only like kings according to the law; lastly, he was a conqueror of the French king, and for this we dislike him less than if he had conquered the French people. How then do we like him? We like him in the play. There he is a very amiable monster, a very splendid pageant. As we like to gaze at a panther or a young lion in their cages in the Tower, and catch a pleasing horror from their glistening eyes, their velvet paws, and dreadless roar, so we take a very romantic, heroic, patriotic, and poetical delight in the boasts and feats of our younger Harry, as they appear on the stage and are confined to lines of ten syllables; where no blood follows the stroke that wounds our ears, where no harvest bends beneath horses' hoofs, no city flames, no little child is butchered, no dead men's bodies are found piled on heaps and festering the next morning—in the orchestra!

So much for the politics of this play; now for the poetry. Perhaps one of the most striking images in all Shakespeare is that given of war in the first lines of the Prologue.

> O for a muse of fire, that would ascend
> The brightest heaven of inventions,
> A kingdom for a stage, princes to act,
> And monarchs to behold the swelling scene!
> Then should the warlike Harry, like himself,
> Assume the port of Mars, and *at his heels*
> *Leash'd in like hounds, should famine, sword, and fire*
> *Crouch for employment.*

Rubens, if he had painted it, would not have improved upon this simile.

The conversation between the Archbishop of Canterbury and the Bishop of Ely relating to the sudden change in the manners of Henry V is among the well-known *Beauties* of Shakespeare. It is indeed admirable both for strength and grace.

It has sometimes occurred to us that Shakespeare, in describing 'the reformation' of the Prince, might have had an eye to himself—

Which is a wonder how his grace should glean it,
Since his addiction was to courses vain,
His companies unletter'd, rude and shallow,
His hours fill'd up with riots, banquets, sports;
And never noted in him any study,
Any retirement, any sequestration
From open haunts and popularity.
*Ely.* The strawberry grows underneath the nettle,
And wholesome berries thrive and ripen best
Neighbour'd by fruit of baser quality:
And so the prince obscur'd his contemplation
Under the veil of wildness, which no doubt
Grew like the summer-grass, fastest by night,
Unseen, yet crescive in his faculty.

This at least is as probable an account of the progress of the poet's mind as we have met with in any of the Essays on the Learning of Shakespeare.

Nothing can be better managed than the caution which the king gives the meddling Archbishop, not to advise him rashly to engage in the war with France, his scrupulous dread of the consequences of that advice, and his eager desire to hear and follow it.

And God forbid, my dear and faithful lord,
That you should fashion, wrest, or bow your reading,
Or nicely charge your understanding soul
With opening titles miscreate, whose right
Suits not in native colours with the truth.
For God doth know how many now in health
Shall drop their blood, in approbation
Of what your reverence shall incite us to.
Therefore take heed how you impawn your person,
How you awake our sleeping sword of war;
We charge you in the name of God, take heed.
For never two such kingdoms did contend
Without much fall of blood, whose guiltless drops
Are every one a woe, a sore complaint
'Gainst him, whose wrong gives edge unto the swords

That make such waste in brief mortality.
Under this conjuration, speak, my lord;
For we will hear, note, and believe in heart,
That what you speak, is in your conscience wash'd,
As pure as sin wtih baptism.

Another characteristic instance of the blindness of human nature to everything but its own interests is the complaint made by the king of 'the ill neighbourhood' of the Scot in attacking England when she was attacking France.

For once the eagle England being in prey,
To her unguarded nest the weazel Scot
Comes sneaking, and so sucks her princely eggs.

It is worth observing that in all these plays, which give an admirable picture of the spirit of the *good old times*, the moral inference does not at all depend upon the nature of the actions, but on the dignity or meanness of the persons committing them. 'The eagle England' has a right 'to be in prey', but 'the weazel Scot' has none 'to come sneaking to her nest', which she has left to pounce upon others. Might was right, without equivocation or disguise, in that heroic and chivalrous age. The substitution of right for might, even in theory, is among the refinements and abuses of modern philosophy.

A more beautiful rhetorical delineation of the effects of subordination in a commonwealth can hardly be conceived than the following:

For government, though high and low and lower,
Put into parts, doth keep in one consent,
Congruing in a full and natural close,
Like music.
——Therefore heaven doth divide
The state of man in divers functions,
Setting endeavour in continual motion;
To which is fixed, as an aim or butt,
Obedience: for so work the honey bees;
Creatures that by a rule in nature, teach
The art of order to a peopled kingdom.

They have a king, and officers of sorts:
Where some, like magistrates, correct at home;
Others, like merchants, venture trade abroad;
Others, like soldiers, armed in their stings,
Make boot upon the summer's velvet buds;
Which pillage they with merry march bring home
To the tent-royal of their emperor;
Who, busied in his majesty, surveys
The singing mason building roofs of gold;
The civil citizens kneading up the honey;
The poor mechanic porters crowding in
Their heavy burthens at his narrow gate;
The sad-eyed justice, with his surly hum,
Delivering o'er to executors pale
The lazy yawning drone. I this infer,—
That many things, having full reference
To one consent, may work contrariously:
As many arrows, loosed several ways,
Fly to one mark;
As many several ways meet in one town;
As many fresh streams meet in one salt sea;
As many lines close in the dial's centre;
So may a thousand actions, once a-foot,
End in one purpose, and be all well borne
Without defeat.

Henry V is but one of Shakespeare's second-rate plays. Yet by quoting passages, like this, from his second-rate plays alone, we might make a volume 'rich with his praise,'

As is the oozy bottom of the sea
With sunken wrack and sumless treasuries.

Of this sort are the king's remonstrance to Scroop, Grey, and Cambridge, on the detection of their treason, his address to the soldiers at the siege of Harfleur, and the still finer one before the battle of Agincourt, the description of the night before the battle, and the reflections on ceremony put into the mouth of the king.

O hard condition; twin-born with greatness,
Subjected to the breath of every fool,
Whose sense no more can feel but his own wringing!

What infinite heart's ease must kings neglect,
That private men enjoy ? and what have kings,
That privates have not too, save ceremony ?
Save general ceremony ?
And what art thou, thou idol ceremony ?
What kind of god art thou, that suffer'st more
Of mortal griefs, than do thy worshippers ?
What are thy rents ? what are thy comings-in ?
O ceremony, show me but thy worth !
What is thy soul, O adoration ?
Art thou aught else but place, degree, and form,
Creating awe and fear in other men ?
Wherein thou art less happy, being feared,
Than they in fearing.
What drink'st thou oft, instead of homage sweet,
But poison'd flattery ? O, be sick, great greatness,
And bid thy ceremony give thee cure !
Think'st thou, the fiery fever will go out
With titles blown from adulation ?
Will it give place to flexure and low bending ?
Can'st thou, when thou command'st the beggar's knee,
Command the health of it ? No, thou proud dream,
That play'st so subtly with a king's repose,
I am a king, that find thee : and I know,
'Tis not the balm, the sceptre, and the ball,
The sword, the mace, the crown imperial,
The enter-tissu'd robe of gold and pearl,
The farsed title running 'fore the king,
The throne he sits on, nor the tide of pomp
That beats upon the high shore of this world,
No, not all these, thrice-gorgeous ceremony,
Not all these, laid in bed majestical,
Can sleep so soundly as the wretched slave ;
Who, with a body fill'd, and vacant mind,
Gets him to rest, cramm'd with distressful bread,
Never sees horrid night, the child of hell :
But, like a lacquey, from the rise to set,
Sweats in the eye of Phoebus, and all night
Sleeps in Elysium ; next day, after dawn,
Doth rise, and help Hyperion to his horse ;
And follows so the ever-running year
With profitable labour, to his grave :
And, but for ceremony, such a wretch,
Winding up days with toil, and nights with sleep,
Has the forehand and vantage of a king.
The slave, a member of the country's peace,
Enjoys it ; but in gross brain little wots,

What watch the king keeps to maintain the peace,
Whose hours the peasant best advantages.

Most of these passages are well known: there is one, which we do not remember to have seen noticed, and yet it is no whit inferior to the rest in heroic beauty. It is the account of the deaths of York and Suffolk.

*Exeter.* The duke of York commends him to your majesty.
*K. Henry.* Lives he, good uncle? thrice within this hour,
I saw him down; thrice up again, and fighting;
From helmet to the spur all blood he was.
*Exeter.* In which array (brave soldier) doth he lie,
Larding the plain: and by his bloody side
(Yoke-fellow to his honour-owing wounds)
The noble earl of Suffolk also lies.
Suffolk first died: and York, all haggled o'er,
Comes to him, where in gore he lay insteep'd,
And takes him by the beard; kisses the gashes,
That bloodily did yawn upon his face;
And cries aloud—*Tarry, dear cousin Suffolk!*
*My soul shall thine keep company to heaven:*
*Tarry, sweet soul, for mine, then fly a-breast;*
*As, in this glorious and well-foughten field,*
*We kept together in our chivalry!*
Upon these words I came, and cheer'd him up:
He smil'd me in the face, raught me his hand,
And, with a feeble gripe, says—*Dear my lord,*
*Commend my service to my sovereign.*
So did he turn, and over Suffolk's neck
He threw his wounded arm, and kiss'd his lips;
And so, espous'd to death, with blood he seal'd
A testament of noble-ending love.

But we must have done with splendid quotations. The behaviour of the king, in the difficult and doubtful circumstances in which he is placed, is as patient and modest as it is spirited and lofty in his prosperous fortune. The character of the French nobles is also very admirably depicted; and the Dauphin's praise of his horse shows the vanity of that class of persons in a very striking point of view. Shakespeare always accompanies a foolish prince with a satirical courtier, as we see in this instance. The comic parts of *Henry V* are very inferior to those of *Henry IV*. Falstaff is dead, and without him, Pistol, Nym, and Bardolph are satellites without a sun. Fluellen the Welshman is the most entertaining character in the piece. He is good natured, brave, choleric, and pedantic. His parallel between Alexander and Harry of Monmouth, and his desire to have 'some disputations' with Captain Macmorris on the discipline of the Roman wars, in the heat of the battle, are never to be forgotten. His treatment of Pistol is as good as Pistol's treatment of his French prisoner. There are two other remarkable prose passages in this play: the conversation of Henry in disguise with the three sentinels on the duties of a soldier, and his courtship of Katherine in broken French. We like them both exceedingly, though the first savours perhaps too much of the king, and the last too little of the lover.

# *Henry VI*

IN THREE PARTS

During the time of the civil wars of York and Lancaster, England was a perfect bear-garden, and Shakespeare has given us a very lively picture of the scene. The three parts of *Henry VI* convey a picture of very little else ; and are inferior to the other historical plays. They have brilliant passages ; but the general ground-work is comparatively poor and meagre, the style ' flat and unraised '. There are few lines like the following :

> Glory is like a circle in the water ;
> Which never ceaseth to enlarge itself,
> Till by broad spreading it disperse to naught.

The first part relates to the wars in France after the death of Henry V and the story of the Maid of Orleans. She is here almost as scurvily treated as in Voltaire's Pucelle. Talbot is a very magnificent sketch : there is something as formidable in this portrait of him, as there would be in a monumental figure of him or in the sight of the armour which he wore. The scene in which he visits the Countess of Auvergne, who seeks to entrap him, is a very spirited one, and his description of his own treatment while a prisoner to the French not less remarkable.

> *Salisbury.* Yet tell'st thou not how thou wert entertain'd.
> *Talbot.* With scoffs and scorns, and contumelious taunts,
> In open-market-place produced they me,
> To be a public spectacle to all.
> Here, said they, is the terror of the French,
> The scarecrow that affrights our children so.

Then broke I from the officers that led me,
And with my nails digg'd stones out of the ground,
To hurl at the beholders of my shame.
My grisly countenance made others fly,
None durst come near for fear of sudden death.
In iron walls they deem'd me not secure :
So great a fear my name amongst them spread,
That they suppos'd I could rend bars of steel.
And spurn in pieces posts of adamant.
Wherefore a guard of chosen shot I had :
They walk'd about me every minute-while ;
And if I did but stir out of my bed,
Ready they were to shoot me to the heart.

The second part relates chiefly to the contests between the nobles during the minority of Henry and the death of Gloucester, the good Duke Humphrey. The character of Cardinal Beaufort is the most prominent in the group : the account of his death is one of our author's masterpieces. So is the speech of Gloucester to the nobles on the loss of the provinces of France by the king's marriage with Margaret of Anjou. The pretensions and growing ambition of the Duke of York, the father of Richard III are also very ably developed. Among the episodes, the tragi-comedy of Jack Cade, and the detection of the impostor Simcox are truly edifying.

The third part describes Henry's loss of his crown : his death takes place in the last act, which is usually thrust into the common acting play of *Richard III*. The character of Gloucester, afterwards King Richard, is here very powerfully commenced, and his dangerous designs and long-reaching ambition are fully described in his soliloquy in the third act, beginning, 'Aye, Edward will use women honourably '. Henry VI is drawn as distinctly as his high-spirited Queen, and notwithstanding the very mean figure which Henry makes as a king, we still feel more respect for him than for his wife.

We have already observed that Shakespeare was scarcely more remarkable for the force and marked contrasts of his characters than for the truth and subtlety with which he has distinguished those which approached the nearest to each other. For instance, the soul of Othello is hardly more distinct from that of Iago than that of Desdemona is shown to be from Aemilia's; the ambition of Macbeth is as distinct from the ambition of Richard III as it is from the meekness of Duncan; the real madness of Lear is as different from the feigned madness of Edgar[1] as from the babbling of the fool; the contrast between wit and folly in Falstaff and Shallow is not more characteristic though more obvious than the gradations of folly, loquacious or reserved, in Shallow and Silence; and again, the gallantry of Prince Henry is as little confounded with that of Hotspur as with the cowardice of Falstaff, or as the sensual and philosophic cowardice of the Knight is with the pitiful and cringing cowardice of Parolles. All these several personages were as different in Shakespeare as they would have been in themselves: his imagination borrowed from the life, and every circumstance, object, motive, passion, operated there as it would in reality, and produced a world of men and women as distinct, as true and as various as those that exist in nature. The peculiar property of Shakespeare's imagination was this truth, accompanied with the unconsciousness of nature: indeed, imagination to be perfect must be unconscious, at least in production; for nature is so. We shall attempt one example more in the characters of Richard II and Henry VI.

The characters and situations of both these persons were so nearly alike, that they would have

[1] There is another instance of the same distinction in Hamlet and Ophelia. Hamlet's pretended madness would make a very good real madness in any other author.

been completely confounded by a commonplace poet. Yet they are kept quite distinct in Shakespeare. Both were kings, and both unfortunate. Both lost their crowns owing to their mismanagement and imbecility; the one from a thoughtless, wilful abuse of power, the other from an indifference to it. The manner in which they bear their misfortunes corresponds exactly to the causes which led to them. The one is always lamenting the loss of his power which he has not the spirit to regain; the other seems only to regret that he had ever been king, and is glad to be rid of the power, with the trouble; the effeminacy of the one is that of a voluptuary, proud, revengeful, impatient of contradiction, and inconsolable in his misfortunes; the effeminacy of the other is that of an indolent, good-natured mind, naturally averse to the turmoils of ambition and the cares of greatness, and who wishes to pass his time in monkish indolence and contemplation.—Richard bewails the loss of the kingly power only as it was the means of gratifying his pride and luxury; Henry regards it only as a means of doing right, and is less desirous of the advantages to be derived from possessing it than afraid of exercising it wrong. In knighting a young soldier, he gives him ghostly advice—

Edward Plantagenet, arise a knight,
And learn this lesson, draw thy sword in right.

Richard II in the first speeches of the play betrays his real character. In the first alarm of his pride, on hearing of Bolingbroke's rebellion, before his presumption has met with any check, he exclaims:

Mock not my senseless conjuration, lords:
This earth shall have a feeling, and these stones
Prove armed soldiers, ere her native king
Shall falter under proud rebellious arms.
. . . . . . .

Not all the water in the rough rude sea
Can wash the balm from an anointed king ;
The breath of wordly man cannot depose
The Deputy elected by the Lord.
For every man that Bolingbroke hath prest,
To lift sharp steel against our golden crown,
Heaven for his Richard hath in heavenly pay
A glorious angel ; then if angels fight,
Weak men must fall ; for Heaven still guards the right.

Yet, notwithstanding this royal confession of faith, on the very first news of actual disaster, all his conceit of himself as the peculiar favourite of Providence vanishes into air.

But now the blood of twenty thousand men
Did triumph in my face, and they are fled.
All souls that will be safe fly from my side ;
For time hath set a blot upon my pride.

Immediately after, however, recollecting that 'cheap defence' of the divinity of kings which is to be found in opinion, he is for arming his name against his enemies.

Awake, thou coward Majesty, thou sleep'st ;
Is not the King's name forty thousand names ?
Arm, arm, my name : a puny subject strikes
At thy great glory.

King Henry does not make any such vapouring resistance to the loss of his crown, but lets it slip from off his head as a weight which he is neither able nor willing to bear ; stands quietly by to see the issue of the contest for his kingdom, as if it were a game at push-pin, and is pleased when the odds prove against him.

When Richard first hears of the death of his favourites, Bushy, Bagot, and the rest, he indignantly rejects all idea of any further efforts, and only indulges in the extravagant impatience of his grief and his despair, in that fine speech which has been so often quoted :

*Aumerle.* Where is the duke my father, with his power?
*K. Richard.* No matter where: of comfort no man speak:
Let's talk of graves, of worms, and epitaphs,
Make dust our paper, and with rainy eyes
Write sorrow in the bosom of the earth!
Let's choose executors, and talk of wills:
And yet not so—for what can we bequeath,
Save our deposed bodies to the ground?
Our lands, our lives, and all are Bolingbroke's,
And nothing can we call our own but death,
And that small model of the barren earth,
Which serves as paste and cover to our bones.
For heaven's sake let us sit upon the ground,
And tell sad stories of the death of Kings:
How some have been depos'd, some slain in war;
Some haunted by the ghosts they dispossess'd;
Some poison'd by their wives, some sleeping kill'd;
All murder'd:—for within the hollow crown,
That rounds the mortal temples of a king,
Keeps death his court: and there the antic sits,
Scoffing his state, and grinning at his pomp!
Allowing him a breath, a little scene
To monarchize, be fear'd, and kill with looks;
Infusing him with self and vain conceit—
As if this flesh, which walls about our life,
Were brass impregnable; and, humour'd thus,
Comes at the last, and, with a little pin,
Bores through his castle wall, and—farewell king!
Cover your heads, and mock not flesh and blood
With solemn reverence; throw away respect,
Tradition, form, and ceremonious duty,
For you have but mistook me all this while:
I live on bread like you, feel want, taste grief,
Need friends, like you;—subjected thus,
How can you say to me—I am a king?

There is as little sincerity afterwards in his affected resignation to his fate, as there is fortitude in this exaggerated picture of his misfortunes before they have happened.

When Northumberland comes back with the message from Bolingbroke, he exclaims, anticipating the result,—

What must the king do now? Must he submit?
The king shall do it: must he be depos'd?

The king shall be contented : must he lose
The name of king ? O' God's name let it go.
I'll give my jewels for a set of beads ;
My gorgeous palace for a hermitage ;
My gay apparel for an almsman's gown ;
My figur'd goblets for a dish of wood ;
My sceptre for a palmer's walking staff ;
My subjects for a pair of carved saints,
And my large kingdom for a little grave—
A little, little grave, an obscure grave.

How differently is all this expressed in King Henry's soliloquy, during the battle with Edwards' party :

This battle fares like to the morning's war,
When dying clouds contend with growing light,
What time the shepherd blowing of his nails,
Can neither call it perfect day or night.
Here on this mole-hill will I sit me down ;
To whom God will, there be the victory !
For Margaret my Queen and Clifford too
Have chid me from the battle, swearing both
They prosper best of all whence I am thence.
Would I were dead, if God's good will were so.
For what is in this world but grief and woe ?
O God ! methinks it were a happy life
To be no better than a homely swain,
To sit upon a hill as I do now,
To carve out dials quaintly, point by point,
Thereby to see the minutes how they run :
How many make the hour full complete,
How many hours bring about the day,
How many days will finish up the year,
How many years a mortal man may live.
When this is known, then to divide the times :
So many hours must I tend my flock,
So many hours must I take my rest,
So many hours must I contemplate,
So many hours must I sport myself ;
So many days my ewes have been with young,
So many weeks ere the poor fools will yean,
So many months ere I shall shear the fleece :
So many minutes, hours, weeks, months, and years
Past over, to the end they were created,
Would bring white hairs unto a quiet grave.

Ah! what a life were this! how sweet, how lovely!
Gives not the hawthorn bush a sweeter shade
To shepherds looking on their silly sheep,
Than doth a rich embroidered canopy
To kings that fear their subjects' treachery?
O yes it doth, a thousand-fold it doth.
And to conclude, the shepherds' homely curds,
His cold thin drink out of his leather bottle,
His wonted sleep under a fresh tree's shade,
All of which secure and sweetly he enjoys,
Is far beyond a prince's delicates,
His viands sparkling in a golden cup,
His body couched in a curious bed,
When care, mistrust, and treasons wait on him.

This is a true and beautiful description of a naturally quiet and contented disposition and not, like the former, the splenetic effusion of disappointed ambition.

In the last scene of *Richard II* his despair lends him courage: he beats the keeper, slays two of his assassins, and dies with imprecations in his mouth against Sir Pierce Exton, who 'had staggered his royal person'. Henry, when he is seized by the deer-stealers, only reads them a moral lecture on the duty of allegiance and the sanctity of an oath; and when stabbed by Gloucester in the Tower, reproaches him with his crimes, but pardons him his own death.

# *Richard III*

Richard III may be considered as properly a stage-play: it belongs to the theatre, rather than to the closet. We shall therefore criticize it chiefly with a reference to the manner in which we have seen it performed. It is the character in which Garrick came out: it was the second character in which Mr. Kean appeared, and in which he acquired his fame. Shakespeare we have always with us: actors we have only for a few seasons; and therefore some account of them may be acceptable, if not to our contemporaries, to those who come after us, if 'that rich and idle personage, Posterity', should deign to look into our writings.

It is possible to form a higher conception of the character of Richard than that given by Mr. Kean: but we cannot imagine any character represented with greater distinctness and precision, more perpectly *articulated* in every part. Perhaps indeed there is too much of what is technically called execution. When we first saw this celebrated actor in the part, we thought he sometimes failed from an exuberance of manner, and dissipated the impression of the general character by the variety of his resources. To be complete, his delineation of it should have more solidity, depth, sustained and impassioned feeling, with somewhat less brilliancy, with fewer glancing lights, pointed transitions, and pantomimic evolutions.

The Richard of Shakespeare is towering and lofty; equally impetuous and commanding; haughty, violent, and subtle; bold and treacherous; confident in his strength as well as in his cunning; raised high by his birth, and higher by his talents and his crimes; a royal usurper, a princely hypocrite, a tyrant and a murderer of the house of Plantagenet.

> But I was born so high:
> Our aery buildeth in the cedar's top,
> And dallies with the wind, and scorns the sun.

The idea conveyed in these lines (which are indeed omitted in the miserable medley acted for *Richard III*) is never lost sight of by Shakespeare, and should not be out of the actor's mind for a moment. The restless and sanguinary Richard is not a man striving to be great, but to be greater than he is; conscious of his strength of will, his power of intellect, his daring courage, his elevated station; and making use of these advantages to commit unheard-of-crimes, and to shield himself from remorse and infamy.

If Mr. Kean does not entirely succeed in concentrating all the lines of the character, as drawn by Shakespeare, he gives an animation, vigour, and relief to the part which we have not seen equalled. He is more refined than Cooke; more bold, varied, and original than Kemble in the same character. In some parts he is deficient in dignity, and particularly in the scenes of state business, he has by no means an air of artificial authority. There is at times an aspiring elevation, an enthusiastic rapture in his expectations of attaining the crown, and at others a gloating expression of sullen delight, as if he already clenched the bauble, and held it in his grasp. The courtship scene with Lady Anne is an admirable exhibition of smooth and smiling villainy. The progress of wily adulation, of encroaching humility, is finely marked by his action, voice and eye. He seems, like the first Tempter, to approach his prey, secure of the event, and as if success had smoothed his way before him. The late Mr. Cooke's manner of representing this scene was more vehement, hurried, and full of anxious uncertainty. This, though more natural in general, was less in character in this particular instance. Richard should woo less as a lover than as an actor—to show his mental superiority, and power of making others the playthings of his purposes. Mr. Kean's attitude in leaning against the side of the stage before he comes forward to address Lady Anne, is one of the most graceful and striking ever witnessed on the stage. It would do for Titian to paint. The frequent and rapid transition of his voice from the expression of the fiercest passion to the most familiar tones of conversation was that which gave a peculiar grace of novelty to his acting on his first appearance. This has been since imitated and caricatured by others, and he himself uses the artifice more sparingly than he did. His by-play is excellent. His manner of bidding his friends 'Good night', after pausing with the point of his sword drawn slowly backward and forward on the ground, as if considering the plan of the battle next day, is a particularly happy and natural thought. He gives to the two last acts of the play the greatest animation and effect. He fills every part of the stage; and makes up for the deficiency of his person by what has been sometimes objected to as an excess of action. The concluding scene in which he is killed by Richmond is the most brilliant of the whole. He fights at last like one drunk with wounds; and the attitude in which he stands with his hands stretched out, after his sword is wrested from him, has a preternatural and terrific grandeur, as if his will could not be disarmed, and the very phantoms of his despair had power to kill.—Mr. Kean has since in a great measure effaced the impression of his Richard III by the superior efforts of his genius in Othello (his master-piece), in the murder-scene in Macbeth, in Richard II, in

Sir Giles Overreach, and lastly in Oroonoko; but we still like to look back to his first performance of this part, both because it first assured his admirers of his future success, and because we bore our feeble but, at that time, not useless testimony to the merits of this very original actor, on which the town was considerably divided for no other reason than because they *were* original.

The manner in which Shakespeare's plays have been generally altered or rather mangled by modern mechanists, is a disgrace to the English stage. The patch-work *Richard III* which is acted under the sanction of his name, and which was manufactured by Cibber, is a striking example of this remark.

The play itself is undoubtedly a very powerful effusion of Shakespeare's genius. The ground-work of the character of Richard, that mixture of intellectual vigour with moral depravity, in which Shakespeare delighted to show his strength—gave full scope as well as temptation to the exercise of his imagination. The character of his hero is almost everywhere predominant, and marks its lurid track throughout. The original play is, however, too long for representation, and there are some few scenes which might be better spared than preserved, and by omitting which it would remain a complete whole. The only rule, indeed, for altering Shakespeare is to retrench certain passages which may be considered either as superfluous or obsolete, but not to add or transpose anything. The arrangement and development of the story, and the mutual contrast and combination of the *dramatis personae*, are in general as finely managed as the development of the characters or the expression of the passions.

This rule has not been adhered to in the present instance. Some of the most important and striking passages in the principal character have been omitted, to make room for idle and misplaced extracts from other plays; the only intention of which seems to have been to make the character of Richard as odious and disgusting as possible. It is apparently for no other purpose than to make Gloucester stab King Henry on the stage, that the fine abrupt introduction of the character in the opening of the play is lost in the tedious whining morality of the uxorious king (taken from another play);—we say *tedious*, because it interrupts the business of the scene, and loses its beauty and effect by having no intelligible connexion with the previous character of the mild, well-meaning monarch. The passages which the unfortunate Henry has to recite are beautiful and pathetic in themselves, but they have nothing to do with the world that Richard has to 'bustle in'. In the same spirit of vulgar caricature is the scene between Richard and Lady Anne (when his wife) interpolated without any authority, merely to gratify this favourite propensity to disgust and loathing. With the same perverse consistency, Richard, after his last fatal struggle, is raised up by some galvanic process, to utter the imprecation, without any motive but pure malignity, which Shakespeare has so properly put into the mouth of Northumberland on hearing of Percy's death. To make room for these worse than needless additions, many of the most striking passages in the real play have been omitted by the foppery and ignorance of the prompt-book critics. We do not mean to insist merely on passages which are fine as poetry and to the reader, such as Clarence's dream, etc., but on those which are important to the understanding of the character, and peculiarly adapted for stage-effect. We will give the following as instances among several others. The first is the scene where Richard enters abruptly to the queen and her friends to defend himself:

*Gloucester*. They do me wrong, and I will not endure it.
Who are they that complain unto the king,
That I forsooth am stern, and love them not ?
By holy Paul, they love his grace but lightly,
That fill his ears with such dissentious rumours :
Because I cannot flatter and look fair,
Smile in men's faces, smooth, deceive, and cog,
Duck with French nods, and apish courtesy,
I must be held a rancorous enemy.
Cannot a plain man live, and think no harm,
But thus his simple truth must be abus'd
With silken, sly, insinuating Jacks ?
*Gray*. To whom in all this presence speaks your grace ?
*Gloucester*. To thee, that hast nor honesty nor grace ;
When have I injur'd thee, when done thee wrong ?
Or thee ? or thee ? or any of your faction ?
A plague upon you all !

Nothing can be more characteristic than the turbulent pretensions to meekness and simplicity in this address. Again, the versatility and adroitness of Richard is admirably described in the following ironical conversation with Brakenbury :

*Brakenbury*. I beseech your graces both to pardon me.
His majesty hath straitly given in charge,
That no man shall have private conference,
Of what degree soever, with your brother.
*Gloucester*. E'en so, and please your worship, Brakenbury.
You may partake of anything we say :
We speak no treason, man—we say the king
Is wise and virtuous, and his noble queen
Well strook in years, fair, and not jealous.
We say that Shore's wife hath a pretty foot,
A cherry lip,
A bonny eye, a passing pleasing tongue ;
That the queen's kindred are made gentlefolks.
How say you, sir ? Can you deny all this ?
*Brakenbury*. With this, my lord, myself have naught to do.
*Gloucester*. What, fellow, naught to do with mistress Shore ?
I tell you, sire, he that doth naught with her,
Excepting one, were best to do it secretely alone.
*Brakenbury*. What one, my lord ?
*Gloucester*. Her husband, knave—would'st thou betray me ?

The feigned reconciliation of Gloucester with the queen's kinsmen is also a masterpiece. One of the finest strokes in the play, and which serves to show as much as anything the deep, plausible manners of Richard, is the unsuspecting security of Hastings, at the very time when the former is plotting his death, and when that very appearance of cordiality and good-humour on which Hastings builds his confidence arises from Richard's consciousness of having betrayed him to his ruin. This, with the whole character of Hastings, is omitted.

Perhaps the two most beautiful passages in the original play are the farewell apostrophe of the queen to the Tower, where the children are shut up from her, and Tyrrel's description of their death. We will finish our quotations with them.

> *Queen.* Stay, yet look back with me unto the Tower ;
> Pity, you ancient stones, those tender babes,
> Whom envy hath immured within your walls ;
> Rough cradle for such little pretty ones,
> Rude, rugged nurse, old sullen play-fellow,
> For tender princes !

The other passage is the account of their death by Tyrrel :

> Dighton and Forrest, whom I did suborn
> To do this piece of ruthless butchery,
> Albeit they were flesh'd villains, bloody dogs,—
> Wept like two children in their death's sad story :
> O thus ! quoth Dighton, lay the gentle babes ;
> Thus, thus, quoth Forrest, girdling one another
> Within their innocent alabaster arms ;
> Their lips were four red roses on a stalk,
> And in that summer beauty kissed each other ;
> A book of prayers on their pillow lay,
> Which once, quoth Forrest, almost changed my mind :
> But oh the devil !—there the villain stopped ;
> When Dighton thus told on—we smothered
> The most replenished sweet work of nature,
> That from the prime creation ere she framed.

These are some of those wonderful bursts of

feeling, done to the life, to the very height of fancy and nature, which our Shakespeare alone could give. We do not insist on the repetition of these last passages as proper for the stage: we should indeed be loath to trust them in the mouth of almost any actor: but we should wish them to be retained in preference at least to the fantoccini exhibition of the young princes, Edward and York, bandying childish wit with their uncle.

# *Henry VIII*

This play contains little action or violence of passion, yet it has considerable interest of a more mild and thoughtful cast, and some of the most striking passages in the author's works. The character of Queen Katherine is the most perfect delineation of matronly dignity, sweetness, and resignation, that can be conceived. Her appeals to the protection of the king, her remonstrances to the cardinals, her conversations with her women, show a noble and generous spirit accompanied with the utmost gentleness of nature. What can be more affecting than her answer to Campeius and Wolsey, who come to visit her as pretended friends.

> ——' Nay, forsooth, my friends,
> They that must weigh out my afflictions,
> They that my trust must grow to, live not here ;
> They are, as all my comforts are, far hence,
> In mine own country, lords.'

Dr. Johnson observes of this play, that 'the meek sorrows and virtuous distress of Katherine have furnished some scenes, which may be justly numbered among the greatest efforts of tragedy. But the genius of Shakespeare comes in and goes out with Katherine. Every other part may be easily conceived and easily written '. This is easily said ; but with all due deference to so great a reputed authority as that of Johnson, it is not true. For instance, the scene of Buckingham led to execution is one of the most affecting and natural in Shakespeare, and one to which there is hardly an approach in any other author. Again, the character of Wolsey, the description of his pride and of his fall, are inimitable, and have, besides their gorgeousness of effect, a pathos, which only the genius of Shakespeare could lend to the distresses of a proud, bad man, like Wolsey. There is a sort of child-like simplicity in the very helplessness of his situation, arising from the recollection of his past overbearing ambition. After the cutting sarcasms of his enemies on his disgrace, against which he bears up with a spirit conscious of his own superiority, he breaks out into that fine apostrophe :

> Farewell, a long farewell, to all my greatness !
> This is the state of man ; to-day he puts forth
> The tender leaves of hope, to-morrow blossoms,
> And bears his blushing honours thick upon him ;
> The third day, comes a frost, a killing frost ;
> And—when he thinks, good easy man, full surely
> His greatness is a ripening—nips his root,
> And then he falls, as I do. I have ventur'd,
> Like little wanton boys that swim on bladders,
> These many summers in a sea of glory ;
> But far beyond my depth : my high-blown pride
> At length broke under me ; and now has left me,
> Weary and old with service, to the mercy
> Of a rude stream, that must for ever hide me.
> Vain pomp and glory of the world, I hate ye !
> I feel my heart new open'd : O how wretched
> Is that poor man, that hangs on princes' favours !
> There is betwixt that smile we would aspire to,
> That sweet aspect of princes, and our ruin,
> More pangs and fears than war and women have ;
> And when he falls, he falls like Lucifer,
> Never to hope again !—

There is in this passage, as well as in the well-known dialogue with Cromwell which follows, something which stretches beyond commonplace ; nor is the account which Griffiths gives of Wolsey's death less Shakespearian ; and the candour with which Queen Katherine listens to the praise of ' him whom of all men while living she hated most ' adds the last graceful finishing to her character.

Among other images of great individual beauty

might be mentioned the description of the effect of Ann Boleyn's presenting herself to the crowd at her coronation.

> ——While her grace sat down
> To rest awhile, some half an hour or so,
> In a rich chair of state, opposing freely
> The beauty of her person to the people.
> Believe me, sir, she is the goodliest woman
> That ever lay by man. Which when the people
> Had the full view of, *such a noise arose*
> *As the shrouds make at sea in a stiff tempest,*
> *As loud and to as many tunes.*

The character of Henry VIII is drawn with great truth and spirit. It is like a very disagreeable portrait, sketched by the hand of a master. His gross appearance, his blustering demeanour, his vulgarity, his arrogance, his sensuality, his cruelty, his hypocrisy, his want of common decency and common humanity, are marked in strong lines. His traditional peculiarities of expression complete the reality of the picture. The authoritative expletive, 'Ha!' with which he intimates his indignation or surprise, has an effect like the first startling sound that breaks from a thunder-cloud. He is of all the monarchs in our history the most disgusting: for he unites in himself all the vices of barbarism and refinement, without their virtues. Other kings before him (such as Richard III) were tyrants and murderers out of ambition or necessity: they gained or established unjust power by violent means: they destroyed their enemies, or those who barred their access to the throne or made its tenure insecure. But Henry VIII's power is most fatal to those whom he loves: he is cruel and remorseless to pamper his luxurious appetites: bloody and voluptuous; an amorous murderer; and uxorious debauchee. His hardened insensibility to the feelings of others is strengthened by the most profligate self-indulgence. The religious hypocrisy, under which he masks his cruelty and his lust, is admirably displayed in the speech in which he describes the first misgivings of his conscience and its increasing throes and terrors, which have induced him to divorce his queen. The only thing in his favour in this play is his treatment of Cranmer: there is also another circumstance in his favour, which is his patronage of Hans Holbein.—It has been said of Shakespeare, 'No maid could live near such a man'. It might with as good reason be said, 'No king could live near such a man'. His eye would have penetrated through the pomp of circumstance and the veil of opinion. As it is, he has represented such persons to the life—his plays are in this respect the glass of history—he has done them the same justice as if he had been a privy counsellor all his life, and in each successive reign. Kings ought never to be seen upon the stage. In the abstract, they are very disagreeable characters: it is only while living that they are 'the best of kings'. It is their power, their splendour, it is the apprehension of the personal consequences of their favour or their hatred that dazzles the imagination and suspends the judgment of their favourites or their vassals; but death cancels the bond of allegiance and of interest; and seen *as they were*, their power and their pretensions look monstrous and ridiculous. The charge brought against modern philosophy as inimical to loyalty is unjust, because it might as well be brought against other things. No reader of history can be a lover of kings. We have often wondered that Henry VIII as he is drawn by Shakespeare, and as we have seen him represented in all the bloated deformity of mind and person, is not hooted from the English stage.

# *King John*

King John is the last of the historical plays we shall have to speak of; and we are not sorry that it is. If we are to indulge our imaginations, we had rather do it upon an imaginary theme; if we are to find subjects for the exercise of our pity and terror, we prefer seeking them in fictitious danger and fictitious distress. It gives a *soreness* to our feelings of indignation or sympathy, when we know that in tracing the progress of sufferings and crimes we are treading upon real ground, and recollect that the poet's 'dream' *denoted a foregone conclusion*—irrevocable ills, not conjured up by fancy, but placed beyond the reach of poetical justice. That the treachery of King John, the death of Arthur, the grief of Constance, had a real truth in history, sharpens the sense of pain, while it hangs a leaden weight on the heart and the imagination. Something whispers us that we have no right to make a mock of calamities like these, or to turn the truth of things into the puppet and plaything of our fancies. 'To consider thus' may be 'to consider too curiously'; but still we think that the actual truth of the particular events, in proportion as we are conscious of it, is a drawback on the pleasure as well as the dignity of tragedy.

*King John* has all the beauties of language and all the richness of the imagination to relieve the painfulness of the subject. The character of King John himself is kept pretty much in the background; it is only marked in by comparatively slight indications. The crimes he is tempted to commit are such as are thrust upon him rather by circumstances and opportunity than of his own seeking: he is here represented as more cowardly than cruel, and as more contemptible than odious. The play embraces only a part of his history. There are however few characters on the stage that excite more disgust and loathing. He has no intellectual grandeur or strength of character to shield him from the indignation which his immediate conduct provokes: he stands naked and defenceless, in that respect, to the worst we can think of him: and besides, we are impelled to put the very worst construction on his meanness and cruelty by the tender picture of the beauty and helplessness of the object of it, as well as by the frantic and heart-rending pleadings of maternal despair. We do not forgive him the death of Arthur because he had too late revoked his doom and tried to prevent it, and perhaps because he has himself repented of his black besign, our *moral sense* gains courage to hate him the more for it. We take him at his word, and think his purposes must be odious indeed, when he himself shrinks back from them. The scene in which King John suggests to Hubert the design of murdering his nephew is a master-piece of dramatic skill, but it is still inferior, very inferior to the scene between Hubert and Arthur, when the latter learns the orders to put out his eyes. If anything ever was penned, heart-piercing, mixing the extremes of terror and pity, of that which shocks and that which soothes the mind, it is this scene. We will give it entire, though perhaps it is tasking the reader's sympathy too much.

*Enter* HUBERT *and Executioner.*

*Hubert.* Heat me these irons hot, and look you stand
Within the arras; when I strike my foot
Upon the bosom of the ground, rush forth
And bind the boy, which you shall find with me,

Fast to the chair: be heedful: hence, and watch.
*Executioner*. I hope your warrant will bear out the deed.
*Hubert*. Uncleanly scruples! fear not you; look to't.—
Young lad, come forth; I have to say with you.

*Enter* ARTHUR.

*Arthur*. Good morning, Hubert.
*Hubert*. Morrow, little Prince.
*Arthur*. As little prince (having so great a title
To be more prince) as may be. You are sad.
*Hubert*. Indeed I have been merrier.
*Arthur*. Mercy on me!
Methinks no body should be sad but I;
Yet I remember when I was in France,
Young gentlemen would be as sad as night,
Only for wantonness. By my Christendom,
So were I out of prison, and kept sheep,
I should be merry as the day is long.
And so I would be here, but that I doubt
My uncle practises more harm to me.
He is afraid of me, and I of him.
Is it my fault that I was Geoffery's son?
Indeed it is not, and I would to heav'n
I were your son, so you would love me, Hubert.
*Hubert*. If I talk to him, with his innocent prate
He will awake my mercy, which lies dead;
Therefore I will be sudden, and dispatch. [*Aside*.
*Arthur*. Are you sick, Hubert? you look pale to-day?
In sooth, I would you were a little sick,
That I might sit all night and watch with you.
Alas, I love you more than you do me.
*Hubert*. His words do take possession of my bosom.
Read here, young Arthur— [*Showing a paper*.
How now, foolish rheum, [*Aside*.
Turning dis-piteous torture out of door!
I must be brief, lest resolution drop
Out at mine eyes in tender womanish tears.—
Can you not read it? Is it not fair writ?
*Arthur*. Too fairly, Hubert, for so foul effect.
Must you with irons burn out both mine eyes?
*Hubert*. Young boy, I must.
*Arthur*. And will you?
*Hubert*. And I will.
*Arthur*. Have you the heart? When your head did but ache,
I knit my handkerchief about your brows,
(The best I had, a princess wrought it me)
And I did never ask it you again;
And with my hand at midnight held your head;

And, like the watchful minutes to the hour,
Still and anon cheer'd up the heavy time,
Saying, what lack you? and where lies your grief?
Or, what good love may I perform for you?
Many a poor man's son would have lain still,
And ne'er have spoke a loving word to you;
But you at your sick service had a prince.
Nay, you may think my love was crafty love,
And call it cunning. Do, and if you will:
If heav'n be pleas'd that you must use me ill,
Why then you must.—Will you put out mine eyes?
These eyes, that never did, and never shall,
So much as frown on you?
*Hubert.* I've sworn to do it;
And with hot irons must I burn them out.
*Arthur.* Oh if an angel should have come to me,
And told me Hubert should put out mine eyes,
I would not have believ'd a tongue but Hubert's.
*Hubert.* Come forth; do as I bid you.
[*Stamps, and the men enter*
*Arthur.* O save me, Hubert, save me! my eyes are out
Ev'n with the fierce looks of these bloody men.
*Hubert.* Give me the iron, I say, and bind him here.
*Arthur.* Alas, what need you be so boist'rous rough?
I will not struggle, I will stand stone-still.
For heav'n's sake, Hubert, let me not be bound!
Nay, hear me, Hubert, drive these men away,
And I will sit as quiet as a lamb:
I will not stir, nor wince, nor speak a word,
Nor look upon the iron angrily:
Thrust but these men away, and I'll forgive you,
Whatever torment you do put me to.
*Hubert.* Go, stand within; let me alone with him.
*Executioner.* I am best pleas'd to be from such a deed.
[*Exit.*
*Arthur.* Alas, I then have chid away my friend.
He hath a stern look, but a gentle heart;
Let him come back, that his compassion may
Give life to yours.
*Hubert.* Come, boy, prepare yourself.
*Arthur.* Is there no remedy?
*Hubert.* None, but to lose your eyes.
*Arthur.* O heav'n! that there were but a mote in yours,
A grain, a dust, a gnat, a wand'ring hair,
Any annoyance in that precious sense!
Then, feeling what small things are boist'rous there,
Your vile intent must needs seem horrible.

*Hubert.* Is this your promise? go to, hold your tongue.
*Arthur.* Let me not hold my tongue; let me not, Hubert;
Or, Hubert, if you will, cut out my tongue,
So I may keep mine eyes. O spare mine eyes!
Though to no use, but still to look on you.
Lo, by my troth, the instrument is cold,
And would not harm me.
*Hubert.* I can heat it, boy.
*Arthur.* No, on good sooth, the fire is dead with grief.
Being create for comfort, to be us'd
In undeserv'd extremes; see else yourself,
There is no malice in this burning coal;
The breath of heav'n hath blown its spirit out,
And strew'd repentant ashes on its head.
*Hubert.* But with my breath I can revive it, boy.
*Arthur.* All things that you shall use to do me wrong.
Deny their office; only you do lack
That mercy which fierce fire and iron extend,
Creatures of note for mercy-lacking uses.
*Hubert.* Well, see to live; I will not touch thine eyes
For all the treasure that thine uncle owns:
Yet I am sworn, and I did purpose, boy,
With this same very iron to burn them out.
*Arthur.* O, now you look like Hubert. All this while
You were disguised.
*Hubert.* Peace! no more. Adieu,
Your uncle must not know but you are dead.
I'll fill these dogged spies with false reports:
And, pretty child, sleep doubtless and secure,
That Hubert, for the wealth of all the world,
Will not offend thee.
*Arthur.* O heav'n! I thank you, Hubert.
*Hubert.* Silence, no more; go closely in with me;
Much danger do I undergo for thee. [*Exeunt.*

His death afterwards, when he throws himself from his prison-walls, excites the utmost pity for his innocence and friendless situation, and well justifies the exaggerated denunciations of Falconbridge to Hubert whom he suspects wrongful of the deed.

There is not yet so ugly a fiend of hell
As thou shalt be, if thou did'st kill this child.
—If thou did'st but consent
To this most cruel act, do but despair:

And if thou want'st a cord, the smallest thread
That ever spider twisted from her womb
Will strangle thee ; a rush will be a beam
To hang thee on : or would'st thou drown thyself,
Put but a little water in a spoon,
And it shall be as all the ocean,
Enough to stifle such a villain up.

The excess of maternal tenderness, rendered desperate by the fickleness of friends and the injustice of fortune, and made stronger in will, in proportion to the want of all other power, was never more finely expressed than in Constance. The dignity of her answer to King Philip, when she refuses to accompany his passenger, 'To me and to the state of my great grief, let kings assemble,' her indignant reproach to Austria for deserting her cause, her invocation to death, 'that love of misery,' however fine and spirited, all yield to the beauty of the passage, where, her passion subsiding into tenderness, she addresses the Cardinal in these words :

Oh father Cardinal, I have heard you say
That we shall see and know our friends in heav'n :
If that be, I shall see my boy again,
For since the birth of Cain, the first male child,
To him that did but yesterday suspire,
There was not such a gracious creature born.
But now will canker-sorrow eat my bud,
And chase the native beauty from his cheek,
And he will look as hollow as a ghost,
As dim and meagre as an ague's fit,
And so he'll die ; and rising so again,
When I shall meet him in the court of heav'n,
I shall not know him ; therefore never, never
Must I behold my pretty Arthur more.
*K. Philip.* You are as fond of grief as of your child.
*Constance.* Grief fills the room up of my absent child :
Lies in his bed, walks up and down with me :
Puts on his pretty looks, repeats his words,
Remembers me of all his gracious parts ;
Stuffs out his vacant garments with his form.
Then have I reason to be fond of grief.

The contrast between the mild resignation of Queen Katherine to her own wrongs, and the wild, uncontrollable affliction of Constance for the wrongs which she sustains as a mother, is no less naturally conceived than it is ably sustained through these two wonderful characters.

The accompaniment of the comic character of the Bastard was well chosen to relieve the poignant agony of suffering, and the cold, cowardly policy of behaviour in the principal characters of this play. Its spirit, invention, volubility of tongue, and forwardness in action, are unbounded. *Aliquando sufflaminandus erat,* says Ben Jonson of Shakespeare. But we should be sorry if Ben Jonson had been his licenser. We prefer the heedless magnimity of his wit infinitely to all Jonson's laborious caution. The character of the Bastard's comic humour is the same in essence as that of other comic characters in Shakespeare; they always run on with good things and are never exhausted; they are always daring and successful. They have words at will and a flow of wit, like a flow of animal spirits. The difference between Falconbridge and the others is that he is a soldier, and brings his wit to bear upon action, is courageous with his sword as well as tongue, and stimulates his gallantry by his jokes, his enemies feeling the sharpness of his blows and the sting of his sarcasms at the same time. Among his happiest sallies are his descanting on the composition of his own person, his invective against 'commodity, tickling commodity', and his expression of contempt for the Archduke of Austria, who had killed his father, which begins in jest but ends in serious earnest. His conduct at the siege of Angiers shows that his resources were not confined to verbal retorts. — The same exposure of the policy of courts and camps, of kings, nobles, priests, and cardinals, takes place here as in the other plays we have gone through, and we shall not go into a disgusting repetition.

This, like the other plays taken from English history, is written in a remarkably smooth and flowing style, very different from some of the tragedies, *Macbeth*, for instance. The passages consist of a series of single lines, not running into one another. This peculiarity in the versification, which is most common in the three parts of *Henry VI*, has been assigned as a reason why those plays were not written by Shakespeare. But the same structure of verse occurs in his other undoubted plays, as in *Richard II* and in *King John*. The following are instances :

> That daughter there of Spain, the Lady Blanch,
> Is near to England ; look upon the years
> Of Lewis the Dauphin, and that lovely maid.
> If lusty love should go in quest of beauty,
> Where should he find it fairer than in Blanch ?
> If zealous love should go in search of virtue,
> Where should he find it purer than in Blanch ?
> If love ambitious sought a match of birth,
> Whose veins bound richer blood than Lady Blanch ?
> Such as she is, in beauty, virtue, birth,
> Is the young Dauphin every way complete :
> If not complete of, say he is not she ;
> And she again wants nothing, to name want,
> If want it be not, that she is not he.
> He is the half part of a blessed man,
> Left to be finished by such as she ;
> And she a fair divided excellence,
> Whose fulness of perfection lies in him.
> O, two such silver currents, when they join,
> Do glorify the banks that bound them in ;
> And two such shores to two such streams made one,
> Two such controlling bounds, shall you be, kings,
> To these two princes, if you marry them.

Another instance, which is certainly very happy as an example of the simple enumeration of a number of particulars, is Salisbury's remonstrance against the second crowning of the king.

Therefore to be possessed with double pomp,
To guard a title that was rich before;
To gild refined gold, to paint the lily,
To throw a perfume on the violet,
To smooth the ice, to add another hue
Unto the rainbow, or with the taper light
To seek the beauteous eye of heav'n to garnish;
Is wasteful and ridiculous excess.

## *Twelfth Night; or, What You Will*

This is justly considered as one of the most delightful of Shakespeare's comedies. It is full of sweetness and pleasantry. It is perhaps too good-natured for comedy. It has little satire, and no spleen. It aims at the ludricous rather than the ridiculous. It makes us laugh at the follies of mankind, not despise them, and still less bear any ill-will towards them. Shakespeare's comic genius resembles the bee rather in its power of extracting sweets from weeds or poisons, than in leaving a sting behind it. He gives the most amusing exaggeration of the prevailing foibles of his characters, but in a way that they themselves, instead of being offended at, would almost join in to humour; he rather contrives opportunities for them to show themselves off in the happiest lights, than renders them contemptible in the perverse construction of the wit or malice of others.—There is a certain stage of society in which people become conscious of their peculiarities and absurdities, affect to disguise what they are, and set up pretensions to what they are not. This gives rise to a corresponding style of comedy, the object of which is to detect the disguises of self-love, and to make reprisals on these preposterous assumptions of vanity, by marking the contrast between the real and the affected character as severely as possible, and denying to those who would impose on us for what they are not, even the merit which they have. This is the comedy of artificial life, of wit and satire, such as we see it in Congreve, Wycherley, Vanbrugh, etc. To this succeeds a state of society from which the same sort of affectation and pretence are banished by a greater knowledge of the world or by their successful exposure on the stage; and which by neutralizing the materials of comic character, both natural and artificial, leaves no comedy at all—but *the sentimental.* Such is our modern comedy. There is a period in the progress of manners anterior to both these, in which the foibles and follies of individuals are of nature's planting, not the growth of art or study; in which they are therefore unconscious of them themselves, or care not who knows them, if they can but have their whim out; and in which, as there is no attempt at imposition, the spectators rather receive pleasure from humouring the inclinations of the persons they laugh at, than wish to give them pain by exposing their absurdity. This may be called the comedy of nature, and it is the comedy which we generally find in Shakespeare.—Whether the analysis here given be just or not, the spirit of his comedies is evidently quite distinct from that of the authors above mentioned, as it is in its essence the same with that of Cervantes, and also very frequently of Moliere, though he was more systematic in his extravagance than Shakespeare. Shakespeare's comedy is of a pastoral and poetical cast. Folly is indigenous to the soil, and shoots out with native, happy, unchecked luxuriance. Absurdity has every encouragement afforded it; and nonsense has room to flourish in. Nothing is stunted by the churlish, icy hand of indifference or severity. The poet runs riot in a conceit, and idolizes a quibble. His whole object is to turn the meanest or rudest objects to a pleasurable account. The relish which he has of a pun, or of the quaint humour of a low character, does not interfere with the delight with which he describes a beautiful image, or the most refined love. The clown's forced jests do not spoil the sweetness of the character of Viola; the same house is big enough to hold Malvolio, the Countess, Maria, Sir Toby, and Sir Andrew Ague-cheek. For instance, nothing can fall much lower than this last character in intellect or morals: yet how are his weaknesses nursed and dandled by Sir Toby into something 'high fantastical', when on Sir Andrew's commendation of himself for dancing and fencing, Sir Toby answers: 'Wherefore are these things hid? Wherefore have these gifts a curtain before them? Are they like to take dust like Mistress Moll's picture? Why dost thou not go to church in a galliard, and come home in a coranto? My very walk should be a jig! I would not so much as make water but in a cinque-pace. What does thou mean? Is this a world to hide virtues in? I did think by the excellent constitution of thy leg, it was framed under the star of a galliard!'—How Sir Toby, Sir Andrew, and the Clown afterwards *chirp over their cups*, how they 'rouse the night-owl in a catch, able to draw three souls out of one weaver'!—What can be better than Sir Toby's unanswerable answer to Malvolio, 'Dost thou think, because thou art virtuous, there shall be no more cakes and ale?' In a word, the best turn is given to everything, instead of the worst. There is a constant infusion of the romantic and enthusiastic, in proportion as the characters are natural and sincere: whereas, in the more artificial style of comedy, everything gives way to ridicule and indifference, there being nothing left but affectation on one side, and incredulity on the other.—Much as we like Shakespeare's comedies, we cannot agree with Dr. Johnson that they are better than his tragedies; nor do we like them half so well. If his inclination to comedy sometimes led him to trifle with the seriousness of tragedy, the poetical and impassioned passages are the best parts of his comedies. The great and secret charm of *Twelfth Night* is the character of Viola. Much as we like catches and cakes and ale, there is something that we like better. We have a friendship for Sir Toby; we patronize Sir Andrew; we have an understanding with the Clown, a sneaking kindness for Maria and her rogueries; we feel a regard for Malvolio, and sympathize with his gravity, his smiles, his cross-garters, his yellow stockings, and imprisonment in the stocks. But there is something that excites in us a stronger feeling than all this—it is Viola's confession of her love.

> *Duke.* What's her history?
> *Viola. A blank, my lord, she never told her love:*
> She let concealment, like a worm i' th' bud,
> Feed on her damask cheek, she pin'd in thought,
> And with a green and yellow melancholy,
> She sat like Patience on a monument,
> Smiling at grief. *Was not this love indeed?*
> We men may say more, swear more, but indeed,
> Our shows are more than will; for still we prove
> Much in our vows, but little in our love.
> *Duke.* But died thy sister of her love, my boy?
> *Viola.* I am all the daughters of my father's house,
> And all the brothers too; and yet I know not.

Shakespeare alone could describe the effect of his own poetry.

> Oh, it came o'er the ear like the sweet south
> That breathes upon a bank of violets,
> Stealing and giving odour.

What we so much admire here is not the image of Patience on a monument, which has been generally quoted, but the lines before and after it. 'They give a very echo to the seat where love is throned'. How long ago it is since we first learnt to repeat them; and still, still they vibrate on the heart, like the sounds which the passing wind draws from the trembling strings of a harp left on some desert shore! There are other passages of not less impassioned sweetness. Such is Olivia's address to

Sebastian whom she supposes to have already deceived her in a promise of marriage.

Blame not this haste of mine: if you mean well,
Now go with me and with this holy man
Into the chantry by: there before him,
And underneath that consecrated roof,
Plight me the full assurance of your faith,
*That my most jealous and too doubtful soul*
*May live at peace.*

We have already said something of Shakespeare's songs. One of the most beautiful of them occurs in this play, with a preface of his own to it.

*Duke.* O fellow, come, the song we had last night.
Mark it, Cesario, it is old and plain;
The spinsters and the knitters in the sun,
And the free maids that weave their thread with bones,
Do use to chaunt it: it is silly sooth,
And dallies with the innocence of love,
Like the old age.

SONG

Come away, come away, death,
And in sad cypress let me be laid;
Fly away, fly away, breath;
I am slain by a fair cruel maid.
My shroud of white, stuck all with yew,
O prepare it;
My part of death no one so true
Did share it.

Not a flower, not a flower sweet,
On my black coffin let there be strown;
Not a friend, not a friend greet
My poor corpse, where my bones shall be thrown:
A thousand thousand sighs to save,
Lay me, O! where
Sad true-love never find my grave,
To weep there.

Who after this will say that Shakespeare's genius was only fitted for comedy? Yet after reading other parts of this play, and particularly the garden-scene where Malvolio picks up the letter, if we were to say that his genius for comedy was less than his genius for tragedy, it would perhaps only prove that our own taste in such matters is more saturnine than mercurial.

*Enter* MARIA.

*Sir Toby.* Here comes the little villain :—How now, my nettle of India ?

*Maria.* Get ye all three into the box-tree : Malvolio's coming down this walk : he has been yonder i' the sun, practising behaviour to his own shadow this half hour : observe him, for the love of mockery ; for I know this letter will make a contemplative idiot of him. Close, in the name of jesting ! Lie thou there ; for here comes the trout that must be caught with tickling.

[*They hide themselves. Maria throws down a letter, and Exit.*]

*Enter* MALVOLIO.

*Malvolio.* 'Tis but fortune ; all is fortune. Maria once told me, she did affect me ; and I have heard herself come thus near, that, should she fancy, it should be one of my complexion. Besides, she uses me with a more exalted respect than any one else that follows her. What should I think on't ?

*Sir Toby.* Here's an over-weening rogue !

*Fabian.* O, peace ! Contemplation makes a rare turkey-cock of him ; how he jets under his advanced plumes !

*Sir Andrew.* 'Slight, I could so beat the rogue :—

*Sir Toby.* Peace, I say.

*Malvolio.* To be Count Malvolio ;—

*Sir Toby.* Ah, rogue !

*Sir Andrew,* Pistol him, pistol him.

*Sir Toby.* Peace, peace !

*Malvolio.* There is example for't ; the lady of the Strachy married the yeoman of the wardrobe.

*Sir Andrew.* Fie on him, Jezebel !

*Fabian.* O, peace ! now he's deeply in ; look, how imagination blows him.

*Malvolio.* Having been three months married to her, sitting in my chair of state,—

*Sir Toby.* O for a stone bow, to hit him in the eye !

*Malvolio.* Calling my officers about me, in my branch'd velvet gown ; having come from a day-bed, where I have left Olivia sleeping.

*Sir Toby.* Fire and brimstone !

*Fabian.* O peace, peace !

*Malvolio.* And then to have the humour of state : and after a demure travel of regard,—telling them, I know my place, as I would they should do theirs,—to ask for my kinsman Toby.—

*Sir Toby.* Bolts and shackles !

*Fabian.* O, peace, peace, peace! now, now.

*Malvolio.* Seven of my people, with an obedient start, make out for him; I frown the while; and, perchance, wind up my watch, or play with some rich jewel. Toby approaches; curtsies there to me.

*Sir Toby.* Shall this fellow live?

*Fabian.* Though our silence be drawn from us with cares, yet peace.

*Malvolio.* I extend my hand to him thus, quenching my familiar smile with an austere regard to control.

*Sir Toby.* And does not Toby take you a blow o' the lips then?

*Malvolio.* Saying—Cousin Toby, my fortunes having cast me on your niece, give me this prerogative of speech;—

*Sir Toby.* What what?

*Malvolio.* You must amend your drunkenness.

*Fabian.* Nay, patience, or we break the sinews of our plot.

*Malvolio.* Besides, you waste the treasure of your time with a foolish knight—

*Sir Andrew.* That's me, I warrant you.

*Malvolio.* One Sir Andrew—

*Sir Andrew.* I knew, 'twas I; for many do call me fool.

*Malvolio.* What employment have we here? [*Taking up the letter.*

The letter and his comments on it are equally good. If poor Malvolio's treatment afterwards is a little hard, poetical justice is done in the uneasiness which Olivia suffers on account of her mistaken attachment to Cesario, as her insensibility to the violence of the Duke's passion is atoned for by the discovery of Viola's concealed love of him.

# *The Two Gentlemen of Verona*

This is little more than the first outlines of a comedy loosely sketched in. It is the story of a novel dramatized with very little labour or pretension; yet there are passages of high poetical spirit, and of inimitable quaintness of humour, which are undoubtedly Shakespeare's, and there is throughout the conduct of the fable a careless grace and felicity which marks it for his. One of the editors (we believe, Mr. Pope) remarks in a marginal note to the *Two Gentlemen of Verona*: 'It is observable (I know not for what cause) that the style of this comedy is less figurative, and more natural and unaffected than the greatest part of this author's, though supposed to be one of the first he wrote'. Yet so little does the editor appear to have made up his mind upon this subject, that we find the following note to the very next (the second) scene. 'This whole scene, like many others in these plays (some of which I believe were written by Shakespeare, and others interpolated by the players) is composed of the lowest and most trifling conceits, to be accounted for only by the gross taste of the age he lived in: *Populo ut placerent.* I wish I had authority to leave them out, but I have done all I could, set a mark of reprobation upon them, throughout this edition'. It is strange that our fastidious critic should fall so soon from praising to reprobating. The style of the familiar parts of this comedy is indeed made up of conceits—low they may be for what we know, but then they are not poor, but rich ones. The scene of Launce with his dog (not that in the second, but that in the fourth act) is a perfect treat in the way of farcical drollery and invention; nor do we think Speed's manner of proving his master to be in love deficient in wit or sense, though the style may be criticized as not simple enough for the modern taste.

*Valentine.* Why, how know you that I am in love?

*Speed.* Marry, by these special marks: first, you have learned, like Sir Protheus, to wreathe your arms like a malcontent, to relish a love-song like a robin-red-breast, to walk alone like one that had the pestilence, to sigh like a schoolboy that had lost his A B C, to weep like a young wench that had buried her grandam, to fast like one that takes diet, to watch like one that fears robbing, to speak puling like a beggar at Hallowmas. You were wont, when you laughed, to crow like a cock; when you walked, to walk like one of the lions; when you fasted, it was presently after dinner; when you looked sadly, it was for want of money; and now you are metamorphosed with a mistress, that when I look on you, I can hardly think you my master.

The tender scenes in this play, though not so highly wrought as in some others, have often much sweetness of sentiment and expression. There is something pretty and playful in the conversation of Julia with her maid, when she shows such a disposition to coquetry about receiving the letter from Proteus; and her behaviour afterwards and her disappointment, when she finds him faithless to his vows, remind us at a distance of Imogen's tender constancy. Her answer to Lucetta, who advises her against following her lover in disguise, is a beautiful piece of poetry.

*Lucetta.* I do not seek to quench your love's hot fire,
But qualify the fire's extremest rage,
Lest it should burn above the bounds of reason.
*Julia.* The more thou damm'st it up, the more it burns;
The current that with gentle murmur glides,
Thou know'st, being stopp'd, impatiently doth rage;
But when his fair course is not hindered,
He makes sweet music with th' enamell'd stones,
Giving a gentle kiss to every sedge
He overtaketh in his pilgrimage:

And so by many winding nooks he strays,
With willing sport, to the wild ocean.[1]
Then let me go, and hinder not my course ;
I'll be as patient as a gentle stream,
And make a pastime of each weary step,
Till the last step have brought me to my love ;
And there I'll rest, as after much turmoil,
A blessed soul doth in Elysium.

If Shakespeare indeed had written only this and other passages in the *Two Gentlemen of Verona*, he would *almost* have deserved Milton's praise of him—

And sweetest Shakespeare, Fancy's child,
Warbles his native wood-notes wild.

But as it is, he deserves rather more praise than this.

[1] The river wanders at its own sweet will.
WORDSWORTH.

# *The Merchant of Venice*

This is a play that in spite of the change of manners and of prejudices still holds undisputed possession of the stage. Shakespeare's malignant has outlived Mr. Cumberland's benevolent Jew. In proportion as Shylock has ceased to be a popular bugbear, 'bated with the rabble's curse', he becomes a half favourite with the philosophical part of the audience, who are disposed to think that Jewish revenge is at least as good as Christian injuries. Shylock is *a good hater*: 'a man no less sinned against than sinning'. If he carries his revenge too far, yet he has strong grounds for 'the lodged hate he bears Anthonio', which he explains with equal force of eloquence and reason. He seems the depositary of the vengeance of his race; and though the long habit of brooding over daily insults and injuries has crusted over his temper with inveterate misanthropy, and hardened him against the contempt of mankind, this adds but little to the triumphant pretensions of his enemies. There is a strong, quick, and deep sense of justice mixed up with the gall and bitterness of his resentment. The constant apprehension of being burnt alive, plundered, banished, reviled, and trampled on, might be supposed to sour the most forbearing nature, and to take something from that 'milk of human kindness', with which his persecutors contemplated his indignities. The desire of revenge is almost inseparable from the sense of wrong; and we can hardly help sympathizing with the proud spirit, hid beneath his 'Jewish gaberdine', stung to madness by repeated undeserved provocations, and labouring to throw off the load of obloquy and oppression heaped upon him and all his tribe by one desperate act of 'lawful' revenge, till the ferociousness of the means by which he is to execute his purpose, and the pertinacity with which he adheres to it, turn us against him; but even at last, when disappointed of the sanguinary revenge with which he had glutted his hopes, and exposed to beggary and contempt by the letter of the law on which he had insisted with so little remorse, we pity him, and think him hardly dealt with by his judges. In all his answers and retorts upon his adversaries, he has the best not only of the argument but of the question, reasoning on their own principles and practice. They are so far from allowing of any measure of equal dealing, of common justice or humanity between themselves and the Jew, that even when they come to ask a favour of him, and Shylock reminds them that 'on such a day they spit upon him, another spurned him, another called him dog, and for these courtesies request he'll lend them so much monies'—Anthonio, his old enemy, instead of any acknowledgement of the shrewdness and justice of his remonstrance, which would have been preposterous in a respectable Catholic merchant in those times, threatens him with a repetition of the same treatment—

> I am as like to call thee so again,
> To spit on thee again, to spurn thee too.

After this, the appeal to the Jew's mercy, as if there were any common principle of right and wrong between them, is the rankest hypocrisy, or the blindest prejudice; and the Jew's answer to one of Anthonio's friends, who asks him what his pound of forfeit flesh is good for, is irresistible:

> To bait fish withal; if it will feed nothing else, it will feed my revenge. He hath disgrac'd me, and hinder'd me of half a million,

laughed at my losses, mock'd at my gains, scorn'd my nation, thwarted my bargains, cool'd my friends, heated mine enemies; and what's his reason? I am a Jew. Hath not a Jew eyes; hath not a Jew hands, organs, dimensions, senses, affections, passions; fed with the same food, hurt with the same weapons, subject to the same diseases, healed by the same means, warmed and cooled by the same winter and summer that a Christian is? If you prick us, do we not bleed? If you tickle us, do we not laugh? If you poison us, do we not die? And if you wrong us, shall we not revenge? If we are like you in the rest, we will resemble you in that. If a Jew wrong a Christian, what is his humility? revenge. If a Christian wrong a Jew, what should his sufferance be by Christian example? why revenge. The villany you teach me I will execute, and it shall go hard but I will better the instruction.

The whole of the trial scene, both before and after the entrance of Portia, is a masterpiece of dramatic skill. The legal acuteness, the passionate declamations, the sound maxims of jurisprudence, the wit and irony interspersed in it, the fluctuations of hope and fear in the different persons, and the completeness and suddenness of the catastrophe, cannot be surpassed. Shylock, who is his own counsel, defends himself well, and is triumphant on all the general topics that are urged against him, and only fails through a legal flaw. Take the following as an instance:

*Shylock.* What judgment shall I dread, doing no wrong?
You have among you many a purchas'd slave,
Which, like your asses, and your dogs, and mules,
You use in abject and in slavish part,
Because you bought them;—shall I say to you,
Let them be free, marry them to your heirs?
Why sweat they under burdens? let their beds
Be made as soft as yours, and let their palates
Be season'd with such viands? you will answer,
The slaves are ours:—so do I answer you:
The pound of flesh, which I demand of him,
Is dearly bought, is mine, and I will have it:
If you deny me, fie upon your law!
There is no force in the decrees of Venice:
I stand for judgment: answer; shall I have it?

The keenness of his revenge awakes all his faculties; and he beats back all opposition to his purpose, whether grave or gay, whether of wit or argument, with an equal degree of earnestness and self-possession. His character is displayed as distinctly in other less prominent parts of the play, and we may collect from a few sentences the history of his life—his descent and origin, his thrift and domestic economy, his affection for his daughter, whom he loves next to his wealth, his courtship and his first present to Leah, his wife! 'I would not have parted with it' (the ring which he first gave her) 'for a wilderness of monkeys!' What a fine Hebraism is implied in this expression!

Portia is not a very great favourite with us, neither are we in love with her maid, Nerissa. Portia has a certain degree of affectation and pedantry about her, which is very unusual in Shakespeare's women, but which perhaps was a proper qualification for the office of a 'civil doctor', which she undertakes and executes so successfully. The speech about mercy is very well; but there are a thousand finer ones in Shakespeare. We do not admire the scene of the caskets; and object entirely to the Black Prince, Morocchius. We should like Jessica better if she had not deceived and robbed her father, and Lorenzo, if he had not married a Jewess, though he thinks he has a right to wrong a Jew. The dialogue between this newly-married couple by moonlight, beginning 'On such a night', &c., is a collection of classical elegancies. Launcelot, the Jew's man, is an honest fellow. The dilemma in which he describes himself placed between his 'conscience and the fiend', the one of which advises him to run away from his master's service and the other to stay in it, is exquisitely humorous.

Gratiano is a very admirable subordinate character. He is the jester of the piece; yet one speech of his, in his own defence, contains a whole volume of wisdom.

*Anthonio.* I hold the world but as the world, Gratiano,
A stage, where every one must play his part;
And mine a sad one.
*Gratiano.* Let me play the fool:
With mirth and laughter let old wrinkles come;
And let my liver rather heat with wine,
Than my heart cool with mortifying groans.
Why should a man, whose blood is warm within,
Sit like his grandsire cut in alabaster?
Sleep when he wakes? and creep into the jaundice
By being peevish? I tell thee what, Anthonio—
I love thee, and it is my love that speaks;—
There are a sort of men, whose visages
Do cream and mantle like a standing pond:
And do a wilful stillness entertain,
With purpose to be drest in an opinion
Of wisdom, gravity, profound conceit;
As who should say, *I am Sir Oracle,*
*And when I ope my lips, let no dog bark!*
O, my Anthonio, I do know of these,
That therefore only are reputed wise,
For saying nothing; who, I am very sure,
If they should speak, would almost damn those ears,
Which hearing them, would call their brothers fools.
I'll tell thee more of this another time:
But fish not, with this melancholy bait,
For this fool's gudgeon, this opinion.

Gratiano's speech on the philosophy of love, and the effect of habit in taking off the force of passion, is as full of spirit and good sense. The graceful winding up of this play in the fifth act, after the tragic business is dispatched, is one of the happiest instances of Shakespeare's knowledge of the principles of the drama. We do not mean the pretended quarrel between Portia and Nerissa and their husbands about the rings, which is amusing enough, but the conversation just before and after the return of Portia to her own house, beginning 'How sweet the moonlight sleeps upon this bank', and ending 'Peace! how the moon sleeps with Endymion, and would not be awaked'. There is a number of beautiful thoughts crowded into that short space, and linked together by the most natural transitions.

When we first went to see Mr. Kean in Shylock we expected to see, what we had been used to see, a decrepit old man, bent with age and ugly with mental deformity, grinning with deadly malice, with the venom of his heart congealed in the expression of his countenance, sullen, morose, gloomy, inflexible, brooding over one idea, that of his hatred, and fixed on one unalterable purpose, that of his revenge. We were disappointed, because we had taken our idea from other actors, not from the play. There is no proof there that Shylock is old, but a single line, 'Bassanio and *old* Shylock, both stand forth',—which does not imply that he is infirm with age—and the circumstance that he has a daughter marriageable, which does not imply that he is old at all. It would be too much to say that his body should be made crooked and deformed to answer to his mind, which is bowed down and warped with prejudices and passion. That he has but one idea, is not true; he has more ideas than any other person in the piece: and if he is intense and inveterate in the pursuit of his purpose, he shows the utmost elasticity, vigour, and presence of mind, in the means of attaining it. But so rooted was our habitual impression of the part from seeing it caricatured in the representation, that it was only from a careful perusal of the play itself that we saw our error. The stage is not in general the best place to study out author's characters in. It is too often filled with traditional common-place conceptions of the part, handed down from sire to son, and suited to the taste of *the great vulgar and the small.*—''Tis an unweeded garden: things rank and gross do merely gender in it!' If a man of genius comes once in an age to clear away the rubbish, to make it fruitful and wholesome, they cry, ''Tis a bad school: it may be like nature, it may be like Shakespeare, but it is not like us'. Admirable critics!

# *The Winter's Tale*

We wonder that Mr. Pope should have entertained doubts of the genuineness of this play. He was, we suppose, shocked (as a certain critic suggests) at the Chorus, Time, leaping over sixteen years with his crutch between the third and fourth act, and at Antigonus's landing with the infant Perdita on the sea-coast of Bohemia. These slips or blemishes, however, do not prove it not to be Shakespeare's; for he was as likely to fall into them as anybody; but we do not know anybody but himself who could produce the beauties. The *stuff* of which the tragic passion is composed, the romantic sweetness, the comic humour, are evidently his. Even the crabbed and tortuous style of the speeches of Leontes, reasoning on his own jealousy, beset with doubts and fears, and entangled more and more in the thorny labyrinth, bears every mark of Shakespeare's peculiar manner of conveying the painful struggle of different thoughts and feelings, labouring for utterance, and almost strangled in the birth. For instance:

> Ha' not you seen, Camillo?
> (But that's past doubt; you have, or your eye-glass
> Is thicker than a cuckold's horn) or heard,
> (For to a vision so apparent, rumour
> Cannot be mute) or thought (for cogitation
> Besides not within man that does not think)
> My wife is slippery? If thou wilt, confess,
> Or else be impudently negative,
> To have nor eyes, nor ears, nor thought.—

Here Leontes is confounded with his passion, and does not know which way to turn himself, to give words to the anguish, rage, and apprehension which tug at his breast. It is only as he is worked up into a clearer conviction of his wrongs by insisting on the grounds of his unjust suspicions to Camillo, who irritates him by his opposition, that he bursts out into the following vehement strain of bitter indignation: yet even here his passion staggers, and is as it were oppressed with its own intensity.

> Is whispering nothing?
> Is leaning cheek to cheek? is meeting noses?
> Kissing with inside lip? stopping the career
> Of laughter with a sigh? (a note infallible
> Of breaking honesty!) horsing foot on foot?
> Skulking in corners? wishing clocks more swift?
> Hours, minutes? the noon, midnight? and all eyes
> Blind with the pin and web, but theirs; theirs only,
> That would, unseen, be wicked? is this nothing?
> Why then the world, and all that's in't, is nothing,
> The covering sky is nothing, Bohemia's nothing,
> My wife is nothing!

The character of Hermione is as much distinguished by its saint-like resignation and patient forbearance, as that of Paulina is by her zealous and spirited remonstrances against the injustice done to the queen, and by her devoted attachment to her misfortunes. Hermione's restoration to her husband and her child, after her long separation from them, is as affecting in itself as it is striking in the representation. Camillo, and the old shepherd and his son, are subordinate but not uninteresting instruments in the development of the plot, and though last, not least, comes Autolycus, a very pleasant thriving rogue; and (what is the best feather in the cap of all knavery) he escapes with impunity in the end.

*The Winter's Tale* is one of the best-acting of our

author's plays. We remember seeing it with great pleasure many years ago. It was on the night that King took leave of the stage, when he and Mrs. Jordan played together in the after-piece of *The Wedding-day*. Nothing could go off with more éclat, with more spirit, and grandeur of effect. Mrs. Siddons played Hermione, and in the last scene acted the painted statue to the life—with true monumental dignity and noble passion; Mr. Kemble, in Leontes, worked himself up into a very fine classical frenzy; and Bannister, as Autolycus, roared as loud for pity as a sturdy beggar could do who felt none of the pain he counterfeited, and was sound of wind and limb. We shall never see these parts so acted again; or if we did, it would be in vain. Actors grow old, or no longer surprise us by their novelty. But true poetry, like nature, is always young; and we still read the courtship of Florizel and Perdita, as we welcome the return of spring, with the same feelings as ever.

*Florizel.* Thou dearest Perdita,
With these fourc'd thoughts, I prithee, darken not
The mirth o' the feast: or, I'll be thine, my fair,
Or not my father's: for I cannot be
Mine own, nor anything to any, if
I be not thine. To this I am most constant,
Tho' destiny say, No. Be merry, gentle;
Strangle such thoughts as these, with anything
That you behold the while. Your guests are coming:
Lift up your countenance; as it were the day
Of celebration of that nuptial which
We two have sworn shall come.
*Perdita.* O lady Fortune,
Stand you auspicious!

*Enter Shepherd, Clown,* MOPSA, DORCAS, *Servants; with* POLIXENES, *and* CAMILLO, *disguised.*

*Florizel.* See, your guests approach.
Address yourself to entertain them sprightly,
And let's be red with mirth.
*Shepherd.* Fie, daughter! when my old wife liv'd upon
This day, she was both pantler, butler, cook;

Both dame and servant: welcom'd all, serv'd all:
Would sing her song, and dance her turn: now here
At upper end o' the table, now i' the middle:
On his shoulder, and his: her face o' fire
With labour; and the thing she took to quench it
She would to each one sip. You are retir'd,
As if you were a feasted one, and not
The hostess of the meeting. Pray you, bid
These unknown friends to us welcome; for it is
A way to make us better friends, more known.
Come, quench your blushes; and present yourself
That which you are, mistress o' the feast. Come on,
And bid us welcome to your sheep-shearing,
As your good flock shall prosper.

*Perdita.* Sir, welcome! [*To Polixenes and Camillo.*
It is my father's will I should take on me
The hostess-ship o' the day; you're welcome, sir!
Give me those flowers there, Dorcas.—Reverend sirs,
For you there's rosemary and rue; these keep
Seeming, and savour, all the winter long:
Grace and remembrance be unto you both
And welcome to our shearing!

*Polixenes.* Shepherdess,
(A fair one are you) well you fit our ages
With flowers of winter.

*Perdita.* Sir, the year growing ancient,
Not yet on summer's death, nor on the birth
Of trembling winter, the fairest flowers o' the season
Are our carnations, and streak'd gilly-flowers,
Which some call nature's bastards: of that kind
Our rustic garden's barren; and I care not
To get slips of them.

*Polixenes.* Wherefore, gentle maiden,
Do you neglect them?

*Perdita.* For I have heard it said
There is an art which in their piedness shares
With great creating nature.

*Polixenes.* Say, there be:
Yet nature is made better by no mean,
But nature makes that mean: so, o'er that art
Which, you say, adds to nature, is an art
That nature makes. You see, sweet maid, we marry
A gentler scion to the wildest stock;
And make conceive a bark of baser kind
By bud of nobler race. This is an art
Which does mend nature, change it rather: but
The art itself is nature.

*Perdita.* So it is.[1]
*Polixenes.* Then make your garden rich in gilly-flowers,
And do not call them bastards.
*Perdita.* I'll not put
The dibble in earth, to set one slip of them ; [1]
No more than, were I painted, I would wish
This youth should say, 'twere well ; and only therefore
Desire to breed by me.—Here's flowers for you ;
Hot lavender, mints, savory, marjoram ;
The marigold, that goes to bed with the sun,
And with him rises, weeping : these are flowers
Of middle summer, and, I think, they are given
To men of middle age. You are very welcome.
*Camillo.* I should leave grazing, were I of your flock,
And only live by gazing.
*Perdita.* Out, alas !
You'd be so lean, that blasts of January
Would blow you through and through. Now my fairest friends.
I would I had some flowers o' the spring that might
Become your time of day ; and yours, and yours,
That wear upon your virgin branches yet
Your maidenheads growing : O Proserpina !
For the flowers now that frighted tho, let'st fall
From Dis's waggon ! daffodils,
That come before the swallow dares and take
The winds of March with beauty : violets dim,
But sweeter than the lids of Juno's eyes,
Or Cytherea's breath ; pale primroses,
That die unmarried, ere they can behold
Bright Phoebus in his strength (a malady
Most incident to maids) ; bold oxlips, and
The crown-imperial ; lilies of all kinds,
The fleur-de-lis being one ! O, these I lack
To make you garlands of ; and my sweet friend
To strow him o'er and o'er.
*Florizel.* What, like a corse ?
*Perdita.* No, like a bank, for love to lie and play on ;
Not like a corse ; or if—not to be buried,
But quick, and in mine arms. Come, take your flowers ;
Methinks, I play as I have seen them do
In Whitsun pastorals : sure this robe of mine
Does change my disposition.
*Florizel.* What you do,

[1]The lady, we here see, gives up the argument, but keeps her mind.

Still betters what is done. When you speak, sweet,
I'd have you do it ever: when you sing,
I'd have you buy and sell so; so give alms;
Pray so; and for the ordering your affairs,
To sing them too. When you do dance, I wish you
A wave o' the sea, that you might ever do
Nothing but that: move still, still so,
And own no other function. Each your doing,
So singular in each particular,
Crowns what you're doing in the present deeds,
That all your acts are queens.

*Perdita.* O Doricles,
Your praises are too large; but that your youth
And the true blood, which peeps forth fairly through it,
Do plainly give you out an unstained shepherd;
With wisdom I might fear, my Doricles,
You woo'd me the false way.

*Florizel.* I think you have
As little skill to fear, as I have purpose
To put you to 't. But come, our dance, I pray.
Your hand, my Perdita: so turtles pair,
That never mean to part.

*Perdita.* I'll swear for 'em.

*Polixenes.* This is the prettiest low-born lass that ever
Ran on the green-sward; nothing she does, or seems,
But smacks of something greater than herself,
Too noble for this place.

*Camillo.* He tells her something
That makes her blood look out: good sooth she is
The queen of curds and cream.

This delicious scene is interrupted by the father of the prince discovering himself to Florizel, and haughtily breaking off the intended match between his son and Perdita. When Polixenes goes out, Perdita says,

Even here undone!
I was not much afraid; for once or twice
I was about to speak; and tell him plainly
The self-same sun that shines upon his court,
Hides not his visage from our cottage, but
Looks on 't alike. Wilt please you, sir, be gone?
[*To Florizel.*
I told you what would come of this. Beseech you,
Of your own state take care: this dream of mine,

Being now awake, I'll queen it no inch further,
But milk my ewes and weep.

As Perdita, the supposed shepherdess, turns out to be the daughter of Hermoine, and a princess in disguise, both feelings of the pride of birth and the claims of nature are satisfied by the fortunate event of the story, and the fine romance of poetry is reconciled to the strictest court-etiquette.

# *All's Well that Ends Well*

*All's Well that Ends Well* is one of the most pleasing of our author's comedies. The interest is, however, more of a serious than of a comic nature. The character of Helen is one of great sweetness and delicacy. She is placed in circumstances of the most critical kind, and has to court her husband both as a virgin and a wife: yet the most scrupulous nicety of female modesty is not once violated. There is not one thought or action that ought to bring a blush into her cheeks, or that for a moment lessens her in our esteem. Perhaps the romantic attachment of a beautiful and virtuous girl to one placed above her hopes by the circumstances of birth and fortune, was never so exquisitely expressed as in the reflections which she utters when young Roussillon leaves his mother's house, under whose protection she has been brought up with him, to repair to the French king's court.

*Helena.* Oh, were that all—I think not on my father,
And these great tears grace his remembrance more
Than those I shed for him. What was he like?
I have forgot him. My imagination
Carries no favour in it, but Bertram's.
I am undone, there is no living, none,
If Bertram be away. It were all one
That I should love a bright particular star,
And think to wed it; he is so above me:
In his bright radiance and collateral light
Must I be comforted, not in his sphere.
Th' ambition in my love thus plagues itself;
The hind that would be mated by the lion,
Must die for love. 'Twas pretty, tho' a plague,
To see him every hour, to sit and draw
His arched brows, his hawking eye, his curls

In our heart's table: heart too capable
Of every line and trick of his sweet favour.
But now he's gone, and my idolatrous fancy
Must sanctify his relics.

The interest excited by this beautiful picture of a fond and innocent heart is kept up afterwards by her resolution to follow him to France, the success of her experiment in restoring the king's health, her demanding Bertram in marriage as a recompense, his leaving her in disdain, her interview with him afterwards disguised as Diana, a young lady whom he importunes with his secret addresses, and their final reconciliation when the consequences of her stratagem and the proofs of her love are fully made known. The persevering gratitude of the French king to his benefactress, who cures him of a languishing distemper by a prescription hereditary in her family, the indulgent kindness of the Countess, whose pride of birth yields, almost without a struggle, to her affection for Helen, the honesty and uprightness of the good old lord Lafeu, make very interesting parts of the picture. The wilful stubbornness and youthful petulance of Bertram are also very admirably described. The comic part of the play turns on the folly, boasting, and cowardice of Parolles, a parasite and hanger-on of Bertram's, the detection of whose false pretensions to bravery and honour forms a very amusing episode. He is first found out by the old lord Lafeu, who says, 'The soul of this man is in his clothes;' and it is proved afterwards that his heart is in his tongue, and that both are false and hollow. The adventure of 'the bringing off of his drum' has become proverbial as a satire on all ridiculous and blustering undertakings which the person never means to perform: nor can anything be more severe than what one of the bystanders remarks upon what Parolles says of himself, 'Is it possible he should know what he is, and be that he is ?' Yet Parolles himself gives the best solution of the difficulty afterwards when he is thankful to escape with his life and the loss of character ; for, so that he can live on, he is by no means squeamish about the loss of pretensions, to which he had sense enough to know he had no real claims, and which he had assumed only as a means to live.

> *Parolles.* Yet I am thankful : if my heart were great,
> 'Twould burst at this. Captain I'll be no more,
> But I will eat and drink, and sleep as soft
> As captain shall. Simply the thing I am
> Shall make me live : who knows himself a braggart,
> Let him fear this ; for it shall come to pass,
> That every braggart shall be found an ass.
> Rust sword, cool blushes, and Parolles live
> Safest in shame ; being fool'd, by fool'ry thrive ;
> There's place and means for every man alive.
> I'll after them.

The story of *All's Well that Ends Well*, and of several others of Shakespeare's plays, is taken from Boccaccio. The poet has dramatized the original novel with great skill and comic spirit, and has preserved all the beauty of character and sentiment without *improving upon* it, which was impossible. There is indeed in Boccaccio's serious pieces a truth, a pathos, and an exquisite refinement of sentiment, which is hardly to be met with in any other prose writer whatever. Justice has not been done him by the world. He has in general passed for a mere narrator of lascivious tales or idle jests. This character probably originated in his obnoxious attacks on the monks, and has been kept up by the grossness of mankind, who revenged their own want of refinement on Boccaccio, and only saw in his writings what suited the coarseness of their own tastes. But the truth is, that he has carried sentiment of every kind to its very highest purity and perfection. By sentiment we would here understand the habitual workings of some one powerful feeling, where the heart reposes almost entirely upon itself, without the violent excitement of opposing duties or untoward circumstances. In this way, nothing ever came up to the story of Frederigo Alberigi and his Falcon. The perseverance in attachment, the spirit of gallantry and generosity displayed in it, has no parallel in the history of heroical sacrifices. The feeling is so unconscious too, and involuntary, is brought out in such small, unlooked-for, and unostentatious circumstances, as to show it to have been woven into the very nature and soul of the author. The story of Isabella is scarcely less fine and is more affecting in the circumstances and in the catastrophe. Dryden has done justice to the impassioned eloquence of the Tancred and Sigismunda; but has not given an adequate idea of the wild preternatural interest of the story of Honoria. Cimon and Iphigene is by no means one of the best, notwithstanding the popularity of the subject. The proof of unalterable affection given in the story of Jeronymo, and the simple touches of nature and picturesque beauty in the story of the two holiday lovers, who were poisoned by tasting of a leaf in the garden of Florence, are perfect masterpieces. The epithet of Divine was well bestowed on this great painter of the human heart. The intervention implied in his different tales is immense: but we are not to infer that it is all his own. He probably availed himself of all the common traditions which were floating in his time, and which he was the first to appropriate. Homer appears the most original of all authors—probably for no other reason than that we can trace the plagiarism no further. Boccaccio has furnished subjects to numberless writers since his time, both dramatic and narrative. The story of Griselda is borrowed from his *Decameron* by Chaucer; as is the Knight's Tale (Palamon and Arcite) from his poem of the Theseid.

## *Love's Labour's Lost*

If we were to part with any of the author's comedies, it should be this. Yet we should be loth to part with Don Adriano de Armado, that mighty potentate of nonsense, or his page, that handful of wit; with Nathaniel the curate, or Holofernes the schoolmaster, and their dispute after dinner on 'the golden cadences of poesy'; with Costard the clown, or Dull the constable. Biron is too accomplished a character to be lost to the world, and yet he could not appear without his fellow courtiers and the king: and if we were to leave out the ladies, the gentlemen would have no mistresses. So that we believe we may let the whole play stand as it is, and we shall hardly venture to 'set a mark of reprobation on it'. Still we have some objections to the style, which we think savours more of the pedantic spirit of Shakespeare's time than of his own genius; more of controversial divinity, and the logic of Peter Lombard, than of the inspiration of the Muse. It transports us quite as much to the manners of the court, and the quirks of courts of law, as to the scenes of nature or the fairyland of his own imagination. Shakespeare has set himself to imitate the tone of polite conversation then prevailing among the fair, the witty, and the learned, and he has imitated it but too faithfully. It is as if the hand of Titian had been employed to give grace to the curls of a full-bottomed periwig, or Raphael had attempted to give expression to the tapestry figures in the House of Lords. Shakespeare has put an excellent description of this fashionable jargon into the mouth of the critical Holofernes 'as too picked, too spruce, too affected too odd, as it were, too peregrinate, as I may call it'; and nothing can be more marked than the difference when he breaks loose from the trammels he had imposed on himself, 'as light as bird from brake', and speaks in his own person. We think, for instance, that in the following soliloquy the poet has fairly got the start of Queen Elizabeth and her maids of honour:

*Biron.* O! and I forsooth in love,
I that have been love's whip;
A very beadle to an amorous sigh:
A critic; nay, a night-watch constable,
A domineering pedant o'er the boy,
Than whom no mortal more magnificent.
This whimpled, whining, purblind, wayward boy,
This signior Junio, giant dwarf, Dan Cupid,
Regent of love-rimes, lord of folded arms,
Th' anointed sovereign of sighs and groans:
Liege of all loiterers and malcontents,
Dread prince of plackets, king of codpieces,
Sole imperator, and great general
Of trotting parators (O my little heart!)
And I to be a corporal of his field,
And wear his colours like a tumbler's hoop!
What? I love! I sue! I seek a wife!
A woman, that is like a German clock,
Still a repairing; ever out of frame;
And never going aright, being a watch,
And being watch'd, that it may still go right?
Nay, to be perjur'd, which is worst of all:
And among three to love the worst of all,
A whitely wanton with a velvet brow,
With two pitch balls stuck in her face for eyes;
Ay, and by heav'n, one that will do the deed,
Though Argus were her eunuch and her guard;
And I to sigh for her! to watch for her!
To pray for her! Go to; it is a plague
That Cupid will impose for my neglect
Of his almighty dreadful little might.
Well, I will love, write, sigh, pray, sue, and groan:
Some men must love my lady, and some Joan.

The character of Biron drawn by Rosaline and

that which Biron gives of Boyet are equally happy. The observations on the use and abuse of study, and on the power of beauty to quicken the understanding as well as the senses, are excellent. The scene which has the greatest dramatic effect is that in which Biron, the king, Longaville, and Dumain, successively detect each other and are detected in their breach of their vow and in their profession of attachment to their several mistresses, in which they suppose themselves to be overheard by no one. The reconciliation between these lovers and their sweethearts is also very good, and the penance which Rosaline imposes on Biron, before he can expect to gain her consent to marry him, full of propriety and beauty.

*Rosaline.* Oft have I heard of you, my lord Biron,
Before I saw you : and the world's large tongue
Proclaims you for a man replete with mocks ;
Full of comparisons, and wounding flouts ;
Which you on all estates will execute,
That lie within the mercy of your wit.
To weed this wormwood from your faithful brain ;
And therewithal to win me, if you please,
(Without the which I am not to be won)
You shall this twelvemonth term from day to day
Visit the speechless sick, and still converse
With groaning wretches ; and your task shall be,
With all the fierce endeavour of your wit,
T' enforce the pained impotent to smile.
*Biron.* To move wild laughter in the throat of death ?
It cannot be : it is impossible :
Mirth cannot move a soul in agony.
*Rosaline.* Why, that's the way to choke a gibing spirit,
Whose influence is begot of that loose grace,
Which shallow laughing hearers give to fools :
A jest's prosperity lies in the ear
Of him that hears it ; never in the tongue
Of him that makes it : then, if sickly ears,
Deaf'd with the clamours of their own dear groans,
Will hear your idle scorns, continue then,
And I will have you, and that fault withal ;
But, if they will not, throw away that spirit,
And I shall find you empty of that fault,

Right joyful of your reformation.
*Biron.* A twelvemonth ? Well, befall what will befall,
I'll jest a twelvemonth in an hospital.

The famous cuckoo-song closes the play ; but we shall add no more criticisms : 'the words of Mercury are harsh after the songs of Apollo '.

## *Much Ado About Nothing*

This admirable comedy used to be frequently acted till of late years. Mr. Garrick's Benedick was one of his most celebrated characters; and Mrs. Jordan, we have understood, played Beatrice very delightfully. The serious part is still the most prominent here, as in other instances that we have noticed. Hero is the principal figure in the piece, and leaves an indelible impression on the mind by her beauty, her tenderness, and the hard trial of her love. The passage in which Claudio first makes a confession of his affection towards her conveys as pleasing an image of the entrance of love into a youthful bosom as can well be imagined.

Oh, my lord,
When you went onward with this ended action,
I look'd upon her with a soldier's eye,
That lik'd, but had a rougher task in hand
Than to drive liking to the name of love;
But now I am return'd, and that war-thoughts
Have left their places vacant; in their rooms
Come thronging soft and delicate desires,
All prompting me how fair young Hero is,
Saying, I lik'd her ere I went to wars.

In the scene at the altar, when Claudio, urged on by the villain Don John, brings the charge of incontinence against her, and as it were divorces her in the very marriage-ceremony, her appeals to her own conscious innocence and honour are made with the most affecting simplicity.

*Claudio.* No, Leonato,
I never tempted her with word too large,
But, as a brother to his sister, show'd

Bashful sincerity, and comely love.
*Hero.* And seem'd I ever otherwise to you?
*Claudio.* Out on thy seeming, I will write against it:
You seem to me as Dian in her orb,
As chaste as is the bud ere it be blown;
But you are more intemperate in your blood
Than Venus, or those pamper'd animals
That rage in savage sensuality.
*Hero.* Is my lord well, that he doth speak so wide?
*Leonato.* Are these things spoken, or do I but dream?
*John.* Sir, they are spoken, and these things are true.
*Benedick.* This looks not like a nuptial.
*Hero.* True? O God!

The justification of Hero in the end, and her restoration to the confidence and arms of her lover, is brought about by one of those temporary consignments to the grave of which Shakespeare seems to have been fond. He has perhaps explained the theory of this predilection in the following lines:

*Friar.* She dying, as it must be so maintain'd,
Upon the instant that she was accus'd,
Shall be lamented, pity'd, and excus'd,
Of every hearer: for it so falls out,
That what we have we prize not to the worth,
While we enjoy it; but being lack'd and lost,
Why then we rack the value; then we find
The virtue, that possession would not show us
Whilst it was ours.—So will it fare with Claudio;
When he shall hear she dy'd upon his words,
The idea of her love shall sweetly creep
Into his study of imagination;
And every lovely organ of her life
Shall come apparel'd in more precious habit,
More moving, delicate, and full of life,
Into the eye and prospect of his soul,
Than when she liv'd indeed.

The principal comic characters in *Much Ado About Nothing,* Benedick and Beatrice, are both essences in their kind. His character as a woman-hater is admirably supported, and his conversion to matrimony is no less happily effected by the pretended story of Beatrice's love for him. It is hard to say which of the two scenes is the best, that of the trick which is thus practised on Benedick, or that in which Beatrice is prevailed on to take pity on him by overhearing her cousin and her maid declare (which they do on purpose) that he is dying of love for her. There is something delightfully picturesque in the manner in which Beatrice is described as coming to hear the plot which is contrived against herself:

> For look where Beatrice, like a lapwing, runs
> Close by the ground, to hear our conference.

In consequence of what she hears (not a word of which is true) she exclaims when these good-natured informants are gone:

> What fire is in mine ears? Can this be true?
>   Stand I condemn'd for pride and scorn so much?
> Contempt, farewell! and maiden pride adieu!
>   No glory lives behind the back of such.
> And, Benedick, love on, I will requite thee;
>   Taming my wild heart to thy loving hand;
> If thou dost love, my kindness shall incite thee
>   To bind our loves up in an holy band:
> For others say thou dost deserve; and I
> Believe it better than reportingly.

And Benedick, on his part, is equally sincere in his repentance with equal reason, after he has heard the grey-beard, Leonato, and his friend, 'Monsieur Love', discourse of the desperate state of his supposed inamorata.

> This can be no trick; the conference was sadly borne.—They have the truth of this from Hero. They seem to pity the lady; it seems her affections have the full bent. Love me! why, it must be requited. I hear how I am censur'd: they say, I will bear myself proudly, if I perceive the love come from her; they say too, that she will rather die than give any sign of affection.—I did never think to marry: I must not seem proud:—happy are they that hear their detractions, and can put them to mending. They say, the lady is fair; 'tis a truth, I can bear them witness: and virtuous;—'tis so, I cannot reprove it: and wise—but for

loving me:—by my troth it is no addition to her wit;—nor no great argument of her folly, for I will be horribly in love with her.—I may chance to have some odd quirks and remnants of wit broken on me, because I have rail'd so long against marriage: but doth not the appetite alter? A man loves the meat in his youth, that he cannot endure in his age.—Shall quips, and sentences, and these paper bullets of the brain, awe a man from the career of his humour? No: the world must be peopled. When I said, I would die a bachelor, I did not think I should live till I were marry'd.—Here comes Beatrice: by this day, she's a fair lady: I do spy some marks of love in her.

The beauty of all this arises from the characters of the persons so entrapped. Benedick is a professed and staunch enemy to marriage, and gives very plausible reasons for the faith that is in him. And as to Beatrice, she persecutes him all day with her jests (so that he could hardly think of being troubled with them at night), she not only turns him but all other things into jest, and is proof against everything serious.

*Hero.* Disdain and scorn ride sparkling in her eyes,
Misprising what they look on; and her wit
Values itself so highly, that to her
All matter else seems weak: she cannot love,
Nor take no shape nor project of affection,
She is so self-endeared.
*Ursula.* Sure, I think so;
And therefore, certainly it were not good
She knew his love, lest she make sport at it.
*Hero.* Why, you speak truth: I never yet saw man,
How wise, how noble, young, how rarely featur'd,
But she would spell him backward: if fair-fac'd,
She'd swear the gentleman should be her sister;
If black, why, nature, drawing of an antick,
Made a foul blot: if tall, a lance ill-headed;
If low, an agate very vilely cut:
If speaking, why, a vane blown with all winds;
If silent, why, a block moved with none.
So turns she every man the wrong side out;
And never gives to truth and virtue that
Which simpleness and merit purchaseth.

These were happy materials for Shakespeare to work on, and he has made a happy use of them.

Perhaps that middle point of comedy was never more nicely hit in which the ludicrous blends with the tender, and our follies, turning round against themselves in support of our affections, retain nothing but their humanity.

Dogberry and Verges in this play are inimitable specimens of quaint blundering and misprisions of meaning ; and are a standing record of that formal gravity of pretension and total want of common understanding, which Shakespeare no doubt copied from real life, and which in the course of two hundred years appear to have ascended from the lowest to the highest offices in the state.

# *As You Like It*

Shakespeare has here converted the forest of Arden into another Arcadia, where they 'fleet the time carelessly, as they did in the golden world'. It is the most ideal of any of this author's plays. It is a pastoral drama in which the interest arises more out of the sentiments and characters than out of the actions or situations. It is not what is done, but what is said, that claims our attention. Nursed in solitude, 'under the shade of melancholy boughs', the imagination grows soft and delicate, and the wit run riot in idleness, like a spoiled child that is never sent to school. Caprice and fancy reign and revel here, and stern necessity is banished to the court. The mild sentiments of humanity are strengthened with thought and leisure; the echo of the cares and noise of the world strikes upon the ear of those 'who have felt them knowingly', softened by time and distance. 'They hear the tumult, and are still'. The very air of the place seems to breathe a spirit of philosophical poetry; to stir the thoughts, to touch the heart with pity, as the drowsy forest rustles to the sighing gale. Never was there such beautiful moralizing, equally free from pedantry or petulance.

> And this their life, exempt from public haunts,
> Finds tongues in trees, books in the running brooks,
> Sermons in stones, and good in everything.

Jaques is the only purely contemplative character in Shakespeare. He thinks, and does nothing. His whole occupation is to amuse his mind, and he is totally regardless of his body and his fortunes.

He is the prince of philosophical idlers ; his only passion is thought ; he sets no value upon anything but as it serves as food for reflection. He can 'suck melancholy out of a song, as a weasel sucks eggs' ; the motley fool, 'who morals on the time', is the greatest prize he meets with in the forest. He resents Orlando's passion for Rosalind as some disparagement of his own passion for abstract truth ; and leaves the Duke, as soon as he is restored to his sovereignty, to seek his brother out, who has quitted it, and turned hermit.

——Out of these convertites
There is much matter to be heard and learnt.

Within the sequestered and romantic glades of the forest of Arden, they find leisure to be good and wise, or to play the fool and fall in love. Rosalind's character is made up of sportive gaiety and natural tenderness : her tongue runs the faster to conceal the pressure at her heart. She talks herself out of breath, only to get deeper in love. The coquetry with which she plays with her lover in the double character which she has to support is managed with the nicest address. How full of voluble, laughing grace is all her conversation with Orlando :

——In heedless mazes running
With wanton haste and giddy cunning.

How full of real fondness and pretended cruelty is her answer to him when he promises to love her 'For ever and a day' !

Say a day without the ever : no, no, Orlando, men are April when they woo, December when they wed : maids are May when they are maids, but the sky changes when they are wives : I will be more jealous of thee than a Barbary cock-pigeon over his hen ; more clamorous than a parrot against rain ; more new-fangled than an ape ; more giddy in my desires than a monkey ; I will weep for nothing, like Diana in the fountain, and I will do that when you are disposed to be merry ; I will laugh like a hyen, and that when you are inclined to sleep.

*Orlando.* But will my Rosalind do so?
*Rosalind.* By my life she will do as I do.

The silent and retired character of Celia is a necessary relief to the provoking loquacity of Rosalind, nor can anything be better conceived or more beautifully described than the mutual affection between the two cousins:

——We still have slept together,
Rose at an instant, learn'd, play'd, eat together,
And wheresoe'er we went, like Juno's swans,
Still we went coupled and inseparable.

The unrequited love of Silvius for Phebe shows the perversity of this passion in the commonest scenes of life, and the rubs and stops which nature throws in its way, where fortune has placed none. Touchstone is not in love, but he will have a mistress as a subject for the exercise of his grotesque humour, and to show his contempt for the passion, by his indifference about the person. He is a rare fellow. He is a mixture of the ancient cynic philosopher with the modern buffoon, and turns folly into wit, and wit into folly, just as the fit takes him. His courtship of Audrey not only throws a degree of ridicule on the state of wedlock itself, but he is equally an enemy to the prejudices of opinion in other respects. The lofty tone of enthusiasm, which the Duke and his companions in exile spread over the stillness and solitude of a country life, receives a pleasant shock from Touchstone's sceptical determination of the question.

*Corin.* And how like you this shepherd's life, Mr. Touchstone?
*Clown.* Truly, shepherd, in respect of itself, it is a good life; but in respect that it is a shepherd's life, it is naught. In respect that it is solitary, I like it very well; but in respect that it is private, it is a very vile life. Now in respect it is in the fields, it pleaseth me well; but in respect it is not in the court, it is tedious. As it is a spare life, look you, it fits my humour; but as there is no more plenty in it, it goes much against my stomach.

Zimmerman's celebrated work on *Solitude* discovers only *half* the sense of this passage.

There is hardly any of Shakespeare's plays that contains a greater number of passages that have been quoted in books of extracts, or a greater number of phrases that have become in a manner proverbial. If we were to give all the striking passages, we should give half the play. We will only recall a few of the most delightful to the reader's recollection. Such are the meeting between Orlando and Adam, the exquisite appeal of Orlando to the humanity of the Duke and his company to supply him with food for the old man, and their answer, the Duke's description of a country life, and the account of Jaques moralizing on the wounded deer, his meeting with Touchstone in the forest, his apology for his own melancholy and his satirical vein, and the well-known speech on the stages of human life, the old song of 'Blow, blow, thou winter's wind', Rosalind's description of the marks of a lover and of the progress of time with different persons, the picture of the snake wreathed round Oliver's neck while the lioness watches her sleeping prey, and Touchstone's lecture to the shepherd, his defence of cuckolds, and panegyric on the virtues of 'an If'.—All of these are familiar to the reader: there is one passage of equal delicacy and beauty which may have escaped him, and with it we shall close our account of *As You Like It*. It is Phebe's description of Ganimed at the end of the third act.

Think not I love him, tho' I ask for him;
'Tis but a peevish boy, yet he talks well;—
But what care I for words! yet words do well,
When he that speaks them pleases those that hear:
It is a pretty youth; not very pretty;
But sure he's proud, and yet his pride becomes him;
He'll make a proper man; the best thing in him
Is his complexion; and faster than his tongue
Did make offence, his eye did heal it up:

He is not very tall, yet for his years he's tall ;
His leg is but so so, and yet 'tis well ;
There was a pretty redness in his lip,
A little riper, and more lusty red
Than that mix'd in his cheek ; 'twas just the difference
Betwixt the constant red and mingled damask.
There be some women, Silvius, had they mark'd him
In parcels as I did, would have gone near
To fall in love with him : but for my part
I love him not, nor hate him not ; and yet
I have more cause to hate him than to love him ;
For what had he to do to chide at me ?

# *The Taming of the Shrew*

*The Taming of the Shrew* is almost the only one of Shakespeare's comedies that has a regular plot, and downright moral. It is full of bustle, animation, and rapidity of action. It shows admirably how self-will is only to be got the better of by stronger will, and how one degree of ridiculous perversity is only to be driven out by another still greater. Petruchio is a madman in his senses; a very honest fellow, who hardly speaks a word of truth, and succeeds in all his tricks and impostures. He acts his assumed character to the life, with the most fantastical extravagance, with complete presence of mind, with untired animal spirits, and without a particle of ill humour from beginning to end.—The situation of poor Katharine, worn out by his incessant persecutions, becomes at last almost as pitiable as it is ludicrous, and it is difficult to say which to admire most, the unaccountableness of his actions, or the unalterableness of his resolutions. It is a character which most husbands ought to study, unless perhaps the very audacity of Petruchio's attempt might alarm them more than his success would encourage them. What a sound must the following speech carry to some married ears!

> Think you a little din can daunt my ears?
> Have I not in my time heard lions roar?
> Have I not heard the sea, puff'd up with winds,
> Rage like an angry boar, chafed with sweat?
> Have I not heard great ordnance in the field?
> And heav'n's artillery thunder in the skies?
> Have I not in a pitched battle heard
> Loud larums, neighing steeds, and trumpets clang?

And do you tell me of a woman's tongue,
That gives not half so great a blow to hear,
As will a chestnut in a farmer's fire ?

Not all Petruchio's rhetoric would persuade more than 'some dozen followers' to be of this heretical way of thinking. He unfolds his scheme for the Taming of the Shrew, on a principle of contradiction, thus :

I'll woo her with some spirit when she comes.
Say that she rail, why then I'll tell her plain
She sings as sweetly as a nightingale ;
Say that she frown, I'll say she looks as clear
As morning roses newly wash'd with dew ;
Say she be mute, and will not speak a word,
Then I'll commend her volubility,
And say she uttereth piercing eloquence :
If she do bid me pack, I'll give her thanks,
As tho' she bid me stay by her a week ;
If she deny to wed, I'll crave the day,
When I shall ask the banns, and when be married.

He accordingly gains her consent to the match, by telling her father that he has got it ; disappoints her by not returning at the time he has promised to wed her, and when he returns, creates no small consternation by the oddity of his dress and equipage. This however is nothing to the astonishment excited by his mad-brained behaviour at the marriage. Here is the account of it by an eye-witness :

*Gremio.* Tut, she's a lamb, a dove, a fool to him :
I'll tell you, Sir Lucentio ; when the priest
Should ask if Katherine should be his wife ?
Ay, by gogs woons, quoth he ; and swore so loud,
That, all amaz'd, the priest let fall the book ;
And as he stooped again to take it up,
This mad-brain'd bridegroom took him such a cuff,
That down fell priest and book, and book and priest.
Now take them up, quoth he, if any list.
*Tranio.* What said the wench when he rose up again ?
*Gremio.* Trembled and shook ; for why, he stamp'd and swore,
As if the vicar meant to cozen him.

But after many ceremonies done,
He calls for wine ; a health, quoth he ; as if
He'd been aboard carousing with his mates
After a storm ; quaft off the muscadel,
And threw the sops all in the sexton's face ;
Having no other cause but that his beard
Grew thin and hungerly, and seem'd to ask
His sops as he was drinking. This done, he took
The bride about the neck, and kiss'd her lips
With such a clamorous smack, that at their parting
All the church echoed : and I seeing this,
Came thence for very shame ; and after me,
I know, the rout is coming ;—
Such a mad marriage never was before.

The most striking and at the same time laughable feature in the character of Petruchio throughout, is the studied approximation to the intractable character of real madness, his apparent insensibility to all external considerations, and utter indifference to everything but the wild and extravagant freaks of his own self-will. There is no contending with a person on whom nothing makes any impression but his own purposes, and who is bent on his own whims just in proportion as they seem to want common-sense. With him a thing's being plain and reasonable is a reason against it. The airs he gives himself are infinite, and his caprices as sudden as they are groundless. The whole of his treatment of his wife at home is in the same spirit of ironical attention and inverted gallantry. Everything flies before his will, like a conjurer's wand, and he only metamorphoses his wife's temper by metamorphosing her senses and all the objects she sees, at a word's speaking. Such are his insisting that it is the moon and not the sun which they see, &c. This extravagance reaches its most pleasant and poetical height in the scene where, on their return to her father's, they meet old Vincentio, whom Petruchio immediately addresses as a young lady :

*Petruchio.* Good morrow, gentle mistress, where away ?

Tell me, sweet Kate, and tell me truly too,
Hast thou beheld a fresher gentlewoman?
Such war of white and red within her cheeks;
What stars do spangle heaven with such beauty,
As those two eyes become that heav'nly face?
Fair lovely maid, once more good day to thee:
Sweet Kate, embrace her for her beauty's sake.
*Hortensio.* He'll make the man mad to make a woman of him.
*Katherine.* Young budding virgin, fair and fresh and sweet,
Wither away, or where is thy abode?
Happy the parents of so fair a child;
Happier the man whom favourable stars
Allot thee for his lovely bed-fellow.
*Petruchio.* Why, how now, Kate, I hope thou art not mad:
This is a man, old, wrinkled, faded, wither'd,
And not a maiden, as thou say'st he is.
*Katherine.* Pardon, old father, my mistaken eyes
That have been so bedazed with the sun
That everything I look on seemeth green.
Now I perceive thou art a reverend father.

The whole is carried on with equal spirit, as if the poet's comic Muse had wings of fire. It is strange how one man could be so many things; but so it is. The concluding scene, in which trial is made of the obedience of the new-married wives (so triumphantly for Petruchio), is a very happy one.—In some parts of this play there is a little too much about music-masters and masters of philosophy. They were things of greater rarity in those days than they are now. Nothing, however, can be better than the advice which Tranio gives his master for the prosecution of his studies:

The mathematics, and the metaphysics,
Fall to them as you find your stomach serves you:
No profit grows, where is no pleasure ta'en:
In brief, sir, study what you most affect.

We have heard the *Honey-Moon* called 'an elegant Katharine and Petruchio'. We suspect we do not understand this word *elegant* in the sense that many people do. But in our sense of the word, we should call Lucentio's description of his mistress elegant :

> Tranio, I saw her coral lips to move,
> And with her breath she did perfume the air :
> Sacred and sweet was all I saw in her.

When Biondello tells the same Lucentio for his encouragement, 'I knew a wench married in an afternoon as she went to the garden for parsley to stuff a rabbit, and so may you, sir'—there is nothing elegant in this, and yet we hardly know which of the two passages is the best.

*The Taming of the Shrew* is a play within a play. It is supposed to be a play acted for the benefit of Sly the tinker, who is made to believe himself a lord, when he wakes after a drunken brawl. The character of Sly and the remarks with which he accompanies the play are as good as the play itself. His answer when he is asked how he likes it, 'Indifferent well ; 'tis a good piece of work, would 'twere done', is in good keeping, as if he were thinking of his Saturday night's job. Sly does not change his tastes with his new situation, but in the midst of splendour and luxury still calls out lustily and repeatedly 'for a pot o' the smallest ale'. He is very slow in giving up his personal identity in his sudden advancement. 'I am Christophero Sly, call not me honour nor lordship. I ne'er drank sack in my life : and if you give me any conserves, give me conserves of beef : ne'er ask me what raiment I'll wear, for I have no more doublets than backs, no more stockings than legs, nor no more shoes than feet, nay, sometimes more feet than shoes, or such shoes as my toes look through the over-leather.—What, would you make me mad ? Am not I Christophero Sly, old Sly's son of Burton-heath, by birth a pedlar, by education a cardmaker, by transmutation a bear-herd, and now by present profession a tinker ? Ask Marian Hacket, the fat alewife of Wincot, if she know me not ; if she say I am not fourteen-pence on the score for sheer ale, score me up for the lying'st knave in Christendom '.

This is honest. ' The Slies are no rogues ', as he says of himself. We have a great predilection for this representative of the family ; and what makes us like him the better is, that we take him to be of kin (not many degrees removed) to Sancho Panza.

## *Measure for Measure*

This is a play as full of genius as it is of wisdom. Yet there is an original sin in the nature of the subject, which prevents us from taking a cordial interest in it. 'The height of moral argument' which the author has maintained in the intervals of passion or blended with the more powerful impulses of nature, is hardly surpassed in any of his plays. But there is in general a want of passion; the affections are at a stand; our sympathies are repulsed and defeated in all directions. The only passion which influences the story is that of Angelo; and yet he seems to have a much greater passion for hypocrisy than for his mistress. Neither are we greatly enamoured of Isabella's rigid chastity, though she could not act otherwise than she did. We do not feel the same confidence in the virtue that is 'sublimely good' at another's expense, as if it had been put to some less disinterested trial. As to the Duke, who makes a very imposing and mysterious stage-character, he is more absorbed in his own plots and gravity than anxious for the welfare of the state; more tenacious of his own character than attentive to the feelings and apprehensions of others. Claudio is the only person who feels naturally; and yet he is placed in circumstances of distress which almost preclude the wish for his deliverance. Mariana is also in love with Angelo, whom we hate. In this respect, there may be said to be a general system of cross-purposes between the feelings of the different characters and the sympathy of the reader or the audience. This principle of repugnance seems to have reached its height in the character of Master Barnardine, who not only sets at defiance the opinions of others, but has even thrown off all self-regard,—' one that apprehends death no more dreadfully but as a drunken sleep; careless, reckless, and fearless of what's past, present, and to come'. He is a fine antithesis to the morality and the hypocrisy of the other characters of the play. Barnardine is Caliban transported from Prospero's wizard island to the forests of Bohemia or the prisons of Vienna. He is the creature of bad habits as Caliban is of gross instincts. He has, however, a strong notion of the natural fitness of things, according to his own sensations—' He has been drinking hard all night, and he will not be hanged that day'—and Shakespeare has let him off at last. We do not understand why the philosophical German critic, Schlegel, should be so severe on those pleasant persons, Lucio, Pompey, and Master Froth, as to call them 'wretches'. They appear all mighty comfortable in their occupations, and determined to pursue them, 'as the flesh and fortune should serve'. A very good exposure of the want of self-knowledge and contempt for others, which is so common in the world, is put into the mouth of Abhorson, the jailer, when the Provost proposes to associate Pompey with him in his office—' A bawd, sir? Fie upon him, he will discredit our mystery'. And the same answer would serve in nine instances out of ten to the same kind of remark, 'Go to, sir, you weigh equally; a feather will turn the scale'. Shakespeare was in one sense the least moral of all writers; for morality (commonly so called) is made up of antipathies; and his talent consisted in sympathy with human nature, in all its shapes, degrees, depressions, and elevations. The object of the pedantic moralist is to find out the bad in everything: his was to show that 'there is some soul of goodness in things evil'. Even Master Barnardine is not left to the mercy of what others think of him ; but when he comes in, speaks for himself, and pleads his own cause, as well as if counsel had been assigned him. In one sense, Shakespeare was no moralist at all : in another, he was the greatest of all moralists. He was a moralist in the same sense in which nature is one. He taught what he had learnt from her. He showed the greatest knowledge of humanity with the greatest fellow-feeling for it.

One of the most dramatic passages in the present play is the interview between Claudio and his sister, when she comes to inform him of the conditions on which Angelo will spare his life.

*Claudio.* Let me know the point.
*Isabella.* O, I do fear thee, Claudio : and I quake,
Lest thou a feverous life should'st entertain,
And six or seven winters more respect
Than a perpetual honour. Dar'st thou die ?
The sense of death is most in apprehension ;
And the poor beetle, that we tread upon,
In corporal sufferance finds a pang as great
As when a giant dies.
*Claudio.* Why give you me this shame ?
Think you I can a resolution fetch
From flowery tenderness ; if I must die,
I will encounter darkness as a bride.
And hug it in mine arms.
*Isabella.* There spake my brother ! there my father's grave
Did utter forth a voice ! Yes, thou must die :
Thou art too noble to conserve a life
In base appliances. This outward-sainted deputy—
Whose settled visage and deliberate word
Nips youth i' the head, and follies doth emmew
As faulcon doth the fowl—is yet a devil.
*Claudio.* The princely Angelo ?
*Isabella.* Oh, 'tis the cunning livery of hell,
The damned'st body to invest and cover
In princely guards ! Dost thou think, Claudio,
If I would yield him my virginity,
Thou might'st be freed ?
*Claudio.* Oh, heavens ! it cannot be.
*Isabella.* Yes, he would give it thee, for this rank offence,
So to offend him still : this night's the time

That I should do what I abhor to name,
Or else thou dy'st to-morrow.
*Claudio.* Thou shalt not do 't.
*Isabella.* Oh, were it but my life,
I'd throw it down for your deliverance
As frankly as a pin.
*Claudio.* Thanks, dear Isabel.
*Isabella.* Be ready, Claudio, for your death to-morrow.
*Claudio.* Yes.—Has he affections in him,
That thus can make him bite the law by the nose ?
When he would force it, sure it is no sin ;
Or of the deadly seven it is the least.
*Isabella.* Which is the least ?
*Claudio.* If it were damnable, he, being so wise,
Why would he for the momentary trick
Be perdurably fin'd ? Oh, Isabel !
*Isabella.* What says my brother ?
*Claudio.* Death is a fearful thing.
*Isabella.* And shamed life a hateful.
*Claudio.* Aye, but to die, and go we know not where ;
To lie in cold obstruction, and to rot ;
This sensible warm motion to become
A kneaded clod ; and the delighted spirit
To bathe in fiery floods, or to reside
In thrilling regions of thick-ribbed ice :
To be imprison'd in the viewless winds,
And blown with restless violence round about
The pendant world ; or to be worse than worst
Of those, that lawless and incertain thoughts
Imagine howling !—'tis too horrible !
The weariest and most loathed worldly life,
That age, ache, penury, and imprisonment
Can lay on nature, is a paradise
To what we fear of death.
*Isabella.* Alas ! alas !
*Claudio.* Sweet sister, let me live :
What sin you do to save a brother's life,
Nature dispenses with the deed so far,
That it becomes a virtue.

What adds to the dramatic beauty of this scene and the effect of Claudio's passionate attachment to life is, that it immediately follows the Duke's lecture to him, in the character of the Friar, recommending an absolute indifference to it.

——Reason thus with life,—
If I do lose thee, I do lose a thing,
That none but fools would keep : a breath thou art,
Servile to all the skyey influences
That do this habitation, where thou keep'st,
Hourly afflict : merely, thou art death's fool ;
For him thou labour'st by thy flight to shun,
And yet run'st toward him still : thou art not noble ;
For all the accommodations, that thou bear'st,
Are nurs'd by baseness : thou art by no means valiant ;
For thou dost fear the soft and tender fork
Of a poor worm : thy best of rest is sleep,
And that thou oft provok'st ; yet grossly fear'st
Thy death, which is no more. Thou art not thyself ;
For thou exist'st on many a thousand grains
That issue out of dust : happy thou art not ;
For what thou hast not, still thou striv'st to get ;
And what thou hast, forget'st : thou art not certain ;
For thy complexion shifts to strange effects,
After the moon ; if thou art rich, thou art poor ;
For, like an ass, whose back with ingots bows,
Thou bear'st thy heavy riches but a journey,
And death unloads thee : friend thou hast none ;
For thy own bowels, which do call thee sire,
The mere effusion of thy proper loins,
Do curse the gout, serpigo, and the rheum,
For ending thee no sooner : thou hast nor youth, nor age ;
But, as it were, an after-dinner's sleep,
Dreaming on both : for all thy blessed youth
Becomes as aged, and doth beg the alms
Of palsied eld ; and when thou art old, and rich,
Thou hast neither heat, affection, limb, nor beauty,
To make thy riches pleasant. What's yet in this,
That bears the name of life ? Yet in this life
Lie hid more thousand deaths ; yet death we fear,
That makes these odds all even.

# *The Merry Wives of Windsor*

*The Merry Wives of Windsor* is no doubt a very amusing play, with a great deal of humour, character, and nature in it: but we should have liked it much better, if any one else had been the hero of it, instead of Falstaff. We could have been contented if Shakespeare had not been 'commanded to show the knight in love'. Wits and philosophers, for the most part, do not shine in that character; and Sir John himself by no means comes off with flying colours. Many people complain of the degradation and insults to which Don Quixote is so frequently exposed in his various adventures. But what are the unconscious indignities which he suffers, compared with the sensible mortifications which Falstaff is made to bring upon himself? What are the blows and buffetings which the Don receives from the staves of the Yanguesian carriers or from Sancho Panza's more hard-hearted hands, compared with the contamination of the buck-basket, the disguise of the fat woman of Brentford, and the horns of Herne the hunter, which are discovered on Sir John's head? In reading the play, we indeed wish him well through all these discomfitures, but it would have been as well if he had not got into them. Falstaff in the *Merry Wives of Windsor* is not the man he was in the two parts of *Henry IV*. His wit and eloquence have left him. Instead of making a butt of others, he is made a butt of by them. Neither is there a single particle of love in him to excuse his follies: he is merely a designing, bare-faced knave, and an unsuccessful one. The scene with Ford as Master Brook, and that with

Simple, Slender's man, who comes to ask after the Wise Woman, are almost the only ones in which his old intellectual ascendancy appears. He is like a person recalled to the stage to perform an unaccustomed and ungracious part; and in which we perceive only 'some faint sparks of those flashes of merriment, that were wont to set the hearers in a roar'. But the single scene with Doll Tearsheet, or Mrs. Quickly's account of his desiring 'to eat some of housewife Keach's prawns', and telling her 'to be no more so familiarity with such people', is worth the whole of the *Merry Wives of Windsor* put together. Ford's jealousy, which is the mainspring of the comic incidents, is certainly very well managed. Page, on the contrary, appears to be somewhat uxorious in his disposition; and we have pretty plain indications of the effect of the characters of the husbands on the different degrees of fidelity in their wives. Mrs. Quickly makes a very lively go-between, both between Falstaff and his Dulcineas, and Anne Page and her lovers, and seems in the latter case so intent on her own interest as totally to overlook the intentions of her employers. Her master, Doctor Caius, the Frenchman, and her fellow servant Jack Rugby, are very completely described. This last-mentioned person is rather quaintly commended by Mrs. Quickly's as 'an honest, willing, kind fellow, as ever servant shall come in house withal, and I warrant you, no tell-tale, nor no breed-bate; his worst fault is, that he is given to prayer; he is something peevish that way; but nobody but has his fault'. The Welsh Parson, Sir Hugh Evans (a title which in those days was given to the clergy) is an excellent character in all respects. He is as respectable as he is laughable. He has 'very good discretions, and very odd humours'. The duel-scene with Caius gives him an opportunity to show his 'cholers and his tremblings of mind', his valour and his melancholy, in an irresistible manner. In the dialogue, which at his mother's request he holds with his pupil, William Page, to show his progress in learning, it is hard to say whether the simplicity of the master or the scholar is the greatest. Nym, Bardolph, and Pistol, are but the shadows of what they were; and Justice Shallow himself has little of his consequence left. But his cousin, Slender, makes up for the deficiency. He is a very potent piece of imbecility. In him the pretensions of the worthy Gloucestershire family are well kept up, and immortalized. He and his friend Sackerson and his book of songs and his love of Anne Page and his having nothing to say to her can never be forgotten. It is the only first-rate character in the play, but it is in that class. Shakespeare is the only writer who was as great in describing weakness as strength.

## *The Comedy of Errors*

This comedy is taken very much from the Menaechmi of Plautus, and is not an improvement on it. Shakespeare appears to have bestowed no great pains on it, and there are but a few passages which bear the decided stamp of his genius. He seems to have relied on his author, and on the interest arising out of the intricacy of the plot. The curiosity excited is certainly very considerable, though not of the most pleasing kind. We are teased as with a riddle, which notwithstanding we try to solve. In reading the play, from the sameness of the names of the two Antipholises and the two Dromios, as well from their being constantly taken for each other by those who see them, it is difficult, without a painful effort of attention, to keep the characters distinct in the mind. And again, on the stage, either the complete similarity of their persons and dress must produce the same perplexity whenever they first enter, or the identity of appearance which the story supposes will be destroyed. We still, however, having a clue to the difficulty, can tell which is which, merely from the practical contradictions which arise, as soon as the different parties begin to speak; and we are indemnified for the perplexity and blunders into which we are thrown by seeing others thrown into greater and almost inextricable ones.—This play (among other considerations) leads us not to feel much regret that Shakespeare was not what is called a classical scholar. We do not think his *forte* would ever have lain in imitating or improving on what others invented, so much as in inventing for himself, and perfecting what he invented,—not perhaps by the omission of faults, but by the addition of the highest excellences. His own genius was strong enough to bear him up, and he soared longest and best on unborrowed plumes.—The only passage of a very Shakespearian cast in this comedy is the one in which the Abbess, with admirable characteristic artifice, makes Adriana confess her own misconduct in driving her husband mad.

*Abbess.* How long hath this possession held the man ?
*Adriana.* This week he hath been heavy, sour, sad
And much, much different from the man he was ;
But, till this afternoon, his passion
Ne'er brake into extremity of rage.
*Abbess.* Hath he not lost much wealth by wreck at sea ?
Bury'd some dear friend ? Hath not else his eye
Stray'd his affection in unlawful love ?
A sin prevailing much in youthful men,
Who give their eyes the liberty of gazing.
Which of these sorrows is he subject to ?
*Adriana.* To none of these, except it be the last :
Namely, some love, that drew him oft from home.
*Abbess.* You should for that have reprehended him.
*Adriana.* Why, so I did.
*Abbess.* But not rough enough.
*Adriana.* As roughly as my modesty would let me.
*Abbess.* Haply, in private.
*Adriana.* And in assemblies too.
*Abbess.* Aye, but not enough.
*Adriana.* It was the copy of our conference :
In bed, he slept not for my urging it ;
At board, he fed not for my urging it ;
Alone it was the subject of my theme ;
In company, I often glanc'd at it ;
Still did I tell him it was vile and bad.
*Abbess.* And therefore came it that the man was mad :
The venom'd clamours of a jealous woman
Poison more deadly than a mad dog's tooth.
It seems, his sleeps were hinder'd by thy railing :
And therefore comes it that his head is light.
Thou say'st his meat was sauc'd with thy upbraidings :
Unquiet meals make ill digestions,
Therefore the raging fire of fever bred :
And what's a fever but a fit of madness ?

Thou say'st his sports were hinder'd by thy brawls :
Sweet recreation barr'd, what doth ensue,
But moody and dull melancholy,
Kinsman to grim and comfortless despair ;
And, at her heels, a huge infectious troop
Of pale distemperatures, and foes to life ?
In food, in sport, and life-preserving rest
To be disturb'd, would mad or man or beast :
The consequence is then, thy jealous fits
Have scar'd thy husband from the use of wits.
*Luciana.* She never reprehended him but mildly,
When he demeaned himself rough, rude, and wildly.—
Why bear you these rebukes, and answer not ?
*Adriana.* She did betray me to my own reproof.

Pinch the conjurer is also an excrescence not to be found in Plautus. He is indeed a very formidable anachronism.

They brought one Pinch, a hungry lean-fac'd villain,
A meer anatomy, a mountebank,
A thread-bare juggler and a fortune-teller,
A needy, hollow-ey'd, sharp-looking wretch,
A living dead man.

This is exactly like some of the Puritanical portraits to be met with in Hogarth.

## *Doubtful Plays of Shakespeare*

We shall give for the satisfaction of the reader what the celebrated German critic, Schlegel, says on this subject, and then add a very few remarks of our own.

'All the editors, with the exception of Capell, are unanimous in rejecting *Titus Andronicus* as unworthy of Shakespeare, though they always allow it to be printed with the other pieces, as the scape-goat, as it were, of their abusive criticism. The correct method in such an investigation is first to examine into the external grounds, evidences, &c., and to weigh their worth; and then to adduce the internal reasons derived from the quality of the work. The critics of Shakespeare follow a course directly the reverse of this; they set out with a preconceived opinion against a piece, and seek, in justification of this opinion, to render the historical grounds suspicious, and to set them aside. *Titus Andronicus* is to be found in the first folio edition of Shakespeare's works, which it was known was conducted by Heminge and Condell, for many years his friends and fellow-managers of the same theatre. Is it possible to persuade ourselves that they would not have known if a piece in their repertory did or did not actually belong to Shakespeare? And are we to lay to the charge of these honourable men a designed fraud in this single case, when we know that they did not show themselves so very desirous of scraping everything together which went by the name of Shakespeare, but, as it appears, merely gave those plays of which they had manuscripts in hand? Yet the following circumstance is still stronger: George Meres, a contemporary and admirer of Shakespeare, mentions *Titus Andronicus* in an enumeration of his works, in the year 1598. Meres was personally acquainted with the poet, and so very intimately, that the latter read over to him his Sonnets before they were printed. I cannot conceive that all the critical scepticism in the world would be sufficient to get over such a testimony.

'This tragedy, it is true, is framed according to a false idea of the tragic, which by an accumulation of cruelties and enormities degenerates into the horrible, and yet leaves no deep impression behind: the story of Tereus and Philomela is heightened and overcharged under other names, and mixed up with the repast of Atreus and Thyestes, and many other incidents. In detail there is no want of beautiful lines, bold images, nay, even features which betray the peculiar conception of Shakespeare. Among these we may reckon the joy of the treacherous Moor at the blackness and ugliness of his child begot in adultery; and in the compassion of Titus Andronicus, grown childish through grief, for a fly which had been struck dead, and his rage afterwards when he imagines he discovers in it his black enemy we recognize the future poet of *Lear*. Are the critics afraid that Shakespeare's fame would be injured, were it established that in his early youth he ushered into the world a feeble and immature work? Was Rome the less the conqueror of the world because Remus could leap over its first walls? Let any one place himself in Shakespeare's situation at the commencement of his career. He found only a few indifferent models, and yet these met with the most favourable reception, because men are never difficult to please in the novelty of an art before their taste has become fastidious from choice and abundance. Must not this situation have had its influence on him before he learned to make higher demands on himself, and by digging deeper in his own mind, discovered the richest veins of a noble metal? It is even highly probable that he must have made several failures before getting into the right path. Genius is in a certain sense infallible, and has nothing to learn; but art is to be learned, and must be acquired by practice and experience. In Shakespeare's acknowledged works we find hardly any traces of his apprenticeship, and yet an apprenticeship he certainly had. This every artist must have, and especially in a period where he has not before him the example of a school already formed. I consider it as extremely probable, that Shakespeare began to write for the theatre at a much earlier period than the one which is generally stated, namely, not till after the year 1590. It appears that, as early as the year 1584, when only twenty years of age, he had left his paternal home and repaired to London. Can we imagine that such an active head would remain idle for six whole years without making any attempt to emerge by his talents from an uncongenial situation? That in the dedication of the poem of Venus and Adonis he calls it 'the first heir of his invention', proves nothing against the supposition. It was the first which he printed; he might have composed it at an earlier period; perhaps, also, he did not include theatrical labours, as they then possessed but little literary dignity. The earlier Shakespeare began to compose for the theatre, the less are we enabled to consider the immaturity and imperfection of a work as a proof of its spuriousness in opposition to historical evidence, if we only find in it prominent features of his mind. Several of the works rejected as spurious may still have been produced in the period betwixt *Titus Andronicus* and the earliest of the acknowledged pieces.

'At last, Steevens published seven pieces ascribed to Shakespeare in two supplementary volumes.

It is to be remarked, that they all appeared in print in Shakespeare's lifetime, with his name prefixed at full length. They are the following :

'1. *Locrine.* The proofs of the genuineness of this piece are not altogether unambiguous ; the grounds for doubt, on the other hand, are entitled to attention. However, this question is immediately connected with that respecting *Titus Andronicus*, and must be at the same time resolved in the affirmative or negative.

'2. *Pericles, Prince of Tyre.* This piece was acknowledged by Dryden, but as a youthful work of Shakespeare. It is most undoubtedly his, and it has been admitted into several of the late editions. The supposed imperfections originate in the circumstance, that Shakespeare here handled a childish and extravagant romance of the old poet Gower, and was unwilling to drag the subject out of its proper sphere. Hence he even introduces Gower himself, and makes him deliver a prologue entirely in his antiquated language and versification. This power of assuming so foreign a manner is at least no proof of helplessness.

'3. *The London Prodigal.* If we are not mistaken, Lessing pronounced this piece to be Shakespeare's, and wished to bring it on to the German stage.

'4. *The Puritan ; or, the Widow of Watling Street.* One of my literary friends, intimately acquainted with Shakespeare, was of opinion that the poet must have wished to write a play for once in the style of Ben Johnson, and that in this way we must account for the difference between the present piece and his usual manner. To follow out this idea, however, would lead to a very nice critical investigation.

'5. *Thomas, Lord Cromwell.*

'6. *Sir John Oldcastle—First Part.*

'7. *A Yorkshire Tragedy.*

'The three last pieces are not only unquestionably Shakespeare's, but in my opinion they deserve to be classed among his best and maturest works. Steevens admits at last, in some degree, that they are Shakespeare's, as well as the others, excepting *Locrine,* but he speaks of all of them with great contempt, as quite worthless productions. This condemnatory sentence is not, however, in the slightest degree convincing, nor is it supported by critical acumen. I should like to see how such a critic would, of his own natural suggestion, have decided on Shakespeare's acknowledged masterpieces, and what he would have thought of praising in them, had the public opinion not imposed on him the duty of admiration. *Thomas, Lord Cromwell,* and *Sir John Oldcastle,* are biographical dramas, and models in this species: the first is linked, from its subject, to *Henry the Eighth,* and the second to *Henry the Fifth.* The second part of *Oldcastle* is wanting; I know not whether a copy of the old edition has been discovered in England, or whether it is lost. *The Yorkshire Tragedy* is a tragedy in one act, a dramatized tale of murder: the tragical effect is overpowering, and it is extremely important to see how poetically Shakespeare could handle such a subject.

'There have been still farther ascribed to him: 1st. *The Merry Devil of Edmonton,* a comedy in one act, printed in Dodsley's old plays. This has certainly some appearances in its favour. It contains a merry landlord, who bears a great similarity to the one in the *Merry Wives of Windsor.* However, at all events, though an ingenious, it is but a hasty sketch. 2nd. *The Accusation of Paris.* 3rd. *The Birth of Merlin.* 4th. *Edward the Third.* 5th. *The Fair Emma.* 6th. *Mucedorus.* 7th. *Arden of Feversham.* I have never seen any of these, and cannot therefore say anything respecting them. From the passages cited, I am led to conjecture that the subject of *Mucedorus* is the popular story of Valentine and Orson; a beautiful subject which Lope de Vega has also taken for a play. *Arden of Feversham* is said to be a tragedy on the story of a man, from whom the poet was descended by the mother's side. If the quality of the piece is not too directly at variance with this claim, the circumstance would afford an additional probability in its favour. For such motives were not foreign to Shakespeare: he treated Henry the Seventh, who bestowed lands on his forefathers for services performed by them, with a visible partiality.

'Whoever takes from Shakespeare a play early ascribed to him, and confessedly belonging to his time, is unquestionably bound to answer, with some degree of probability, this question: who has then written it? Shakespeare's competitors in the dramatic walk are pretty well known, and if those of them who have even acquired a considerable name, a Lilly, a Marlow, a Heywood, are still so very far below him, we can hardly imagine that the author of a work, which rises so high beyond theirs, would have remained unknown.'—*Lectures on Dramatic Literature*, vol. ii, page 252.

We agree to the truth of this last observation, but not to the justice of its application to some of the plays here mentioned. It is true that Shakespeare's best works are very superior to those of Marlow, or Heywood, but it is not true that the best of the doubtful plays above enumerated are superior or even equal to the best of theirs. *The Yorkshire Tragedy*, which Schlegel speaks of as an undoubted production of our author's, is much more in the manner of Heywood than of Shakespeare. The effect is indeed overpowering, but the mode of producing it is by no means poetical. The praise which Schlegel gives to *Thomas, Lord Cromwell*, and to *Sir John Oldcastle*, is altogether exaggerated. They are very indifferent compositions, which have not the slightest pretensions to rank with *Henry V* or *Henry VIII*. We suspect that the German critic was not very well acquainted with the dramatic contemporaries of Shakespeare, or aware of their general merits; and that he accordingly mistakes a resemblance in style and manner for an equal degree of excellence. Shakespeare differed from the other writers of his age not in the mode of treating his subjects, but in the grace and power which he displayed in them. The reason assigned by a literary friend of Schlegel's for supposing *The Puritan: or, the Widow of Watling Street*, to be Shakespeare's, viz. that it is in the style of Ben Jonson, that is to say, in a style just the reverse of his own, is not very satisfactory to a plain English understanding. *Locrine*, and *The London Prodigal*, if they were Shakespeare's at all, must have been among the sins of his youth. *Arden of Feversham* contains several striking passages, but the passion which they express is rather that of a sanguine temperament than of a lofty imagination; and in this respect they approximate more nearly to the style of other writers of the time than to Shakespeare's. *Titus Andronicus* is certainly as unlike Shakespeare's usual style as it is possible. It is an accumulation of vulgar physical horrors, in which the power exercised by the poet bears no proportion to the repugnance excited by the subject. The character of Aaron the Moor is the only thing which shows any originality of conception; and the scene in which he expresses his joy 'at the blackness and ugliness of his child begot in adultery', the only one worthy of Shakespeare. Even this is worthy of him only in the display of power, for it gives no pleasure. Shakespeare managed these things differently. Nor do we think it a sufficient answer to say that this was an embryo or crude production of the author. In its kind it is full grown, and its features decided and overcharged. It is not like a first imperfect essay, but shows a confirmed habit, a systematic preference of violent effect to everything else. There are occasional detached images of great beauty and delicacy, but these were not beyond the powers of other writers then living. The circumstances which inclines us to reject the external evidence in favour of this play being Shakespeare's is, that the grammatical construction is constantly false and mixed up with vulgar abbreviations, a fault that never occurs in any of his genuine plays. A similar defect, and the halting measure of the verse are the chief objections to *Pericles of Tyre*, if we except the far-fetched and complicated absurdity of the story. The movement of the thoughts and passions has something in it not unlike Shakespeare, and several of the descriptions are either the original hints of passages which Shakespeare has engrafted on his other plays, or are imitations of them by some contemporary poet. The most memorable idea in it is in Marina's speech, where she compares the world to ' a lasting storm, hurrying her from her friends '.

## *Poems and Sonnets*

Our idolatry of Shakespeare (not to say our admiration) ceases with his plays. In his other productions he was a mere author, though not a common author. It was only by representing others, that he became himself. He could go out of himself, and express the soul of Cleopatra; but in his own person, he appeared to be always waiting for the prompter's cue. In expressing the thoughts of others, he seemed inspired; in expressing his own, he was a mechanic. The licence of an assumed character was necessary to restore his genius to the privileges of nature, and to give him courage to break through the tyranny of fashion, the trammels of custom. In his plays, he was 'as broad and casing as the general air'; in his poems, on the contrary, he appears to be 'cooped, and cabined in' by all the technicalities of art, by all the petty intricacies of thought and language, which poetry had learned from the controversial jargon of the schools, where words had been made a substitute for things. There was, if we mistake not, something of modesty, and a painful sense of personal propriety at the bottom of this. Shakespeare's imagination, by identifying itself with the strongest characters in the most trying circumstances, grappled at once with nature, and trampled the littleness of art under his feet: the rapid changes of situation, the wide range of the universe, gave him life and spirit, and afforded full scope to his genius; but returned into his closet again, and having assumed the badge of his profession, he could only labour in his vocation, and conform himself to existing models. The thoughts, the passions, the words which the poet's pen, 'glancing from heaven to earth, from earth to heaven', lent to others, shook off the fetters of pedantry and affectation; while his own thoughts and feelings, standing by themselves, were seized upon as lawful prey, and tortured to death according to the established rules and practice of the day. In a word, we do not like Shakespeare's poems, because we like his plays: the one, in all their excellences, are just the reverse of the other. It has been the fashion of late to cry up our author's poems, as equal to his plays: this is the desperate cant of modern criticism. We would ask, was there the slightest comparison between Shakespeare, and either Chaucer or Spenser, as mere poets? Not any.—The two poems of *Venus and Adonis* and of *Tarquin and Lucrece* appear to us like a couple of ice-houses. They are about as hard, as glittering, and as cold. The author seems all the time to be thinking of his verses, and not of his subject,—not of what his characters would feel, but of what he shall say; and as it must happen in all such cases, he always puts into their mouths those things which they would be the last to think of, and which it shows the greatest ingenuity in him to find out. The whole is laboured, up-hill work. The poet is perpetually singling out the difficulties of the art to make an exhibition of his strength and skill in wrestling with them. He is making perpetual trials of them as if his mastery over them were doubted. The images, which are often striking, are generally applied to things which they are the least like: so that they do not blend with the poem, but seem stuck upon it, like splendid patch-work, or remain quite distinct from it, like detached substances, painted and varnished over. A beautiful thought is sure to be lost in an endless commentary upon it. The speakers are like persons who have both leisure and inclination to make riddles on their own situation, and to twist and turn every object or incident into acrostics and anagrams. Everything is spun out into allegory; and a digression is always preferred to the main story. Sentiment is built up upon plays of words; the hero or heroine feels, not from the impulse of passion, but from the force of dialectics. There is besides, a strange attempt to substitute the language of painting for that of poetry, to make us *see* their feelings in the faces of the persons; and again, consistently with this, in the description of the picture in *Tarquin and Lucrece*, those circumstances are chiefly insisted on, which it would be impossible to convey except by words. The invocation to Opportunity in the *Tarquin and Lucrece* is full of thoughts and images, but at the same time it is overloaded by them. The concluding stanza expresses all our objections to this kind of poetry:

> Oh! idle words, servants to shallow fools;
> Unprofitable sounds, weak arbitrators;
> Busy yourselves in skill-contending schools;
> Debate when leisure serves with dull debaters;
> To trembling clients be their mediators:
> For me I force not argument a straw,
> Since that my case is past all help of law.

The description of the horse in *Venus and Adonis* has been particularly admired, and not without reason:

> Round-hoof'd, short-jointed, fetlocks shag and long,
> Broad breast, full eyes, small head, and nostril wide,
> High crest, short ears, straight legs, and passing strong,
> Thin mane, thick tail, broad buttock, tender hide
> Look, what a horse should have he did not lack,
> Save a proud rider on so proud a back.

Now this inventory of perfections shows great knowledge of the horse; and is good matter-of-fact poetry. Let the reader but compare it with a speech in the *Midsummer Night's Dream* where Theseus describes his hounds—

And their heads are hung
With ears that sweep away the morning dew—

and he will perceive at once what we mean by the difference between Shakespeare's own poetry, and that of his plays. We prefer the *Passionate Pilgrim* very much to the *Lover's Complaint.* It has been doubted whether the latter poem is Shakespeare's.

Of the Sonnets we do not well know what to say. The subject of them seems to be somewhat equivocal; but many of them are highly beautiful in themselves, and interesting as they relate to the state of the personal feelings of the author. The following are some of the most striking:

## CONSTANCY

Let those who are in favour with their stars
Of public honour and proud titles boast,
Whilst I, whom fortune of such triumph bars,
Unlook'd for joy in that I honour most.
Great princes' favourites their fair leaves spread,
But as the marigold in the sun's eye;
And in themselves their pride lies buried,
For at a frown they in their glory die.
The painful warrior famous'd for fight,
After a thousand victories once foil'd,
Is from the book of honour razed quite,
And all the rest forgot for which he toil'd:
Then happy I, that love and am belov'd,
Where I may not remove, nor be removed.

## LOVE'S CONSOLATION

When in disgrace with fortune and men's eyes.
I all alone beweep my outcast state,
And trouble deaf heaven with my bootless cries,
And look upon myself, and curse my fate,
Wishing me like to one more rich in hope,
Featur'd like him, like him with friends possess'd,
Desiring this man's art, and that man's scope,
With what I most enjoy contented least;
Yet in these thoughts myself almost despising,
Haply, I think on thee,—and then my state
(Like to the lark at break of day arising

From sullen earth) sings hymns at heaven's gate ;
  For thy sweet love remember'd, such wealth brings
  That then I scorn to change my state with kings.

## NOVELTY

My love is strengthen'd, though more weak in seeming ;
I love not less, though less the show appear :
That love is merchandiz'd, whose rich esteeming
The owner's tongue doth publish every where.
Our love was new, and then but in the spring,
When I was wont to greet it with my lays ;
As Philomel in summer's front doth sing,
And stops his pipe in growth of riper days :
Not that the summer is less pleasant now
Than when her mournful hymns did hush the night,
But that wild music burthens every bough,
And sweets grown common lose their dear delight.
  Therefore, like her, I sometimes hold my tongue,
  Because I would not dull you with my song.

## LIFE'S DECAY

That time of year thou mayst in me behold
When yellow leaves, or none, or few, do hang
Upon those boughs which shake against the cold,
Bare ruin'd choirs, where late the sweet birds sang.
In me thou see'st the twilight of such day
As after sunset fadeth in the west ;
Which by and by black night doth take away,
Death's second self, that seals up all in rest.
In me thou see'st the glowing of such fire,
That on the ashes of his youth doth lie,
As the death-bed whereon it must expire
Consum'd with that which it was nourish'd by.
  This thou perceiv'st, which makes thy love more strong,
  To love that well which thou must leave ere long.

In all these, as well as in many others, there is a mild tone of sentiment, deep, mellow, and sustained, very different from the crudeness of his earlier poems.